‖‖‖‖‖‖‖‖‖‖‖‖
♡ **W9-BWU-711**

GRANDPARENTS' QUEST

A

JAPAN

DIARY

BY
THOMAS N. DRAKE

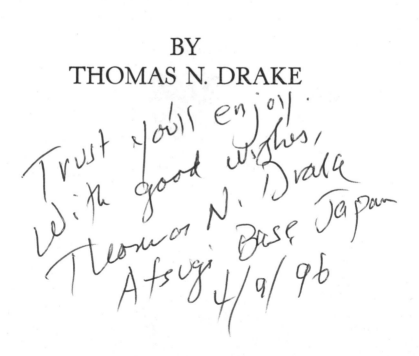

Trust you'll enjoy.
With good wishes,
Thomas N. Drake
Atsugi Base Japan
4/9/96

© 1996 by Thomas N. Drake

All rights reserved. No part of this book may be reproduced
without the express written permission of the copyright holder.
Permission is hereby granted to legitimate literary reviewers to
reproduce excerpts in their reviews.

International Standard Book Number:
1-885487-08-10
Library of Congress Catalogue Card Number:
94-074572
Printed in the United States of America

Published in 1996 by

Brownell & Carroll, Inc. Publishers
3901 Mac Arthur Blvd. Suite 200
Newport Beach, California 92660
1-800-643-6604

DEDICATION

This book is dedicated to my wife, Carolyn Matsuda Drake, whose birthday became its centerpiece and raison d'etre; and also to my granddaughter, Monica Lea Drake, age eight, who figures prominently in the narrative describing her grandmother's birthday, and for the prominent place both have in the heart of this writer.

Thomas Norman Drake
Paradise, California

ACKNOWLEDGEMENTS

The author and his wife are everlastingly in the debt of three people in Japan who played prominent roles as go- betweens during what the reader will discern was a formidable undertaking. Without the intercessive efforts of two of these folks, and the translation ability of the third, our quest might well have gone uncompleted.

The first and foremost is Mr. Tokujiro "Thomas" Seyama, a distinguished man who will always be remembered for his kind intervention and capable dialogue at the crucial beginning of our arduous pursuit. In a country where the two of us were extended many acts of kindness by friends and relatives — as well as from perfect strangers — Mr. Seyama's name is accorded top recognition!

The second person who was to prove a virtual godsend to us was an employee of a hotel in the remote outskirts of a city called *Suzuka*. Miss Matsuo was an American student at Ohio

State University, working her summer vacation months at the hotel and, being fluent in both English and Japanese, was an invaluable translator of the thoughts and emotions of these two American guests. She aided us through what we thought were insurmountable hurdles to achieve our quest, the object of which turned out to be but a five minute walk from that hospitable hotel! Yet, however close, without this young lady's ability to translate English into Japanese for a third party, we might well have been "stranded on Base indefinitely. Fortunately, she brought us "home."

That third party was the hotel manager, a lady of great dignity and tenacity of will (as the reader will discover). I am truly sorry not to have noted this resolute person's name in a journal which was partly written in a second floor room of her comfortable hotel. I hope to be forgiven that omission. If travel takes you to Japan, you will do well to stop at the Suzuka International Hotel, where you will perhaps meet the manager and gain a full understanding of her strength of character.

It was she, together with our dear friend, Mr. Seyama, and surprise-acquaintance, Miss Matsuo, to whom our heartfelt thanks will be directed every time we think of a certain granddaughter living in a distant village called *Suzuka-Shi*.

PREFACE

side from letters and postcards, this retiree hasn't subscribed to the writing habit. Even those letters and cards are dreaded occupations - things to be put off with foreboding. Yet, from the outset of a month-long trip to Japan, I began to set down the daily comings and goings my wife and I experienced with friends and family.

After filling the pages of one notebook and commencing another, I began to chronicle the most important event of our month in Japan — the odyssey of American grandparents to find a granddaughter who was taken there to live.

And once past the inordinately troublesome task of *finding* her, there began the excruciatingly vexing business involved to even *see* our granddaughter! Those events, written on a certain birthday and dated May 31st, became the heart and soul of this narrative (indeed, the only reason now that this diary is being read by others).

If having done so, I have tweaked the reader's funny bone in places — or emoted concern and anger in others — it will have been a worthwhile labor. And if I have done nothing more than to satisfy a natural curiosity for a peek at the pages of another's diary, this also gives me some satisfaction. I have savored the many hours spent transferring voluminous notes into typewritten pages — and now a once dreaded task has become almost pleasant.

CHAPTER 1

unday, May 8:

"Packing these blamed suitcases is the worst part of any trip," I tell my wife on this early morning, with all the last minute humdrum of things to do. There is the hot water heater to turn off, laundry-room water valves to close, clock and light timer-switches to activate — and a few other mundane things we must do before embarking on a trip of this length. Almost five weeks will be consumed before we return to our retirement home in Paradise, California.

But at this moment, toting the luggage from hallway to car is of prime concern (dear wife will never let me forget the time we drove off on a long trip to leave behind a white cosmetic bag in the hall). "What in tarnation did you stuff in this humongous gray bag? It's so heavy my ears are tapering upwards! I'm getting too old to handle freight the size and weight of this, Carolyn."

"Calm down, Tom," chastens the wife. "That particular bag

contains the set of books you seek to donate to a museum in Japan, and your other travel, language and dictionary books. And you're not 'too old' — just too *lazy!* My goodness — You haven't reached sixty-four yet, silly Grandpa."

That 'silly grandpa' moniker Carolyn uses rubbed off on a granddaughter we seek to see in Japan (Monica frequently mimicked that same appellation in response to Gramp's tomfoolery, employed periodically to induce a spate of giggles from that dear child).

A last minute check of the car reveals nothing has been overlooked. The luggage is intact — four suitcases and two hand-carrys — the maximum permissible for air transit.

So we set out down Skyway, the main street through this hamlet of some 25,000 souls, situated in the northern reaches of California's Sierra-Nevada, 2,000 feet above sea level.

"Whew - I'm perspiring already," I tell my wife, who looks cool as a cucumber as we wend our way across a complicated series of back roads leading to the I-5 Freeway. Then we accelerate to speed us to our daughter's home in one of the fastest-growing cities in the U.S.A. - San Jose.

Carolyn flicks on the car radio, which picks up KGO, a powerful AM station beamed from San Francisco, 180 miles distant. "Bernie Ward is on, Tom. Let's listen."

Bernie is a popular talk show host of a program he calls "God Talk." As we have no church affiliation, tuning in to Bernie Ward on Sunday mornings is our 'church.' This guy has an Irish gift of gab, and his interchanges with telephone callers are sometimes enlightening, sometimes hilarious — like now: This popular man is verbally jousting with a loquacious lady — a regular caller and strong Mormon named Bev. Bernie finally breaks off with, "No need to ask you to call again to raise hell with me, Bev — that's a certainty — but I do ask that you have a happy Mother's Day."

I'm anxious to reach our family in San Jose, but must stop

now to gas up at a station next to the Nut Tree Restaurant — a popular tourist-trap along Interstate-80.

Carolyn levers the seat back, all set to take a good nap. "No one to talk with, all by myself," I hum the title song of *Ain't Misbehavin'*, a delightful musical Carolyn and I took in on a trip to San Francisco's Curran Theatre, and I am lost in a reverie of thinking ahead to the trip abroad that awaits. "…just me and my ra-di-o…."

This trip, as I have mentioned, is an odyssey to find and visit our first grandchild — a granddaughter whom we have neither seen nor heard from in two years, since she was abruptly taken from the U.S. to live with her mother, and her mother's parents in Japan.

The mother's name is Miyoko, and she married our son, David, at the American Embassy in Tokyo in September of 1983. He had been working at the Atsugi, Japan naval-air facility from 1980 on. Their daughter, Monica Lea Drake, was born in the U.S. Naval Hospital on the island of Guam, July 28, 1985.

The marriage, according to our son, was happy at the outset, and Miyoko was a caring, loving wife and mother. Then, some years later in the spring of 1987, while this family of three were residing on the outskirts of the picturesque city of San Diego, something transformed Miyoko's thought processes. From that time on, this marriage was fraught with turbulence — within a short time thereafter — destined to fail.

"That singing of yours woke me right up," the wife states now as she repositions her car seat. "Why don't we listen to the Japanese language tape I bought last week?"

"Okay…since you don't appreciate good music, here goes!"

"Funny," muses Carolyn, "the label on this says *Japanese At A Glance*. Since when does one *glance* with the ears?"

"By the same method you just gave a *passing* glance to

your husband's singing, dear."

The tape commences: "Japanese pronunciation is relatively simple, especially for English speakers. Although there are regional dialects, most people will understand the standard (Tokyo) dialect presented here. Good morning (pause) *"O-HAHyoh goh ZAH-ee-mahs* (pause)."

"*O-HAH-yoh* · gimme a bowl of mush."

"Quit that, Tom! *Shush....you're* mixing me up."

The tape proceeds with frequently used expressions, then some questions and question words. The speakers are, alternatively, male and female.

When the tape arrives at a section for the introduction of cardinal numbers, Carolyn is suitably bored by the counting procedure. After reaching "twenty-seven" (pause) *"NEE jooshe CHEE,"* Carolyn breaks off to query, "Wasn't David twenty-seven when he met us in Tokyo our very first trip to Japan?"

"Twenty-seven and single — and I wish he'd stayed that way until he met the right girl."

Carolyn rests now with her almond eyes closed as the tape rolls right along. By now, it has reached the numeral 90: "Ninety." (pause) *"KYOO joo."*

It was easy to tune this thing out mentally and reflect on the past...

...yes, it *has* been eleven years since our son David greeted us on June 30, 1983, at Tokyo's Narita Airport. He'd become adept at maneuvering his car over there, and drove us safely to his tiny apartment near where he worked then, as now — a sprawling naval air base called *Atsugi,* sandwiched between the sprawling metropolises of Tokyo and Yokohama.

Carolyn and I were introduced to David's steady girlfriend, a slightly built lady his same age, named Miyoko. She seemed nice enough and, little did we realize then, that this lady would bring so much grief to bear upon our lives here in

America.

"One-hundred" (pause) "*hyah-KOO.*" At this juncture, my wife ejects the tape. "Tom," she asks, "do you recall that we had definite hints that something was a bit off balance with Miyoko's personality from the outset?"

"Yeah, honey...remember how she pouted when David didn't ask her to join the three of us during a week-long vacation to southern Japan to visit your dad's relatives? After all, they weren't married then, so her attitude was uncalled for."

"I wasn't thinking of that in particular, Tom. My concern was how strangely reticent she was, scarcely speaking a word in our presence. She always seemed such an inward-looking lady."

"Introvertish she was, babe, but at least her smile seemed pleasant. And we've discussed before how, at David's apartment, she would spend interminable hours reclusively perusing stacks of shopping catalogues. Remember?"

Some of Miyoko's traits were an enigma before, and continued to baffle us later on, during their marriage. Not once during a long span of years spent in the U.S. did she ever call us by our names — and never addressed us as "Dad" or "Mom."

This had always puzzled Carolyn and me, especially since we had hosted a number of Japanese exchange students in our home, who were quick to fix us with a 'Mom" or 'Dad' designation (then, upon returning to their homes in Japan, they would write us — employing the salutory greeting: "Dear American Dad and Mom").

It is an overcast and windy day, this eighth of May; yet no rain falls to spoil a grand picnic in the company of our daughter and family in San Jose. This is a real Mother's Day treat for Carolyn — and a bonus for this fortunate hubby to join in, as we revel in precious moments spent with two adorable grandsons and a princess of a granddaughter.

"What better way to spend Mother's Day," opines Carolyn

at the end of a picnic shared with son-in-law Larry's parents (who drove up from Salinas as we drove south from Paradise). The barbecue and accompanying dishes were superlative, even though this writer's horseshoes and table-tennis play were not.

Before retiring, Carolyn and I look at family photographs displayed on the wall, and spot granddaughter Monica in several of them. "Too bad she and David weren't here for that glorious picnic, honey," Carolyn sighs. "It would have been a special 'icing on the cake' for this Mother's Day."

Our daughter overhears this remark from the kitchen, where she is administering the finishing touches to cleaning the tiled countertops. "Are you guys fairly assured of seeing Monica in Japan?"

"Only time will tell, Andrea," her dad responds. "David hasn't. *But it will truly break our hearts if we don't.*

CHAPTER 11

onday, May 9:

Our daughter and son-in-law both teach intermediate school, so they depart early this morning, and we journey on to spend three long-awaited days in the company of my wife's family (two brothers, two sisters and her widowed mother), all of whom reside in the Los Angeles area.

That distance will take us the better part of seven hours. Carolyn and I are concerned that repairs are still proceeding on the highways and bridges ripped asunder by a terrible earthquake some months before. In fact, we will drive very near the epicenter of that quake to reach Mom Matsuda's home near Culver City, just off the Santa Monica Freeway, an area dealt severe blows by these unpredictable spasms of the earth.

Having watched a late movie on television last night, Carolyn's eyes are heavy and she sleeps soundly at my side. After a snooze of several hours, she awakens as we make tracks along this straight-as-an-arrow, unscenic stretch of the I-5 freeway. "Where are we, Tom? How long did I sleep?"

"Practically since we left Andrea's, honey. We're about ready to head up the 'grapevine' and see some hills instead of this blamed flat and featureless country."

"Oh my, I'm sleepy," dear Carolyn yawns, ready to resume her slumber.

"Ain't misbehavin' - I'm saving my love for youuuuu...."

"If you're going to sing, Tom, I'll insert that Japanese language tape again."

But in no time, this teasing spouse drifts off to leave me thinking about things incidental to the quest of these grandparents to see a granddaughter who dwells on the opposite shore of this Pacific Ocean (although its salt water washes both coasts, it's still an incomprehensible bridge of ocean)....

The reader will recall that Monica's mother abstained from the practice of greeting Carolyn or me by name — yet what a *shocking* greeting lay in store for us when Miyoko phoned from her San Diego condo one July day in 1989!

I was working then in the real estate business, and Carolyn was taking her turn running an antique shop co-op. We returned home to find a loud screaming and sobbing Miyoko on the telephone answering service.

We were aware that David had flown to Norfolk, Virginia, to undergo some technical training for two weeks. Yet, here was Miyoko, screaming on the telephone that David had left her for 'no telling where,' and asking that we phone her right away, as she wanted to bring Monica to our home and talk with us.

Carolyn phoned Miyoko and found her in near hysterics, so I phoned in reservations for mother and daughter to take a plane from San Diego to Sacramento. We fortunately knew of a neighbor of theirs, and Carolyn reached him by phone. This kind fellow was willing to do the favor of driving Miyoko and Monica to the airport.

Early the following day, I drove one hundred miles south to the Sacramento Airport to greet them. I was happy to see Monica her usual, bubbly self — seemingly unaffected by her mother's disturbed mindset — thank God.

While driving north, I tried to calm and placate my daughter-in-law. "The nature of David's present position takes him away from home on occasional trips of no more than two week's duration," I explained, "and those trips are generally shorter when his tasks accrue to naval facilities in California."

"I am sorry. I don't know why . . . I just thought something wrong. Something very wrong," Miyoko responded.

Then, when she closed her eyes, I thought, *Oh, good...perhaps she will settle down now and cease acting so pitifully upset.*

Four-year-old Monica's eyes were alert and anxious, and I tried to distract their anxieties by singing a nursery rhyme to Monica. This dear hadn't had much of a chance to focus on things childlike, so I served up one of her favorites: "The Itsy-Bitsy Spider."

"The itsy-bitsy spider climbed up the water spout..."

"Wait, Grandpa. I sing with you."

Monica gleefully joined in to make it a soprano-baritone duet while her mother sat, unsmiling and transfixed, with arms folded across her bosom. She seemed to be searching for the right words to express her thoughts, and finally interjected, "Maybe I wrong about things. I think we go home now."

That said, Miyoko started to open the car door while I was driving on Highway 70 just south of Marysville! Needless to say, that action startled me no end, and I was glad to quickly observe that the car doors were locked from within!

Upon reaching home, it was readily discernible to Carolyn that Miyoko's mental state was anything but healthy. Miyoko didn't sleep that night (although she and Monica were provided comfortable pillows to share a large bed with Carolyn), and instead, constantly paced the floor like a caged animal. Indeed, her strange behavior appeared that she dare not close her eyes this night or some dreadful creature would materialize!

Several times Carolyn took her arms to gently lead Miyoko back to bed while reassuring, "There's nothing to be frightened of. As you know, I have phoned David to ask that he get an okay to leave Norfolk and come here quickly, as you seem very ill."

My wife slipped into the living room after one of these missions, to whisper: "Tom. What's to be done? Miyoko's arms are so rigid, and her face so agitated, it's frightening!"

"Are we almost there, Tom?"

"Yikes, Carolyn — you startled me! I didn't realize you were awake. I was lost in a sea of thought while you dozed — reminiscing of that time I drove south for a different reason."

Although my beloved looks her alert self, that statement confuses her, so she inquires, "What trip south, Tom? I don't understand."

"That journey I made to the Sacramento Airport to pick up Miyoko and Monica while David was away at Norfolk."

"I get you now. She left us a startling message on our answering machine, requesting an emergency visit with us. And what a dreadful series of episodes followed!"

"How true. Miyoko's actions were inexplicable. You and I know precious little about aberrant states of mind. As educators, we've undertaken courses in child psychology, but the awfulness of that nightmare in progress called for the services of a physician or — better yet — a psychiatrist!"

My wife is fully awake, and adds, "How awful it is to remember Miyoko pacing the floor of our house and peering out the windows, expecting some hobgoblin or Frankenstein monster to grab her. That girl's face was a mask of fear and uncertainty, for sure."

"She seemed to be hallucinating that some varmint — what did you call it — a 'hobgobollin' was out to get her, honey. God only knows what Miyoko was thinking then. But something was radically out of kilter, and those were dark days for the two of us."

"You've forgotten Monica, Tom. I will always be concerned, yet hopeful, that Monica will grow up without her mother's sick behavior affecting her."

"Let's hope that the grandparents Monica stays with in Japan are capable of providing a pleasant and worry-free environment," I add.

"And. . .that whatever paranoia Miyoko suffers has been cured. Well dear, I see we've almost reached my mom's house. How nice her front yard looks."

"Yup. Mom Matsuda will be peering out the window to look for her hobgoblin daughter and her Frankenstein monster son-in-law to arrive and kill the engine."

With the engine 'killed' and the parking brake set, Carolyn and I embrace this alert lady of eighty-four years, beaming at us now....

CHAPTER III

There are too many episodes of interim stopoffs in this diary to include. It would be folly to parade these relatives through the pages here, so the real focus will be on one particular relative — a granddaughter — and secondarily, to share the hazards and joys of travel in Japan. Permit me now a few asides which, indirectly, keep to the topic.

First of all, not all these relatives have been good and kind. Take my brother-in-law Jim, from the city of Torrance, for instance. He had the unmitigated gall to suggest, "Tom, the tickets for your flight to Japan must have been heavily discounted. I note that your arrival date in Tokyo is on Friday the thirteenth, the universal bad luck day."

Perhaps that remark smarts simply because there is some truth to it. "But Jim," I point out. "Our travel agent booked us for the twelfth of May. Can I help it if the plane crosses the International Date Line somewhere over the Pacific Ocean, and —

voila ala presto — the date mysteriously (and not by *my* design) changes to Friday the thirteenth?!"

At least my Japanese-American mother-in-law doesn't tease me. Rather, she teases that it is, upon our arrival to her home, to be a propitious time to dine together on a platter of sashimi and sushi. Mom knows full well that I dearly love these concoctions, which have caught on with so many Americans now as to be downright pricey. Her sashimi is the freshest tuna available, from a supermarket that caters to the palates of Japanese-Americans in her area. It costs $14.95 per pound, yet this generous and understanding mom knows that, at whatever price, it is unavailable back in my rural hometown of Paradise (for sashimi aficionados, *maguro* (tuna), is truly 'paradise'). "What better way to prepare us for a trip to Japan, Mom?" I thank her.

"I sure hope you and Carolyn get to see Daddy's sister over there, Tom."

'Daddy' was her husband and my pal of many years before he departed our company at age eighty-four, just four springs ago. "Here's to your memory, Pop," is my toast at this table." We miss you. And, hopefully, in a few weeks your daughter and I will manage to see your sister in Japan, still going strong at age ninety-five."

That evening we join other family members and friends at a restaurant. Reservations have been made at a nearby Japanese place for this occasion. A kimono-clad waitress greets us after we are seated at two long tables joined together to accommodate our group. She pours tea and then takes each of our orders in turn, jotting them down in Japanese. While she slips away to the kitchen to apprise the chef of our desires, a second waitress — seeing that the first has neglected to pick up our menus — pauses at my post on the left to inquire if we are ready to order. When l respond in her native language, *"Mou, chuumon shimashita* (we've already ordered)," she does a double-take surprised to hear a Caucasian speaking Japanese in this fashion.

I suppose I should take the time to explain my familiarity with *Nihongo* (Japanese language)....

Upon enrolling at the University of Southern California in September of 1952, I was advised that, to secure a degree there, it would be necessary to include a foreign language in my course curriculum, as I had neglected to take one while in high school. That school in the rural Missouri of my youth offered nothing but Latin, and every kid there knew *full well* that, "Only girls study Latin." Now I come to know, *full well*, that I'd tragically erred in that perception — and must hit the books for four semesters.

Ouch. But what language? I wondered, then asked hopefully, "Would it be okay to take Spanish-I for one semester, Italian-I the next, and finish with a flourish of Portugese-I and French-I the subsequent semesters? I know it will be a tough job to study so many different languages, but I'm willing and able... or, at least *willing*."

Actually, my reasoning was that, by narrowing the playing field to four Romance Languages —each with a beginning semester shot — I'd 'lighten the load,' as it were.

Well, that idea went for naught when I was promptly informed, "You must stick with *one* language, and continue with it for *four* semesters.

"Ach du leiber," I gasped. "Two *years*!?!"

This led me to elect Spanish-I for a thrice-weekly, one hour session. Observing that Japanese-I was offered at night school (or University College as described at USC), I made one of the luckiest moves at this point in my life by signing up for Japanese-I also, taught twice weekly from seven to nine-thirty p.m.

After struggling with Spanish-I, and scraping by with a 'C-' final grade, I decided to drop *Espanol* at semester's end. That blamed class had many students — hence more competition for grades. Marv Goux, the football player in the seat next me in Spanish-I, was even provided with a tutor to help him along the way!

As a member of the Trojan Marching Band, I was to share the same football field as this dude (well, at half time, anyway). But do you think my otherwise able band director, Tommy Walker, had the foresight to provide tutors for *his* 'players'? *Nada es posible* (no way, Jose) — the only phrase remembered from Spanish-I.

Japanese-I, however, was inhabited by a small number of aspirants in that language. The class was comprised mostly of middle-aged, daytime workers, seeking knowledge to increase their business or foreign trade connections. And, because the class was small, the instructor provided more individualized help.

Prospering from those generous doses of help — wonder of wonders — at semester's end, this fledgling student was awarded an 'A' grade. One can readily understand my decision to drop the musical-like *Espanol* for *Nihon-go*. Subsequent semesters saw grades fall (but assuredly not tumble) to a 'B', then a 'B-'. In this way, I'd completed my penance for having skipped foreign languages in high school.

Then, having later married an attractive lady my age (Whittier College's Homecoming Queen of 1952), I was able to maintain some degree of fluency through the years, in that Carolyn was from a Japanese-American family background.

Carolyn and her two sisters and brothers, however, scarcely remember the Spanish and French undertaken in high school. And, having been American born, they had no particular interest in studying to learn Japanese either, since both parents were fluent in English.

Caucasians, I've discovered, can get away with speaking broken Japanese to native speakers. Yet those same Japanese are less tolerant of one of their own race who does likewise. Knowing this, dear Carolyn has been circumspect and hesitant to express herself in Japanese. She does, however, comprehend much of what is spoken — indeed, more so than a husband who has made it a study.

Her mom and dad have enjoyed my frequent banterings in their second language, and laugh heartily when I abuse it — such as when I say I must 'launder' my hands before dining, instead of employing the proper word for 'wash'.

Concerning the Japanese language: It is of interest to note that Japanese people assiduously appropriate English words into Japanese. It confounds the imagination to understand why they embrace and employ so many of our words when, in truth, they have perfectly adequate words for those nouns, verbs or adjectives in Japanese! They are insatiable importers of these so-called 'loan words,' and there are literally hundreds of them. But the subsequent distortion of their pronunciation, under the constraints of the Japanese phonetic system, makes for a wonderment of English loan words such as *besuto* (best), *besuto-ten* (best ten) and *besutoseraa* (best seller)! And while I single out this aspect of language as being strangely amusing, it is not in the same league as the diabolical kind of strangeness which came over our former daughter-in-law from Japan....

Up to this point, I have managed to spare my sisters an account of those behavioral changes of Miyoko preceding the divorce from son, David. We live miles apart, so visits with Kay and Ginny are infrequent. Not so Carolyn's younger sis, Jeanne; and now the topic of Miyoko arises, particularly as it relates to Monica being yanked out of school in San Diego and taken to Japan. The child's American family, like Aunt Jeanne, had no foreknowledge that her mother would stoop to such measures. "We were of the opinion that it was mutually agreed for Monica to remain in the U.S.," Carolyn reminisces.

"You have had some restless nights over that," Jeanne tells her sister in recollection of this. "How deceitful!"

"Yes, but nowhere near the restless nights we both had when Miyoko went absolutely bonkers two of the three nights she spent with us," I interject. "With David back, the third night was reasonably calm, and we were able to catch up on some needed sleep. But, oh, that second night!"

"Miyoko, as on the first night, periodically arose from bed to pace the floor," Carolyn picks up the threads. "The outside door and patio doors were double-locked, to prevent another calamity, such as when this sick lady launched herself at a paving contractor across the street in the crazy notion that he was her husband."

"Or a veritable disaster if Miyoko were to leave by the patio deck sliding doors, as that deck sits so high off the ground below," I add. "And that night, as before, from a living room couch 'bed,' I felt like some woebegone sentry serving compulsory duty when sleep was a preferred choice. But dear little Monica at least seemed to sleep well, and she was eating heartily of her grandmother's home cooking."

"And, Jeanne, Tom and I were to learn some months later that the poor child was nearly starved by the reclusive inaction of her mother to prepare anything for either of them!" Carolyn continues. "Miyoko was undergoing another period of sporadic depression even though, reportedly, she had surmounted this, following several weeks of hospitalization and prescription drugs."

"In fact, David felt things were going well enough for him to drive to a naval air facility near Fresno to teach a computer training class," I add, "but that was a mistake."

"Why? What happened? I don't remember hearing that part," quizzes Jeanne, while working on some handicraft items (which is her hobby), but listening intently to our discourse.

"Alarmed that Monica had not appeared in her daughter's

kindergarten class for several days, a kind neighbor in Dave and Miyoko's condo complex paid a visit to Miyoko to inquire of Monica," I explain, "and it was fortuitous that this neighbor and Miyoko both spoke and understood Japanese. She sensed something was wrong, and returned with a gift of food for them."

"I don't know if it was helpful that Mrs. Kayanuma spoke Japanese, Tom. Remember what Monica was to later tell her dad?"

"Oh, good grief, yes. After classmate, Sayuri, left with her mother, would you believe Miyoko threw the food away! Monica reported that her mom said it was poisoned!"

"What a terrible state she must have been in to think that of a lady Tom and I met the previous December at a school program put on for the children's family members."

"Carolyn and I thought it deplorable for Monica to hear such weird tales from her mother. God knows what else that poor child heard."

"Anyway," Carolyn concluded, "the next time we visited in San Diego we met this neighbor and thanked her for her thoughtfulness and gave little Sayuri a gift."

"I only hope you two will be able to visit Monica and check on her welfare," Jeanne remarks while putting her sewing things away for the evening. "C'mon Gussie and Koala (the family cats), let's go upstairs to bed."

CHAPTER IV

Patient reader, if you're still there, I do apologize for having left you stranded at a Japanese restaurant in Los Angeles to stray other paths — some distant others of recent vintage.

If you'll allow, I'd like to return. Not because the food was so special (it wasn't), but the place had an interesting machine, which took up so much space along the rear wall that one couldn't help noticing. It's called a *karaoke,* and for those of you who live so far back in the 'boonies' (like this writer) that you have not heard of this unusual fad imported from Japan, I will enlighten:

For starters, *karaoke* is a device that is compatible with establishments where alcoholic beverages are dispensed. You are not likely to find one reposing in a coffee or ice cream shop. The *karaoke aficionado* — when suitably bolstered by his or her favorite hooch — is given a microphone to sing along to whatever instrumental number is selected from a menu of offerings. The mike is connected to an amplifier/speaker system, and a large TV screen displays the lyrics of the song, highlighting each word as it progresses. This facilitates one's ability to synchronize words and orchestral accompaniment. Thus aided by the *karaoke*, even the most ungifted vocalist becomes a star (and, if not careful, a *falling* star).

Please forgive again, as I promised to keep to the subject of Japan. Yet here I am on a Tokyo-bound airplane, singling out two episodes in this diary that drift from the topic but bear on such fundamental changes in our American scene as to, I hope, be worthy of your interest.

My wife's mother has been a baby-sitter to little ones for a number of years, and maintains that this keeps her young. I think it must be true for she *is* still young at eighty-four, both in mind and spirit.

So as the sun comes up, Mom's doorbell rings, and a sleepy tot is ushered inside to be gently tucked away on one of the living room couches. It is four-year-old Karen, whose parents commute to their Los Angeles workplaces from far-off Lancaster. This involves a one-way trip of one-and-a-half hours — longer if traffic is congested. How sad that this family (or any other, for that matter) must drive so far simply because more remote cities, such as Lancaster, offer affordable housing. How sad that a young child must be rousted from bed for such an early reville.

When Karen wakes, she remembers Carolyn and me from past visits, and says, "Hi, Tom." This casual, American-style informality of children addressing elders by their first names is a shocking aspect of our culture to the Japanese. One's surname is always customary for children to use when addressing their parent's friends. But Carolyn and I like it; and give Karen a welcome hug (which is another affront to Japanese culture, where a bow is the greeting of choice).

One of the books I've packed is *"Jyakku To Mame No Ki,"*

a Japanese version of "Jack and the Beanstalk." I fetch it forth and read to Karen, who sits and listens attentively as I read each sentence in Japanese, then translate it into English.

My mother-in-law is amused, and listens in, ready to correct my accent if necessary, and I thank her. "Mom, this is good practice for what I hope will be a reunion reading session in Japan with eight-year-old Monica."

The *Ki* (pronounced key) in the title, means 'tree,' and I can accept that, as perhaps the Japanese language may lack a separate word for 'stalk,' as in 'beanstalk.' I can't, however, fathom why a *chicken* has been substituted to lay the golden eggs, instead of the magical goose employed for that task in the English version! But sure enough, it's a bird-word of a different color, as is the picture on the back cover of the book I read to Karen.

(Did I just write *back cover*? Well, that is yet another difference of things Japanese; it wasn't an anachronism. You see, Japanese books commence at the back, where ours end, and they end where ours begin. This serves to torment me, especially when I'm actually *in* Japan, with the notion that perhaps I have been doing things backwards all my life, and am just now realizing it!)

Carolyn's sister, Jeanne, was our designated driver to take us to the Los Angeles Airport. This younger sister has been close for years, and spent her last year of high school living with us. She thinks her country-girl, elder sister should have her nails done before departing for Japan, so we embark on a drive to Inglewood, close to the airport, where they each have a manicure, expertly done by a Vietnamese practitioner of that art.

With nothing to read while waiting there for them, I look about and observe several table and floor fans put to work to blow away the potent fumes of nail polish paints and cleaners. But an even more visible sign that there are other threats to one's safety here, are the barred doors and windows. So many of these shops have taken on these prison-like characteristics, they bear mute testimony to the fact that Los Angeles and its environs are fearful, crime-ridden areas, fraught with potential danger.

My wife displays her fingers to me as I sit on a couch with a newspaper in hand. But since it's printed in Vietnamese, this is a hopeless cause. "He does good work, Tom. I told him to move to our town, and he replied: 'Sounds like good place. But if I leave here, your sister get angry'"

Jeanne turns to Carolyn, and comments: "That's right Carolyn. Don't you try and steal Tien from me the way Miyoko stole Monica."

After a long, reflective pause, Jeanne looks deeply in her sister's eyes and tells her for the umpteenth time: "Gosh, Carolyn, I hope you and Tom get to see that granddaughter in Japan."

CHAPTER V

hursday, May 12: Out over the broad, blue Pacific:

As our jumbo jet soars swiftly with the sun, we experience no nightfall whatsoever on this twelfth day of May. While in flight we cross the aforementioned International Date Line and bid *sayonara* to Thursday, the 12th - to bid fair (we hope) to Friday the 13th.

Our flight was delayed by three-quarters of an hour, and a neighbor across the aisle is disgruntled. She says to us in heavily accented English, "My family meeting me Tokyo to take me Yokohama must wait long. *Dah-May* (Nuts!)!"

Carolyn and I think *dah-may* also, knowing that our son will suffer a long wait due to this delay. We are glad Isabel and the baby don't await; considering the bulk of our luggage, there isn't room in a small car for these dears to greet us at the airport.

"Tom, I brought along some photo albums filled with pictures of Monica's summer sojourn with us. Even if we don't find her, it will be good to share these with friends and relatives. Two of our former exchange students got to know Monica, you know."

"You mean Takanori one summer, and Tomomi another, don't you? Dear Tomo was like a little mother to our grand-daughter."

Carolyn then went on to animatedly recall the time a photographer from our *Paradise Post* newspaper happened upon Monica at the tennis courts. "While we played a set of doubles with friends that morning, Monica was hitting a beach ball against the fence with her small racquet."

I laugh, "That photographer was amused at her oversized 'tennis' ball being swatted by her undersized racquet. And how neat it was for friends to clip and save copies of that picture, honey. But that photo and all the others taken of Monica offer scant comfort for the real McCoy."

"What do you mean, exactly?"

"Oh, the reality struck home that we have ample photographic memories. But the fact that she was removed bodily from our family, perhaps against her will, is a hurtful memory — a *dismal* memory!"

This is a tiresomely long airplane flight to Tokyo, and Carolyn now sleeps fitfully while a movie is shown. Although not much of a movie fan, I enjoy the distraction of this film which stars two of my favorite actors — Jack Lemmon and Walter Matthau — and watch to its conclusion.

After the movie, an interesting on-screen display appears, showing our aircraft's location, air speed and estimated time of arrival. It periodically updates information and flickers to different modes. Now, I perceive a map of Japan with an asterisk popping on and off alongside the name *Hakodate*, a city on the northernmost Japanese Island of Hokkaido. I'm at a loss to explain this, unless it is to reassure us that this aircraft can seek to land there, if unable to make Tokyo on (gulp, gasp) Friday *the 13th.*

In any event, the display drew my attention away from more reflection of what occurred when our family first had strong misgivings that a daughter-in-law from the country we are about to enter, was not of sound mind — and the marriage to our son crashed.

"What crashed?" asks my wife with a start!

"Oh, nothing, honey. I must have mumbled something aloud. I'm sorry. But it is good to see you awake. We're about ready to land. Look out the window and observe the largest city in all Japan."

CHAPTER VI

Friday, May 13 — Day one in Japan:
 Customs clearance is a relative breeze. Never have I seen more uniformed employees in an airport, with help (English-speaking!) at virtually every corner. The Los Angeles Airport by way of contrast, is a sterile wilderness where that facility's employee availability is concerned. "So this is how these ingenuous people have solved the problem of unemployment in Japan," I muse to Carolyn.

It's so good to meet and greet our faithful son David with unabashed American hugs. He looks great, and is anxious, after his long wait here, to hit the road. As his mother and I have no yen money yet, David pays the parking fee.

Carolyn is extended the honor of sitting next to her son at the left front of the car while he wends his way out to the main highway heading south. *What's she doing sitting on the left* (you may ask)? Well, just as with Japanese books, everything is reversed-opposite here.

37

This particular driver-passenger, seat reversal induces some consternation in dad from the rear seat. Slouched comfortably against a handbag 'pillow,' I am momentarily startled to look between the front seats and puzzle: *Holy Smokes! What is my wife doing driving in Japan — and passing cars from the right side, yet?!*

I am roused to sit straight up, and see the straight of things. "What a crazy notion your dad just had, Son. While resting, I thought your mother was at the wheel. I must have been half asleep. Let's see...the steering wheel is on the right; the driver is on the right; one passes on the right. Am *I* right?"

You'll just have to relax and adjust over here, Tom, I tell myself, then puzzle to my wife and son, "I wonder if the locals commence eating their meals with dessert?" It's too much to sort out. This reverse order of things, combined with losing the whole night of May 12th boggles my mind.

So I drop it, and affect a super-talkative stance with dear and faithful son, attempting to summarize a year's worth of happenings since we last met. But this doesn't pan out any better. "Ease up, Tom," Carolyn justly cautions. "Dave needs to concentrate on finding the way."

Indeed, we are nearing one of the world's largest metropolises, and our super-highway has become super-congested to a point where driving is a tortuous business. The toll fees for using this highway are tortuous, too, amounting to a yen equivalent of $25 — $50 for son's roundtrip this day!

But his mother and I are assuredly grateful for being chauffeured, and will be only to happy to reimburse him. And what if these highways *aren't* free, as in California? At least these Japanese highways are free of the horrendous crimes occurring daily on those roads, where drive-by shootings and car highjackings are sadly omnipresent!

Our adorable daughter-in-law, Isabel, and one-year-old Kirby greet us at the door while David muscles our luggage into what his parents observe to be a commodious, two-bedroom apartment. The greeting we get from the downstairs neighbor's dog is not a welcoming one; she sets up quite a howl at these strangers who deign to invade her premises.

Dear little babe, Kirby, makes up to us easily. She responds with giggles at her grandpa's silly antics. I also introduce the *lah-dah-dah-dah* melody employed back through many years when greeting her father and his sister. And now, it continues to serve as a catalyst to enlist the attention of grandkids such as this dear little one-year-old.

Carolyn and I have eaten such quantities of food on the plane that we disdain the sight of any more. "My guess is that the flight crew outdid themselves for running late," I surmise.

David leaves for a nearby McDonald's to bring home a take-out of burgers and fries. It is obvious from the way Kirby relishes those french fries that this perky grandchild has already become McDonald's-addicted. The golden arch points the way up to heaven for the children of the world, where clown, Ronald McDonald, greets them, instead of ol' St. Peter.

Carolyn managed to sleep well during our flight. Isabel, however, is tired from a long day at the bank. "Fridays are busy days, as the bank stays open longer. I'll put Kirby to bed and say good night. Then you can have some peace and quiet." Izzie says this while giving David a saucy look, and adds, "But my lucky husband started vacation time today."

That left David together with his mom and dad — a propitious time to inquire of Monica. "I haven't had time off to travel to visit her, Mom and Dad. Traveling in Japan is very expensive, as you're going to find. Train tickets eat up a lot of money, as does the cost of dining and lodging."

"Yes, but what about telephoning?" his mother asks.

"I've tried that a few times, but Miyoko and her parents — where Monica lives — have apparently instructed her to speak only Japanese. She giggles on the phone and tells me the fib that she's forgotten English. That child has been brainwashed in more ways than one."

"That's rotten to the core, Son. Remember that pane of glass Miyoko kicked in at our front entry?" I ask, in recollection of some bizarre behavior exhibited by his ex-wife. "Well, I finally took the door down several weeks ago, and had it fitted with plasticized glass. It's an antique door, you see, and since the glass man couldn't sleeve in a small piece of glass framed by solder, he bent a piece of plastic. It looks like a regular pane of glass there at the bottom of the door."

"Yeah. My ex was a *pane* all right," David puns, and yawns, "I'm getting sleepy. There are some photo albums to the right of the couch you might enjoy thumbing through. Good night, all."

"The poor guy is uncomfortable talking about Monica," Carolyn suggests as our son closes the bathroom door. "It's so sad he's up against an unyielding rock named Miyoko."

My night owl wife is wide awake, and she proceeds to look at photographs, while I kiss her good night to conk out in the guest room next to Kirby's. I hope her grandpa's snores won't cause the poor dear to dream that she is watching "Wild Animal World" on the television . . . .

But before Grandpa drifts off, he harks back in time to the scene where the glass entry door just alluded to was first shattered. That occurred the second day of Miyoko's stay at our home while awaiting David's return from Norfolk....

I left for my real estate office feeling haggard from the loss of sleep resultant from Miyoko's alarms. She continuously paced the floor, peering out of the windows with hallucinogenic visions of some kind or other. That restless behavior had taken its toll on Carolyn and me. But this was minor compared with what was to transpire the next day.

A home was under construction across from ours. When Miyoko saw a worker engaged in paving the driveway she took off on a dead run across the street, right through a section of damp concrete that the worker was spraying with a water hose to obtain an aggregate finish!

Carolyn quickly followed to catch up and try to lead Miyoko home. "It was all I could do to hold my daughter-in-law by the arm to guide her away from that bewildered man," Carolyn was to apprise me later. "For one so slightly built, Miyoko is surprisingly strong," she added in an account of this astonishing happening. "Tom, that poor, deluded lady was convinced the cement worker was her *husband*!! You should have seen her strain and tug at my arm, all the while raging, 'No, no, no - I want go back see my husband!'"

With great difficulty, Carolyn managed to steer her to our entry door. Miyoko balked there like a recalcitrant horse and tried to bolt back up the driveway! When Carolyn sought to prevent an embarrassing, return encounter with the paving contractor, a frenzied kick of Miyoko's shoe broke a pane of glass on our front door.

Further struggle resulted in another swift kick, this time to shatter a glass pane in an antique cabinet situated just inside the entry. The first chance Carolyn could manage, under these hysterical conditions, she phoned my real estate office to inform me, "Tom, this is urgent. You have to help me. I was able to reach our son by phone at Norfolk — but there is no way for David to reach us until tomorrow. And his wife is raising absolute havoc!"

Both of my wife's statements were unfortunately true. David must fly to Sacramento and get a rental car — and Miyoko's behavior pattern was fast evolving from strange to bizarre! But, having heard this distressing news, I quickly phoned a close neighbor to take him into my confidence.

"It's embarrassing to tell you this, Casey, but Carolyn needs your help until I can break away from the office. Our daughter-in-law has come to visit, and must be having a nervous breakdown. As soon as a colleague is rounded up to assist here at N.C.P., I'll scoot right home."

After enlisting the aid of an office standby, I returned to see my wife and neighbor looking on apprehensively while Miyoko ate a bowl of cereal and milk with trembling hands. "You must try to get some food inside you, Miyoko," Carolyn stressed as calmly as possible. "Going without food and sleep is causing you to act in a manner that grievously worries us."

...which is assuredly part of the problem, I think. One cannot go from thin to gaunt and still think clearly.

As a park was nearby my office, offering a quiet and serene setting for a picnic lunch, Carolyn hurriedly prepared and packed one. Our kind neighbor volunteered to accompany us to the park while Carolyn got a needed respite. "I don't know if we can wait for David to get here from Norfolk," she whispered to Casey and me while Miyoko was in the bathroom."

"You're right, babe. Our next step, if matters degenerate further, is the police — or a hospital."

"*Or both*," my beleaguered wife asserts.

After the picnickers were sequestered at a redwood table in the park —with little Monica delighted at the prospect of play and a picnic lunch — I drove the short distance to my office to make plans for an early departure.

This involved an assist from a fellow realtor, and while I was on the phone, Casey came rushing to the door. My good neighbor is hardly what one would call a 'spring chicken,' so I was concerned to see him looking fatigued and so out of breath.

"Tom!" he exclaimed, "she's taken the baby and run off up the hill in the vicinity of the Lutheran Church. And since she grabbed up the baby, I was hesitant to try to stop her. She's too young and athletic for this old guy to restrain, Tom. What next?!"

I rushed to pick up the phone where the party had been kept on hold. "Get down here fast, Bobby. Roger is out on a call, and I have an emergency. I'll lock the door and hang out the 'Be Back Soon' sign. Thanks, guy — see you."

Determined to leave, no matter what, I didn't wait for an answer, and hurriedly stuffed papers in a briefcase while telling my neighbor, "Poor guy — you don't deserve this. I owe you one — or two — or *three* favors. It's piling up!"

And it was, one-two-three, back to the park. Potato chips had been scattered everywhere when Miyoko abruptly ended what should have been a pleasant picnic under towering pine and fir trees in Paradise. Now I must go in search for this mother whose head is filled with unknown demons. But where? That was the next question. "I'll head on up towards the church, Casey. What a day! I sincerely appreciate your help."

"Good luck, Tom. While you're gone, I'll repack the picnic lunch and playthings in the car. I feel so sorry for that poor child being a party to her mother's erratic behavior."

'Erratic' is too mild an adjective, I muse, while hustling on up the hill. *'Crazy' is the word!* I found a side door open at this quaint old church, and entered to find Miyoko standing in the aisle between pews. Monica was still in her arms, cradled tightly, her little face flushed on this warm day. Miyoko had the attention of a perplexed cleaning woman, whose tasks, like mine, had been disrupted.

"I can't quite make out what the lady is saying," the woman reports. "I thought perhaps she must be a Vietnamese, mixed up in some sort of trouble, and wants to pray here in the church."

"I'm sorry. This is my daughter-in-law and my grandchild," I explain. "She is distraught because her husband has been away, working on the East Coast. We hope she will improve when he returns tomorrow."

Miyoko had been carrying Monica all this time, which was no easy task for someone so slight. "There's no reason why Monica can't walk, Miyoko. You must be tired. Here — I'll take her, if you like..."

With that, Miyoko pulled away abruptly. Fortunately, since she was in a weakened state and Monica was so heavy, she made no further attempts to run off.

I made it home with a disappointed Monica and her sullen mother, then walked our neighbor to the door, thanking him again for his help in this emergency. "What's wrong with that woman, Tom? I've never seen anything like it. But, listen — if you need any further help, don't hesitate to ask me."

Carolyn's rest period from this ongoing turmoil was thus terminated, and she used all the persuasive powers of the school teacher she is to get Miyoko to calm down. "You will be seeing David tomorrow," appealed my wife. "You must think of your daughter and what your actions are putting her through."

Miyoko countered defiantly, "I always think my daughter! It's her father who not think of her. That the problem!"

CHAPTER VII

aturday, May 14 — Atsugi Base, Japan:
Day two in Japan beckons, and turns out to be a super one. Baby Kirby, sleeps in until almost seven, and we all hop into Dave's Mazda to visit a golf course restaurant, called (what else?) *The Nineteenth Hole. A* breakfast buffet is the featured attraction on Saturdays and, believe you me, it lives up to its billing.

We see youthful and middle-age members of both the U.S. and Japanese military here. One may be seated anywhere, but it is curious to note that the Japanese and their guests sit apart on the far side of this restaurant, and the Americans seem to prefer to be seated with their own group on the opposite side. My guess as to this volunteer segregation is that it's a problem inherent in language communication. Wrong guess, as David, explains, "You see, there's not a lot of camaraderie between the two groups who jointly share this military defense facility."

Small wonder; I've heard it is difficult for Japanese to savvy the American sense of humor. In fact, little emphasis is placed on even *having* a capacity for humor. I read where a poll was taken by a newspaper asking what qualities prospective brides and grooms deem desirable in their mates. 'A sense of humor' failed to even *make* that list! Rather, such qualities as being 'earnest, sincere, and trustworthy' were at the top.

(Contrast that with the American proclivity to espouse a sense of humor as being so desirable that many comedians have achieved wealth beyond measure for theirs. Indeed, one can cite from a litany of many: Bob Hope, Bill Cosby and Jack Benny — the teams of Laurel and Hardy, Martin and Lewis, George Burns and Gracie Allen; and these to name just a few.)

No matter the seating arrangement, we all dine exceedingly well this morning. Our granddaughter, Kirby, has a good appetite for a one-year-old. There is nothing that doesn't seem to please the palate of this infant, whether in the vegetable, poultry, meat or seafood department, and she chows down on everything placed before her.

I learn from my wife that a dear exchange-student friend of ours named Hirokazu phoned last night. He said he'd gotten my letter announcing this visit, but said he'd struck out when he called the telephone number I gave him for our son's Atsugi Base apartment (although it works fine for us to use that number when dialing direct from our home in California). "But for some strange reason," our son explains, "when phoning here in Japan, one must be routed through an exchange at the Yokosuka Naval Air Station many miles away."

Nonetheless, Hirokazu persisted, and got through and spoke with Carolyn, to say he wants to see us, and desires to travel here for a visit today. We eagerly anticipate a reunion with this fine young man we last saw eleven years ago when he was a university student in Tokyo. Hirokazu is now thirty, and for some years has been working close to his home in *Shizuoka.*

David joined in on the phone conversation to provide directions here.

So it was that this neat fellow, accompanied by his shy and quiet girlfriend, Hiromi, arrived at the Main Gate after a two-hour trip in a Toyota Landcruiser. David was surprised to see a vehicle that large, and told us, "Not many of these are seen in this area. The streets outside Atsugi are so narrow that smaller vehicles and motorcycles are preferred."

We enjoyed a long chat and took many photos. Hirokazu had forgotten his camera, but Dave was able to pick up one of the disposable models at the PX (the military Post Exchange — a type of department store that sells almost everything but groceries).

After lunch at the CPO Club, we toured David's office complex, where he works for the Department of Defense, in a library replete with thick repair manuals. His job involves logging computerized data and keeping track of repair and maintenance schedules for various aircraft used by both Japanese and American military at this facility.

We then say good-bye to our Shizuokan friends, and arrange to meet them again when we next speed south on the bullet train. A week from Tuesday is marked on our calendar for the special day when we will have a reunion with the Mori family, a date set in recognition of Hirokazu's day off from work.

CHAPTER VIII

Sunday, May 15 — Atsugi Naval Air Station, Japan:

Light rain is falling as I awaken to greet the morning. I observe this from the sliding door that leads to a small balcony just large enough to accommodate a barbecue, a bag of charcoal and the usual cooking accouterments for barbecuing - a spatula, king-sized fork and the like. There isn't much space for onlookers here in the 'patio;' perhaps three or four could stand shoulder to shoulder at the iron railing set in the concrete deck to prevent a downwards tumble of perhaps fifteen feet.

The cawing of numerous ravens breaks the early morning silence. I don't readily ascertain from their 'conversations' whether they like this rain or not. I assuredly don't, as we had contemplated some tennis later on. Before leaving this lofty perch, I see even loftier buildings in the near distance. Located there are several apartment complexes, perhaps a dozen stories high. As for this apartment we share with son and family, it is a four-plex of two stories — two up, and two down.

Although daylight out, my wife and host family sleep soundly — or almost so — for there are snores emanating from the master bedroom. *This has got to be my son,* I think. *Isabel is an alto, and the perpetrator of this noisy business is obviously a baritone.*

It is a curious thing that daylight comes earlier here than in California; the sun rises at an earlier time and, conversely, disappears from the horizon sooner than there. The old wristwatch reassures me that nothing is amiss (a watch David gifted me with ten years ago when he was a single man with money to spare). A glance at a wall clock, attests that it is, indeed, but five a.m. *Good grief, Charley Brown,* I ponder. *What the deuce are you doing up at this unholy hour — jet lag or not?*

Alerted to the earliness of the morning (despite the daylight outside giving off conflicting signals), I tread softly through the living room into the kitchen, determined to leave undisturbed the peaceful slumber of my compatriots. Tiptoeing about the large kitchen and attached dining room, I make a pot of tea, then get comfortable in a chair to sip and read a magazine I bought yesterday at the base bookstore. The PX, Post Office, Bank, and various shops like the bookstore, are conveniently located in one area here.

The magazine purchase of yesterday, brought to mind other purchases made there eleven years ago, when Carolyn and I made our first trip here. Our son's apartment was very different then, located a mile or so from the base, and quite small. In fact, it was so tiny that this kitchen where I sit reminiscing is as large as that entire apartment. And the patio just described is about the same size as that kitchen. Since there was no room for a washer and dryer, it was necessary to tool over to the base and feed coin-operated machines at the laundromat when the clothes hamper filled up.

Now, we've 'come up in the world,' with an inside washer and dryer, plus a fine daughter-in-law and one-year-old, grandkid with whom to share these commodious appointments with number-one son. *Vive la difference!* Carolyn and I should be so lucky! But, enough of this. I'll soon feel like the characters who invite you to dinner, only to gain a captive audience to sit through several carrousels of film slides of the happy couple waving at the camera from some vacation haunt. Better now, that I move on to describe this strange magazine.

But, before that, permit me to describe the bookstore lady who cashiered there in July of '83, a grumpy, very unaccommodating person, as I recall. But, as just stated, we *have* come up in the world. That lady is no longer present (and I secretly hope she's been transferred to a new assignment in Afghanistan). Her replacement is a kind and courteous lady. For example, when I asked, "Will it be okay to exchange this book on baby care if my son and his wife already have it?" she readily assented, explaining that I only had to return it with the receipt.

Being a skeptical sort of person born in the 'Show Me' State of Missouri, I wonder if this is really a government-hired cashier's good-natured response, or if it has something to do with Bill Clinton's campaign promise to tighten the screws down on all government employees, thus making them more responsible to the taxpayers, so to speak. I decide that issue in favor of this bookstore clerk's common decency and hospitality — traits which cannot be easily mandated and implemented from such a high office.

The water for my tea boils while sorting out this thing, and I peruse a unique magazine called *Mangajin*. That is not a typo as you will see. *Mangajin* is a word made from two Japanese words: *manga*, for the highly popular comic/cartoon books here, and *jin*, meaning people. It strikes me that *Mangajin* has a dual meaning — a play on words, as it were — since it is so similar to the English word 'magazine.' Strangely enough, it is not pub-

lished over here, but is the product of a U.S. publisher in
Marietta, Georgia!

In any event, it a hugely entertaining guide to Japanese
pop culture and language. It is written in English, and contains
a variety of topical subjects, such as one article on *Pachinko*, a
Japanese pinball game. So many are obsessed with it here that I
recently quipped to Carolyn, "This is not only the land of the
Rising Sun; it is also the Land of the Rising Pachinko Parlors."

There are other articles, equally noteworthy, such as an
American's perception of Japanese life-styles and diet, and another author's assessment of the varying degrees of politeness
employed in spoken Japanese. Also included in this issue are
several classic American comic strips, featuring cartoonist, Bill
Watterson's *Calvin and Hobbes*, and Gary Larson's *The Far
Side*.

The various sequences of these American comic strips
have explanatory translations into Japanese. One can thus learn
that, when Calvin lets go with a noisy burp (written as *BU-
URRP!*), it is best translated into its Japanese equivalent expression (made longer, I suppose, for the emphasis of how a *true*
belch should come across in print) as: *Geppu-geppu-geppu!*
This is certainly enlightening in a much different way than my
Japanese professor envisioned back at USC.

The bulk of this thick magazine has English translations
of a number of quite lengthy 'comic book' scenes, depicting
such strangeness that I now perceive them to be tragi-comic.
One, for instance, depicts a poor, bumbling office worker who is
tricked and lured into what he believes will be an encounter on
a park bench with a beautiful lady. Her photo and voice tape
have been provided by a rascally-looking individual, called
warau sayrusman (bad salesman), who arranges this liason. The
poor fool of an office worker drools over the recorded entreaties
of 'his lady,' while he has her snapshot in hand. In a delirium to
meet this beauty, he discovers that the object of his desire is

nothing more than a fake, life-sized doll, which his unscrupulous agent positioned on a park bench in the moonlight. It's a case of sheer *lunar-lunacy*. When my son later sees the pages of these Japanese comics with words of Japanese translated into English, he tells me: "Gee, Dad, this is a different approach to learning Japanese."

Having finished that episode, I hear the sounds of a genuine live doll. Babe Kirby is wide awake, and entreats Grandpa to pick her up. Grandpa is willing, but one whiff tells him how sweet it is that Grandma has awakened to change the little dickens. Soon, the whole family is summoned into the kitchen to sample the fried tortilla and cheese breakfast Isabel prepares. Nothing tastes better (certainly not toast) than soft tortillas fresh from the frying pan.

Intermittent rain has put a damper on plans to put Kirby in her stroller and take her to the tennis courts next door to watch her mom and dad team up against her grandpa and grandma — a sight which guarantees more laughs in the space of an hour than two full weeks for a Wimbledon spectator.

The rain is so misty light and warm, that David asks, "Mom and Dad, what say we hike over to the recreation hall and play some ping-pong? I promise not to beat you too badly." David lies. He trounces us both, and I am nearly exhausted from chasing the ping-pong ball back and forth over this large room, where others are shooting pool.

Our son hasn't even worked up a sweat, and now leads us to a gymnasium outfitted with every type of Nautilus exercise machine imaginable — a virtual torture chamber for one not acclimated to these contraptions designed by the warped mind of a mad scientist! David patiently makes sure that his mom is strapped in one properly while I watch on and reflect, *Do you suppose it possible that he still remembers the agony perpetuated on him by his mother during the birthing process? If so, what a remarkable memory! Is this rascal seeking to get even here?!*

We finally return home, and Kirby seems miffed that we hadn't taken her with us. This baby relishes every opportunity to travel. "But it's wet out, little rug-rat, her Dad tries to explain, "and besides, you would have witnessed the spectacle of your grandpa being mowed down at the ping-pong table."

"Hmmph," I respond to that dig. "You had the home court advantage. So be quiet and start the barbecue. What little rain might blow in your balcony will merely serve to make the chicken smoke and taste all the better."

That forecast came true. The barbecued chicken, basted to perfection, was enjoyed by all. And I couldn't help but reflect how American-like Carolyn's and my lives have been to this point, even though we are residing somewhere between Tokyo and Yokohama. (This is why, dear reader, I haven't included more than one-third of our experiences actually recorded in this diary, for you've undoubtedly spent similar moments yesterday and today, and likely will tomorrow.)

We are anxious to see the other world — outside the Main Gate — and somewhere in that world to find and spend some moments with a lost, but not forgotten granddaughter named Monica Lea Drake.

CHAPTER IX

Monday, May 16 — Atsugi Base, Japan:

I knew it was a mistake to take a long, delicious nap after the large meal that inspired that nap. As a result, here I am, up at 3:00 a.m. studying and writing.

Today is our first opportunity to go with David to secure temporary-residence passes for Atsugi Base. These will enable us to exit and return unescorted by Dave or Izzie — a real plus when they go back to work after their vacation time is over.

It is also our first opportunity to exchange some traveler's checks for American 'greenbacks' and Japanese 'yen-backs' at the bank. These two objectives accomplished, we continue with Dave and Izzie on a drive to Camp Zama, a trip of approximately one-half hour, along narrow streets lined with shops of all descriptions. There is also the constant and worrisome traffic of cars, trucks, pedestrians and bicyclists — with all except the pedestrians maneuvering on the *wrong* side of the street. You couldn't pay me to drive here.

Our mission to Camp Zama, a large U.S. Army base, is to visit and shop at the large post-exchange store located there. The newly-issued identity passes Carolyn and I have look official; still, they don't gain admission here, and we must be escorted by Dave and Isabel.

It turned out to be mostly window-shopping, but we did buy a new battery for the camera, although the clerk who changed it for us ruined most of the film inside (or so we found later at the photo shop at the Atsugi Navy base). Our sharp-eyed son discovered another curiosity when the first photos were developed after replacing the battery; they all bore the date-year, 1985!

"There must be some truth to the Army and Navy being at odds with each other, Son. The army sure did a number on this navy camera you gave your mother."

"No problem, Dad. I'll fix the date by pressing this button with my pen. There — now your future photos will be brought up to date."

"Thanks, Son. Too bad there isn't a recessed button for one to press to set things right with the Army and Navy."

On the return drive home, David took a detour to show us the apartment and neighborhood where he lived when we visited him eleven years ago. Nothing had changed; there were still the same little family-run establishments, and the Farmer's Market on the corner. And —wow — did son's ex-habitat look small!

There is very little rural, open space. All these small towns, each with their own name — *Ebina, Yamato, Sagami,* and on and on — lie side by side without any defined boundary lines, thus blending into one urban mass of dwellings and businesses (not unlike Los Angeles, where Hollywood, Burbank, Monterey Park, Gardena, Torrance, Culver City and countless other entities merge under the L.A. umbrella).

The only difference here is that the streets are so narrow and the shops so tiny, that one has the illusion of traveling about in a small town.

In our small town of Paradise, California, there must be as many as fifteen shops catering to a public who likes to shop for second-hand goods. Most are privately owned. Two that I know of — Hospice and Salvation Army — are non-profit stores. Besides these, there is a lively trade going on continuously with 'garage sales.' The *Paradise Post's* classified ads are filled with these (and Paradise is no different than thousands of other American cities where commerce with an infinite variety of used goods flourishes).

I simply make mention of this now because the Japanese have no such affection for 'recycled' washers, dryers, television and stereo equipment, kitchenware — and the list is endless when one considers what is discarded from one American home only to be resold to another. You are out of luck here in Japan if shopping for used goods is your forte. Of these myriads of shops one encounters while traveling about here, one never sees second hand shops or garage sales.

This helps me better understand our son's first wife, Miyoko. David told his mother, "I know you are being practical and kind when you give Miyoko all kinds of clean, almost-new dresses and sweaters for her, and baby clothes for Monica. Yet, Japanese people seem to disdain anything but brand new merchandise. She was raised to consider it an insult to be given anything used, Mom. So I end up giving your gifts of this kind to our non-Japanese friends — and it breaks my heart knowing that it's quality stuff." This is just one of many cultural differences to ponder.

Incidentally, Carolyn visited the nursery (officially called The Child Development Center), and was impressed with Kirby's 'teacher,' Ms. Ruby. This lady, born and raised in the Phillipines, is very gregarious, and obviously loves little babes of pre-school age. She is assigned five one-year-olds, and treats all as if they were her very own. The 'classroom' is cheerful, and the activities, inside and out, are appealing — so much so to Kirby that, according to her dad, "You should see how eager Kirby is to go to school each weekday morning."

"And how disappointed she is when the weekend arrives and she can't go," chimes in her mother (Kirby's fretting grandparents are relieved to hear these comforting testimonials).

We appreciate that David has scheduled some vacation time this week. Without such a fine and capable driver, and the car he maintains fastidiously, we would be in a bind. The main gate of this facility is quite distant, and the nearest train station we will begin making use of, *Sagami-Otsuka,* is several miles distant.

Our daughter-in-law Isabel is an example of all that is right with humanity; she is outgoing and personable — a fun lady to be around. Izzy likes people and enjoys her job at the bank. I enjoy her wry sense of humor. She now tells me, as we are set to venture forth again, "Gee, Dad, I know you're not that fond of shopping, but you are in for it today! Your son's about to take us all for some more shopping this afternoon to visit every Japanese department store around here — and he knows them *all*. Dave loves to browse in the electronics sections — that man drools over computer stuff — and I have to watch that he doesn't try to buy a lap-top before Christmas."

This lady is a jewel. "Thanks for pointing this out, Izzie. Being forewarned is being forearmed. I will cancel my participation in this shopping business right now."

Which is what I did. "I'll ride as far as the main street with you, Son, then please drop me off. I plan to walk about and observe what changes, if any, have taken place since you brought your mother and me here in 1983. Enjoy your shopping."

I meander down a broad avenue whose sidewalk is lined with dozens of cherry trees. It must have been a magnificent sight to behold them in full bloom last month. There are several anti-quated jet and prop-driven aircraft on display near the main gate. Each bears a plaque in honor of these old 'bird's' achievements when serving as mainstays of the U.S. Fleet in bygone days.

And, as I come upon a large *torii* gate, the top of which reminds of a sway-back horse, it called to mind another plaque. It was here, underneath the *torii* gate, that a staff photographer from the Atsugi Military Newspaper posed David with parents who were on hand then. Number-one son was being honored as the 'Sailor of the Quarter.' Then, with proud parents looking on, a photo was taken of the Commander of Air Fleet WestPac presenting David with an impressive plaque of wood and bronze. These two photos appeared in the base newspaper.

The main purpose of this facility is to maintain and fly fleets of patrol planes and helicopters, as well as serve as a home base to the flight and support staff of a large aircraft carrier, when porting at Yokusuka between sea duty.

I then retraced my steps to the familiar bookstore, where I browsed a long while, eventually purchasing two books. I also splurged on a map booklet, whose price seemed excessive at $6.99, but may come in handy when Carolyn and I set out on our own to travel many miles south.

The weather is pleasant, so I sit outdoors at a circular table with benches located in the center of Atsugi's Americanized 'commercial district.' The PX is to the right, a 7-11-type store dead ahead, and several small shops on the left, one of which catches my eye, because it is a photo shop. "This place will come in handy when we process the rolls of film as they roll off our camera 'assembly line,' I think aloud.

Without Dave's and Izzie's presence to sign me in the PX — a building off-limits to this civilian — I gaze about elsewhere. The McDonald's just across the street offers carte-blanche admission, but I dislike the idea of going there, and am content to sit here a spell and read.

While engrossed in an interesting book by Dr. H. Kindaichi, one of Japan's most famous linguists, entitled *The Japanese Language*, my attention is momentarily distracted by several little tots of Granddaughter Monica's age who amuse themselves while munching on their takeout burgers and fries. I focus on their actions, and become immediately lost in a reverie of wondering what she might be doing this day at a home somewhere to the south in a town called *Suzuka*.

I'm unable to locate *Suzuka* on the map I just purchased. *This nation is so congested with cities and towns that, apparently, only the larger place names are noted*, I think, and put away map and books to take another walk to survey other sights this clear and sunny day, so much more humid than I'm used to back home. A bowling alley comes into view, with a sign at its open door spelling out a warning in both English and Japanese: 'Be Cautious — Wet Floor.' An Oriental cleaning lady is busy with mop and bucket. It's of note that all the workers laboring with the ongoing maintenance of streets and buildings, as this person toiling at the bowling alley, are all Japanese. The picture one has of American GI's catching all the unlucky laboring details, isn't reality hereabouts.

Warned off from a look at the bowling establishment, I turn the corner and come upon the C.P.O Club where we lunched Saturday with our guests from Shizuoka, Hirokazu and Hiromi. Not being particularly hungry, I give the dining area a wide berth, where waitresses not busy at the moment sit and chat at a table along the far wall. A swinging door leads from the dining room to a spacious bar area visible thru the window.

I enter this door to see a regulation pool table, a dart board area and a wall of gambling machines. Las Vegas-style 'one-armed bandits' are legal at U.S. military stations abroad. Inasmuch as they only take nickels and quarters, they are not placed here to accommodate big spenders, as in Nevada casinos.

These 'bandits' entice merely to empty one's pockets in

dribbling amounts. So I dribble in the pocket change left over from my bookstore purchases, and these few nickels and quarters are consumed without reward, lights flashing on and off in a seeming frenzy to invite me to keep on feeding these machines of insatiable appetite!

"The heck with you greedy things," I snarl at these *bandidos*. In fact, I make a face at the whole wall of the 'hold-up artists,' and saunter over to the bar in expectation of getting something tangible for my money there.

I'll be hornswoggled if the short, white-aproned Filipino guy behind the bar isn't making a face at me. He leans over, face changing from a half-scowl to a grin, and whispers behind a cupped hand, "Listen, podner, if you don't remove your cap in here, you'll have to buy the bar a drink."

"Oh sure, of course," I reply, pretending that I might be forgetful. But heaven forbid that I let this dude, who introduces himself as Nick, think me some greenhorn fresh out of Bootcamp! I'm twice his age, and a Korean Vet, to boot. I doff the offending cap and smooth out my white hair, then tell Nick, with the haughtiest of airs, "What say you slide me a mug of draught beer, pal."

"You're outta luck," Nick responds, giving me that I-know-a-greenhorn-when-I- see-one look of his again. "We serve bottles or cans here; care for a bottle of Budweiser?"

I nod yes, polish off that bottle and order one more for good measure. But that was it! *No genuine draught beer — no more patronage at this joint,* think I (and, what the heck if it *is* reserved for CPO ratings and above!). *Shucks,* I feel like telling this barkeep, *anyone and his mother can drink bottles of beer right out of their own refrigerator. So why bother come here to your honky-tonk joint?* But I took pity on Nick and didn't say anything. Besides, this fellow was too busy with other customers down at the end of the counter to notice if I had. Without so much as a good-bye, I put my cap on before leaving — merely to show who's boss! Sauntering casually out of the swinging door, the danged thing rebounds and almost slams this customer up against the popcorn machine!

The walk home was refreshing, but longer than I bargained for; I got lost and ended up out by the golf course, before stopping to ask for directions. *Well, by this time, David must be home with the family,* I hope, while finding the trail.

Carolyn returned home from shopping with ingredients which she wove into a tasty lasagna dish. We're all smiles — well, not *all*. Kirby is cross, and from her highchair vantage point, looks askance and surly at her gramp's head (she seems to be scowling at the cap he wears at the table).

What a day! Some cowboys sleep with their boots on, it is reputed. Well, listen up podner —this one went to bed this evening with his *cap* on, not bedeviled in the least by Nick the bartender's admonitions (or the grandkid's; lacking Nick's ability with words, the rascal nonetheless scolds Gramps with the most amazing and accusatory face!).

I surrender, and toss the ol' cap in the kid's playpen.

CHAPTER X

Tuesday, May 17, Atsugi Base, Japan:

Wide awake at 3:00 a.m. My internal clock is out of synch — and no wonder. By the process of counting back seven hours it is possible to figure out what the time is in California, and I deduce that it is 8:00 p.m. there. *No wonder I'm wide awake*, but I dare not mention this business to number one son when he awakens. I know what that boy's salty response will likely be — probably, something like, "Well, Dad, you're the only one with this problem, so, I guess the rest of us are gonna have to fix *your* clock."

Ah, well, so be it. The book store purchases will provide a suitable diversion to spend these moments of solitude. What solitude? Kirby starts up a howl and Isabel bounces out of bed to almost knock me down as she sails into the kitchen to fetch Baby a bottle. The wailing from the next room ceases as soon as that bottle is inserted in the wee one's wee mouth. I peek in at her and the smell of wee-wee assaults the olfactory senses, so I scurry back to my books and cup of tea.

I return to Professor Kindaichi's fascinating book, *The Japanese Language*. It has been translated and annotated by Umeyo Hirano. From it, I learn two satirical Japanese poems called *Haiku*. *Haiku* employs but three short lines, each faithful to a prescribed construct: Five syllables for the first line; seven for the second; five in the third.

Haiku writing has caught on with American schoolchildren and is frequently introduced in grade school, at around the 4th or 5th grade. Kids that age shun the effort necessary to produce long compositions as being a tedious exercise, but embrace haiku for its limit of three short lines.

The 'restriction' to only three lines into 5-7-5 syllable sentences is appealing to children. They think, "Hot dog, this is fun writing and easy math," as their #2 lead pencils busily produce a *haiku* (and often two or more). Truly, the Japanese haiku is just the trick for kids with short attention spans.

So, just why is Grandpa turning his attention span to haikus at this early hour? you ask. Well, let's not be sarcastic, dear reader. These are *sophisticated haiku* — just the trick for sophisticated grandpas with short attention spans.

The typical, kid's haiku might go something like this:

My mother is nice (5)
She makes delicious cookies (7)
Sis and I snarf down! (5)

The two entertaining my interest are called *senryuu haiku* (satirical haiku), and I work at committing them to memory, *A piece of cake*, I think, due their brevity. Also, the second sentences of both *haiku* are the same:

Shitsunen to   It sounds better
ieba kikiyoi   To say "lapse of memory"
monowasure.   Rather than "forgetfullness."

Sakkaku to	It sounds better
ieba kikiyoi	To say "an erroneous perception"
kanchigai.	Rather than "a misunderstanding."

It is still very early; no one stirs. The two subject *haikus* have been committed to memory to serve at some later date, perhaps to share with a Japanese friend or acquaintance. It seems a natural inclination for almost all people — be they Japanese, Hungarian, Greek, or Russian — to enjoy another's use of their language. Indeed, I have heard that the French don't merely enjoy, but *demand* their mother tongue be employed. The unfortunate rogue who fails in this gets a one-way ticket to the nearest guillotine, a victim of what they call, their *fait accompli.*

So these tidbits of trivia gleaned from here and there come in handy, you see. The tennis hackers in our group of (mostly) retirees back home repair to a coffee shop after play has ended. There, the latest jokes in circulation are disseminated for that group's amusement. I have heard so many of these, served up with our coffee or tea, that I regret not having written them down as suitable fodder for a second book, to be entitled: *Tennis Court Diary — The Senior Citizens' Best.*

Speaking of tennis, that's precisely what's on the menu this morning. And since the weather report forecasts much warmth and humidity, David, Carolyn and I arrive at the courts at 6:45 a.m., swack balls 'til 8:00, then return home.

But a single bath serves our dwelling here, therefore, being senior (or, truthfully, the one sweating the most), I get the nod for first up in the shower. Then, while Dave and Carolyn clean up, I slip away to visit Kirby's nursery school.

I thought this alert child would be all atwitter to see her gramps, but she is at play on a blue gym mat and continues to focus on that, hardly giving Grandpa more than a passing glance (and that, perhaps, only to note if he has removed his hat indoors in this pre-school room of hers). At any rate, Gramps is *old hat*, any way you slice it, in this little pumpkin's eyes. Yet, as a newcomer to this fraternity of one-year-olds, the other four do break away from their play to give Kirby's grandfather the once-over.

It's an interesting phenomenon that personality-types are established at such a tender age as this. Two little girls are quite forward, toddling over to take the stranger by his hand, but a third girl, kneeling next to Kirby, exhibits reticence. She's content to stay put, and view this stranger from a comfortable distance (if her classmates are so inclined to take it upon themselves to act the role of official greeters, that is *their* business!) and the only other child concerned shies completely away from this stranger in his midst, hanging tightly to the hem of Ms. Ruby's dress, as she admonishes, "It's okay, Joe. This is Kirby's grandfather who visits us." Gramps sits briefly on the mat next to this precious little grandkid. He knows he must soon part company with her, and return home thousands of miles distant to the east.

Re-reading this last line inspires the reaction: *What gives?* Japan *is* the Far East! I must remember to correct the erroneous perception of neighbors in California, who were incorrectly taught that Japan is situated in the Far East. As one who's traveled here from California, I now bear testimony that this country, lies in the Far *West* — and anyone who testifies to the contrary, just plain lies — period!

As promised earlier, numerous contradictions in terms lie in wait to befuddle this hapless sojourner to the East...er...West, and this latest business is just one of them. Anyway, I bid goodbye to Ms. Ruby and her little charges. The two who took my hand at the outset of this visit now act as though they are entitled to leave with me, and I must tell them, "Nothing doing little kids. Ms. Ruby should stand you in the corner for trying to play hooky like this."

Ms. Ruby laughs, and quickly aids in removing these clinging ones to facilitate my retreat. Even my dear Kirby has no such designs, and Joe — absolutely not. He still clings to the security blanket of Ms. Ruby's abundant skirt.

Back at the apartment, Carolyn is anxious to embark on another adventure outside the main gate. David has garnered his mother's undivided attention by offering to introduce her to a multi-storied department store in the neighboring city of Yamato. After being a non-participant in their travels of yesterday, I consent to join in this foray, but must first ask, "Son, have you or Isabel received a phone call or letter from anyone at the U.S. Embassy in Tokyo?"

Son's reply: "Negative, Dad; no calls or letters either. Why?" In response to this query, I produce a copy of a letter sent to Ambassador Walter Mondale, sent because I admire this distinguished man — and also because I've brought something on this trip which, I trust, someone on his staff will find a suitable home for in Japan. That letter, to wit, reads:

April 24, 1994
Dear Ambassador Mondale,
I will be in the Tokyo area from May 14, until the 15th of June, during which time my wife and I will be visiting our son, David, who is in the employ of the Department of Defense at nearby Atsugi Naval Air Base.

The point of this letter is to inform you, sir, that for many years we have had in our possession a set of exceedingly well-preserved and intricately bound books, delineating all of the cartography of 1920 Japan in a set of eleven volumes. These should rightfully be given a place in a museum or library (see photographs enclosed).

As a gesture of goodwill, my wife and I would like to utilize the auspices of your good office to donate these books to a Japanese library or museum (the new Meiji Museum in Tokyo, for instance, may wish to display this collection).

Please advise me at the earliest, via one or your staff mem-
bers, as to your thinking in this matter. This can be done by a
telephone message or letter to my son, whose address and
phone number you will find listed below.
    Yours respectfully,
    Thomas N. Drake

David's phone rang as I finished reading a copy of that letter aloud, and I conjecture, "This is some kind of coincidence. I
bet that's someone from the Embassy now."

Not so. It turns out to be someone from Dave's office, requesting his help in solving some pressing problem. I hear my
son reply in a brusque and brash manner (which he surely
hasn't learned from his 'old man'), "Heck no — I'm on vacation.
You guys are competent to straighten that out." Then he asks
the party on the line to hold a second and turns to us to ask,
"Would you mind waiting in the car while I make a brief stop-
over at my office, Mom and Dad?"

"No problem," I am quick to reply, knowing that our ulti-
mate destination this morning is a shopping expedition.

So, while Carolyn finishes reading a newspaper on the
couch and Dave shaves, I use the phone and manage to get
through to the Embassy, where I am shifted from one secretary
to another, and yet a third. None of them have any knowledge of
my letter to Ambassador at Large, Walter Mondale, who is
larger than life, when one considers that he served as our
nation's Vice President under B̶i̶l̶l̶y̶ *Jimmy* Carter.

It wasn't until I reached home a month later, that I discovered a letter sent me there as follows:

May 17, 1994
Dear Mr. Drake:
Ambassador Mondale has asked me to thank you for your
kind offer to donate your historic Japanese map books to a Japa-

*nese recipient. We are querying libraries and museums, but
have not yet found an appropriate one.*

*Although your proposal is a generous one, it strikes me
that the books would be rarer, and therefore more highly valued, in America. California is in the forefront of Japanese education, and you might find that a high school or university close
to home would be very pleased to receive these books.*

Sincerely,
Arthur Zegelbone
Cultural Attache

Mr. Zegelbone's idea that this collection of books we've
carefully packed and brought with us to Japan, "would be rarer
in America" is strange. And the idea of these books being,
"more highly valued in the U.S." strikes me as equally strange.

In any event, it is now our intention to carry them with us
to Shizuoka when we visit the Mori Family. It was there some
eleven years ago, that Mr. Mori had been kind enough to take
time away from a busy work schedule to introduce Carolyn and
me to the Mayor of Shizuoka. He gave us some nice gifts after
we had tea with him at City Hall, and we hope our books will
find a nice home in one of the libraries or museums of that fair
city.

While driving with David to his office, I tell him of the
change of plans with respect to these books, and ask that he remind me to pack them with the luggage I will take when his
mother and I journey on via the bullet train next week. I also reflect that I must use the larger of two bags to accomplish this,
when I preferred the smaller. *Que sera, sera . . . .*

CHAPTER XI

ednesday, May 18, Atsugi Base, Japan:

The *faux pas* with my phone contact with the Embassy yesterday morning was but one in a series. As the day progressed, nothing seemed to go right. While we drove to Yamato to check out a department store, David kept snaring his mom's attention with such remarks, as, "This is the largest store of its kind around here. It has tons of stuff, including all kinds of grocery items. There is even a movie theatre in the building."

Said building, however, was closed this day, which took us to a 'Plan B' drive to a K-Mart type store with aisles of clothing and things that we didn't need. Carolyn tried on hat after hat while her son and husband looked on, proffering compliments for some, or, "Oh, no, where did you find *that* bowl of fake fruit?" until the poor dear couldn't make up her mind, and moved on to other aisles.

Nothing excited us and, aside from a few postcards purchased, we left empty handed. We were disappointed not to see the store David had raved about, and our faces must have shown it. Number-one son was quick to whet our appetites for a new adventure. "All aboooard. I will now drive you to a terrific sushi bar that Isabel and I love; you won't believe the variety!"

We eagerly went that direction and parked, but wasn't necessary to exit the car to see that it, too, was closed! We ended up back on the base, eating at a canteen catering to Japanese workers there (the ramen noodles were *blah*).

The evening meal barbecued at home caused all to smile, satisfied that this day at least ends well. But what a mistake it was to have napped so soon after dinner. It only made worse my already out-of-synch internal clock — to where it became an 'infernal' clock. By 9:15 my family retired just as I awakened from that nap and, wide awake, I read the newspaper and started in on another book to pass the time.

It was disheartening to recollect that all our dinner had been consumed. The refrigerator was bereft of any leftovers, and my 'hunger clock' began to tick unmercifully. It was useless to contemplate a raid on the 'fridge,' and if McDonalds hadn't shut down for the night I'd have jogged over there to order up something — *anything!*

Yet, by midnight, a welcoming sleep tranquilized a growling stomach into growling snores. But, around 4:00, Kirby's yowls rent the air, and I am wide awake and hungry again. At least I have a temporary ally in Isabel, who is awake to prepare Kirby a bottle. She lends me a sympathetic ear, and suggests, "Well, why don't you have a bowl of cereal, Dad? There's plenty of milk."

"Are you kidding, Izzie? I just dreamt that I was eating shredded wheat, and when I woke up half the mattress was gone!"

Izzie is too sleepy to make any sense of that last remark. She merely yawns and says, "Sorry there's no shredded wheat, but if you look in the cupboard there are other kinds, Dad. Goodnight."

I scout out the postcards bought yesterday and begin to write the folks back home. Six cards bring home the message, each one alike:

Dear___, I'm wide awake at 9:00 p.m. your time — but the heck of it is, it's four in the morning over here and I'm slowly starving to death. Please send a CARE package to this address or you may never hear from me again. Love, Tom

Actually, there is much to be cheerful about. Tomomi, a former exchange student of ours, phoned yesterday in response to our invitation. She reported, "I will come visit with my mother tomorrow at ten o'clock. I will bring my tennis racquet on the train and I want play you if you can please meet us train station where I phone again."

Tomo-chan (*chan* after a name takes the place of the name suffix *san*, when used for young persons and, curiously, the very elderly as well) played tennis with us during two visits to our home in the U.S. — once as a high-schooler, the other while on a semester break from college.

Tomomi is now working long, weary days at a travel agency in Kawasaki, involving long train commutes from her home in Yokohama. Her voice sounded tired on the phone but, nonetheless, this is Wednesday, Tomo-chan's only day off from work, and this 'daughter' needs a break. She wants to play tennis.

It will be good to see this charming, somewhat tomboyish young lady again. Tomo's last letter to us told about a visitor from New Zealand who stayed at her home, as is the custom in Japan and America, to promote visits to learn about each other's cultures and make new friends. "She does not like sightseeing in Japan," Tomomi said in her letter, "because she thinks we must walk so far every day to catch trains."

That bit about walking is certainly valid. If, for no other

reason, Japanese people stay fit, it is as a result of the walking they do — a requisite part of daily life here. The vast majority of Japanese are acculturated to the walking habit. One sees grade school children, their little satchels in hand, walking to and from school. Middle, high, and university teens are seen in large numbers as they walk to and from train stations. One sees no yellow school buses here. The electric trains function as their means of student transportation.

Indeed, the vast majority of the citizenry, young and old, accomplish their travel by train, necessitating long or short hikes, as the case may be, to the train stations. Most stations are either elevated or underground subways, which involves an even more strenuous walk, as it's uphill and downhill. Many of these train station stairways have so many steps that they provide suitable practice for one who pursues the sport of mountain climbing.

America, contrariwise, is an auto-driven culture. Whether to work or play - to the supermarket or church, or a convenience store a short block or two away — Americans must employ their gas-powered vehicles for transport. The scene outside most American high schools, before and after school, is one of school buses belching diesel smoke - or numerous vehicles of those students who disdain the bus as being too *bourgeois* (fit for underclass freshmen or sophomores, perhaps). This fact of life in America will likely continue as long as the price of gasoline is relatively cheap.

Of all the varied commercial enterprises one sees lining the streets and boulevards in Japan, one is not likely to come across the 'fitness centers' that have sprouted up in every town across the American landscape. With the kind of walking Japanese do, who needs a treadmill or stairstepper? The irony of this is — Americans drive to their fitness centers *by car!*

Tomomi phones again to relate that her and her mother's

arrival will be delayed until noon. She phones again from the Sagami Otsuka train station, and David and I drive there, a short distance taking ten minutes. Tomomi is the same buoyant, smiling person we knew, and we meet her mother, Mrs. Sudo, for the first time. She is an attractive, fine featured lady, who appears younger than the forty-eight years her impetuous and guileless daughter reveals as her age. We later learn that her husband died when Tomomi and her younger sister were only seven and five.

Kirby seems delighted to have company as we join in an exchange of pleasantries with our guests, and these friends are so dear that Carolyn doesn't hesitate to communicate in her broken English/Japanese. They've brought a bag of gifts in pretty wrappings, and Kirby thinks it's Christmas all over again. She unwraps a box of cookies, baked special for infants like her, and my resourceful wife, in anticipation of the Japanese ritual of gift-giving, now produces some presents for our guests, apologizing that they are so plainly wrapped in comparison with theirs.

It is warm on the tennis court as David partners with Tomo against Carolyn and me in the first set, then son and his mom versus Tomomi and me the next. Mrs. Sudo looks on for awhile, but then seeks a place away from this midday sun. She finds shade in the adjacent park and watches the children at play there.

The afternoon sun beats down on us, and Tomomi's face is turning pink from this outdoor activity; she and mother are very fair-complected, while David and his parents are sun-bronzed. These tans of ours were not intentionally sought, but are a result of long hours spent playing tennis, such as is underway now.

The appreciation of what constitutes beauty, differs markedly where skin color is concerned. In Japan, a woman's fair complexion is regarded as a sign of beauty, whereas the ideal in America is for skin to be tanned a golden brown. One sees Japanese women protecting their faces with wide-brimmed hats during summery days such as this one. And, before venturing out in full sun, many women carry raised parasols. This cultural habit of sun-avoidance is probably a wise one, given the warnings one hears more and more — that prolonged exposure to the sun with the objective of a healthy tan is anything but healthy! So we hope Tomomi is not burnt from the sun (at least not to the extent she's been 'burnt' in this tennis match, as she had difficulty matching our more experienced game play).

This afternoon we take our guests to the dinner club adjoining the golf course, where, in addition to expected golf activity on the acres of lush green grass, we observe that some swimsuited American women are (naturally) *sunbathing* in lawn chairs.

We encourage our guests to order steak, knowing how cost-prohibitive meat dishes are in their country. Dining here, courtesy of a U.S. military base, prices are modest in comparison.

Afterwards, Tomomi and her mother are fascinated to watch Carolyn put coins in the poker machines and, after some initial success, she hands them some quarters to join in a unique experience, unseen outside the confines of U.S. bases ('bandits' of this sort are outlawed in Japan). Of course, there are numerous *Pachinko* parlors (alluded to in an earlier chapter), but the impetus to play *pachinko* machines is to win pots of metal balls which one can exchange for novelty-item prizes.

We return home to Dave and Izzie's apartment for a short visit, where Mrs. Sudo surprises us with some well-spoken English words. It was an enjoyable conversation with a delightful mother and her daughter, but it is time to say good-bye for now, and David drives them to the Sagami-Otsuka Rail Station.

CHAPTER XII

Thursday, May 19:

The highlight of this day is a trip to Yokosuka, one-hundred miles southeast. Here we drive into the largest of all naval bases in Japan, a sprawling complex of buildings. The U.S. aircraft carrier, *Independence,* is berthed here presently. As we drive by that huge vessel, I suggest, "Why don't you take us on a tour of that monster, Son?"

"No, Dad, I have a better idea. You are about to see the largest PX in the world. Every imaginable product, both Western and Oriental can be found inside."

David hasn't forgotten that his mom's birthday is coming soon, and he tells her, "I brought you here to look for something Isabel and I can buy for your birthday, Mom, so find something really special."

After browsing through a mile of *objets d'art* made from porcelain, glass, brass, etc., on level one, we ascend to level two where Carolyn spies that 'something special.' A huge table of lovely kimonos lights up her eyes. Some have been hung on racks designed to flare out the beautiful robes and attract customers such as we. These kimonos are the genuine article, not the typical ones manufactured for foreign trade. Yards of expensive fabric go into these kimonos, and they can be very expensive. We are told that it is not unusual for a silk kimono to sell for the princely sum of a thousand dollars and more. Therefore, there is a bustling rental trade similar to the tuxedo rental shops back home, as they are used for ceremonial occasions such as weddings or festivals.

These, however, are not brand new, yet look unused, and their prices are only a fraction of the original price when bought new. Carolyn selects a beautiful kimono in a striking pattern, and at seventy American dollars it is a true bargain. A wooden display stand provides the finishing touch, and David looks much pleased as he carries these to the cashier for payment. He tells an equally pleased mother, "This is your combination Mother's Day/Birthday gift, Mom. I hope you like."

"I'm tickled pink," smiles his mother, an expression used by Americans of all skin colors — white, brown, black and yellow — to express a feeling of happiness. If only a benevolent God could somehow change us all to *pink* — instead of the primary, secondary, and mixed colors we come in — then perhaps the species Homo sapiens could achieve a truly non-racist Paradise on Earth.

I also like our son's gift to his mother — 'tickled pink' that the folks in Japan eschew second-hand items, enabling Carolyn to acquire a bargain of a lovely kimono to take back with her to America.

David drives us to a newly opened restaurant complex called *Main Street U.S.A. Food Court.* Baby Kirby has been patient thus far, enjoying her stroller ride about the Yokosuka Base PX, but now she has that 'enough is enough' look and starts to yowl. This is her way of explaining, if she could talk, "I'm hungry, you guys. This bottle is getting older than an antique vendor's wares, and I need some solid food."

Main Street U.S.A. Food Court is just the thing to cool Kirby's temper. This restaurant is divided up into various food service counters which offer a choice of Chinese, Mexican, and German fare. It is crowded with other hungry people who look over the menu signs posted above each counter while waiting in line to order. I latch onto a hard-to-find table, and ask Carolyn to order for me while I sit with this now cherubic granddaughter, observing a vast throng of people who, like us, are transported into a Pavlovian desire to sample what is aromatically enhancing the air.

After feasting on a mixture of international foods, shared from each other's tray, we return to the toll highway. Dave and Izzie are up front and Kirby, sharing the rear seat with her doting grandparents, quickly becomes a dozing granddaughter.

At home now, our son and daughter nap in the late afternoon while I make some diary entries and Carolyn watches TV. Whatever my wife watches fails to sustain her interest, and she dozes off, dreaming of a certain early birthday gift. I need some exercise before joining this household siesta, so embark on one of my many strolls taken for fun and exercise.

Before reaching home I stop in the commissary grocery and pick up a large frozen pizza. Beer is not offered for sale here I am informed, so after placing the pizza in the microwave oven I borrow my son's car and drive half a mile or so to the base liquor store. Stacked up front are high-rise cases of various brands of beer to take out, but all feel warm to the touch. *Warm pizza, yes,* I muse, *but warm beer? No way Jose!*

Thankfully, there are refrigerated cartons at the rear, and I buy a six-pack of San Miguel which, at the price of $3.30, represents yet another of today's bargain purchases. Back home, with state and federal 'sin' taxes and, as with this Philippine brand, import-duty tax, this six-pack would likely cost double. So, I double up and buy two!

Carolyn had awakened from the couch before my departure, and was surprised of my intent to use the car for this trip. "Tom, I thought you said you'd *never* drive in Japan."

"Yes, babe, I vowed never to do this in a land where the driver's seat and thoroughfares are opposite. Yet, while Dave and Izzie sleep, I don't want to disturb them." So it was, like many New Year's vows of the past, I broke this vow for good measure (and good beer).

Dave is up when I return; obviously, the aroma of a combo-pizza taken from the microwave oven has brought him 'round. As he rubs sleep from his eyes, this fresh progeny of mine gives me a dirty look and remarks, "Darn, Dad. Your California license doesn't cut it over here. You have to take a special exam to be licensed here. Too bad you weren't picked up — there would have been more pizza for me."

Seeing that his scolding countenance slowly lightens into a grin as he lectures me, I offer up no rebuttal, and slice up the pizza....

CHAPTER XIII

riday, May 20, Atsugi Base, Japan:

I am up at 6:00 a.m. after an uninterrupted, full night's sleep. "Honey," I sigh, "it's taken me a full week to orient to this Oriental time difference, but I slept well last night. Apparently that jet-lag business is history."

"You're a strange one. How could you? Kirby was a real fussbudget last night. Her crying kept us *all* awake."

Somehow I managed to sleep right through, undisturbed by this baby's noisy protestations; but hearing of them, I don't dare brag what a good sleep I enjoyed, as I breakfast with a sleepy-looking son. David has been asked to work today to help sort out some details for a pending inspection. He leaves at 7:30, and I walk Kirby to her nursery school.

I visit with her 'class' while they breakfast on pancakes and sausage, which Ms. Ruby slices into bite-sized pieces and lathers with syrup. I help her clean up afterwards, and discover as many pancake morsels on the floor as had entered the five little mouths.

Ms. Ruby thanks me and says, "You seem to enjoy children, so maybe you would like to be a grandfather volunteer in some classes."

"Sounds fine, Ms. Ruby, and today is a good day for it, since my son has been called in to work half a day."

A receptionist escorts me to two classrooms and introduces me to the teachers and aides. "The children will be happy. Nine o'clock is a good time for you to read to them."

Since both teachers are from the Philippines, they readily understand my parting comment: "Like MacArthur — I shall return." This affords time to trot home and check in with Carolyn before returning promptly at nine to sign on board with Ms. Cheri's class of four-year-olds. The children sit crosslegged on a carpet while their adoptive grandpa reads *Jack and the Beanstalk* to them. Then, it's time to move on to Ms. Lena's group and do likewise. Both groups of children are attentive, their little eyes aglow, and I read slowly, fanning out each page, so they may view the book's colorful illustrations.

When the teachers and aides try to thank me, I reply, "There's no need for that; I should thank you. It has been a fun activity for this grandpa."

Carolyn is watching TV when I return, but doesn't seem to mind the interruption while I relate the details of this volunteer stint. "When I looked into the animated eyes of those kids, I couldn't help but think of our own granddaughter, Monica," I tell her.

"We must take some books to read to her," she replies, in expectation of a visit with a child she clearly remembers as one who loves to be read to. "She's no doubt reading on her own by now, however," Carolyn muses.

"Yeah, but the question is, does Monica still use English? She's lived here in Japan two years, you know."

The answer to that perplexing question will be provided to these grandparents the next day...

CHAPTER XIV

aturday, May 21, Atsugi Base Japan:

    I'm up at the unholy hour of 1:00 a.m. making a few diary entries while snacking from the refrigerator. Isabel and Carolyn were both coughing during the night; my wife attributes hers to an allergy. The baby does some coughing in her sleep every night, too, but seems well as can be in the morning, although I noted a number of kids at her preschool with the sniffles yesterday.

Back to bed and up again at 6:00 a.m., when I slip out to take a long walk to the Seabee area where I observe another tennis court. What a strange court surface this is, covered by some type of sturdy, plastic material, perhaps one-half inch in height and honeycombed for drainage.

Returning to the apartment, I can't resist Dixie's entreaties to be petted, so pause for a visit, then decide to unleash her for a walkabout. Dixie's owner was placing some things in his van and commented, "I'm getting some stuff ready for the festival and picnic the Filipino community is having later today. It's going to be under a shady grove of trees near the baseball field. Come over and be my guest."

So, after showering, I suggest to my family that we go there together, but Izzie begs off. "No, Dad. You were the one invited. The rest of us wouldn't feel right tagging along."

It was their loss, for it was a super picnic of barbecued shishkebabs complemented by a variety of seafood salads and vegetable dishes — all prepared in delectable style. Preschool teacher Ms. Cheri greets me, as do two small tots who remark upon my having read to them. As I sit holding a paper plate of goodies, one precocious and polite little fellow introduces me to his parents by saying, "This is our grandpa visitor who read us *Jack and Beanstalk*."

The real focus of this day is on an older youth. Takanori Seyama, our former exchange student, has a day off from work, and we will pick him up at Sagami Otsuka Station. David transports us there to greet this slender twenty-one-year-old. Unlike Tomomi, this lad is shy when Carolyn and I hug him. Dave, who met Takanori previously in San Diego, gives the lad a military handshake.

Takanori has been to our home in California on two occasions. The first time he came by himself to gain experience with conversational English. On the second visit, he brought his entire family — father, mother, and kid-sister, Satoko.

Takanori-kun (*kun* is used as a name suffix with males) grins shyly as we make English conversation, apparently too rapid for him to assimilate, and he cocks his head, as if seeking the words to reply. This communication business is obviously difficult. I decide, also, that he is more like his mother — a quiet, but ever-smiling type. His dad, however, thrives on conversation, and after years of study Mr. Seyama is quite fluent in English.

We are anxious to know exactly what our 'son' is doing now that his university days are behind him, and learn that he works in Tokyo at a large investment firm. As with many Japanese companies, he lives there in a dormitory provided by his firm at minimal expense. The provision of dormitory room and board for unmarried employees is a standard feature of large Japanese businesses. Takanori-kun tells us, "I only see my mother and father and sister on weekends or national holidays."

After exchanging gifts and taking photographs, Carolyn makes him lunch, exclaiming, "Your American mom has to fatten you up, skinny guy."

Takanori is not shy about eating, and afterwards asks to use the telephone. He wants to call his dad to tell him he has arrived safely here via the network of trains from his firm in Tokyo. Mr. Seyama wasn't home, but his son leaves a message on the answering service. We chat awhile and the phone rings. David answers it and converses with Mr. Seyama in English, then passes the phone to Takanori, and Japanese becomes the vehicle for some rapid conversation between father and son. Takanori summons me from the living room to the kitchen phone and says, "My father wants talk with you."

With Takanori standing by to retake the phone, Mr. Seyama is insistent that we accompany his son to their home. "I am busy at the moment with a client from King's School, so I am sorry that I can't pick you and Carolyn up to drive you here. But please come on the train with my son and have dinner with us, then I will drive you back."

So, unexpectedly, Carolyn and I are off on a train jaunt to Yokohoma, escorted by another able 'son' who knows his way around over here, but leaving behind a disappointed son and his wife (originally, we were to have baby-sat Kirby while they went to the movies this evening).

This trip to visit the Seyama family isn't part of today's schedule. We were planning to see them in two weeks, when they will take us to the resort area of Hakone, which promises to be a marvelous opportunity for Carolyn and me to stay in a gorgeous countryside setting. "We can play tennis and enjoy the hot-springs spa in Hakone," Mr. Seyama informed us over the phone.

Unplanned or not, this evening has equally marvelous opportunities. Carolyn talks with me as we head to Yokohama Station on the train with Takanori, and suggests, "Since Mr. Seyama is fluent in both English and Japanese, we should tell him about Monica, and ask that he phone her mother about our wish to visit our granddaughter."

"Wow, that's a great idea, honey! Let's do it. Seyama-San will make a perfect go-between in this matter!"

We arrive at the Seyama's home which, being near the Yokohama train station, causes us to realize that, although this home is not palatial, it has been built on very expensive ground. The closer to the heart of commercial areas, such as this, the more dear becomes the cost of acquiring land there. I reflect that this is one more instance of the Japanese way of life being in contradiction to ours. With American cities in decay, those affluent enough to leave the cities behind — whether they be New York, Chicago or Los Angeles, indeed, all over our land — flee to the safe sanctuary of suburban enclaves.

Although never having been bombed to the ground like their Japanese counterpart cities, American cities are crumbling under the weight of other problems. These problems relate to racism, the disparity between 'haves' and 'have-nots' and, most significantly, the mentality of the 'haves' to abandon their cities for flight to the hinterlands called 'suburbs.'

Mrs. Seyama greets us at the door. This is a westernized family, so handshakes and hugs take the place of bows. We greet Mr. Seyama, who is presently engaged with some clients.

Takanori escorts us into the kitchen, where his mother is busily preparing the dinner and, from the looks of this table of foods and condiments, a meal one is not likely to forget soon!

Carolyn offers help, but Mrs. Seyama won't hear of it. She tells Takanori to show us around, and this dutiful son obliges. He further escorts us through a sliding door off the kitchen onto a large veranda of potted plants, a hibachi barbecue/smoker, and a pull-out line for drying clothes or sunning bedding. (The airing of futon mattresses is a widespread cultural practice. From train windows, one can observe miles and miles of apartments, condos and single-family homes, with their futon bedding hung out to air on sunny days.)

We see that this home is built on a split-level foundation, and there is a drop of perhaps fifteen feet off this rear porch veranda. Takanori points to a parking area below, and says, "There my father's car."

"That's a BMW isn't it?" I query. "Why, I thought your dad drove a Mercedes, or at least we have a photograph in an album back home with you and him standing in front of a black Mercedes."

"No. Last car, a Benz. Now my father likes BMW." Carolyn and I think not everything is different here in Japan. Affluence motivates people the world over for the ostentatious acquisition of luxury automobiles.

Within ten minutes, two young lady clients of Mr. Seyama ('Tom,' to us) are escorted to the door. Tom retired from a high-level executive position with Singapore Air Lines, and embarked upon a second career as a representative for the King's School of London, a language and field trip program for Japanese students in Britain.

While Mrs. Seyama (or Michiyo-San) labors with the creation of culinary delights in the kitchen, Mr. Seyama (I will refer to him formally to avoid confusion with your author's name) bids us be seated on the couch, and asks what we would like to drink. Carolyn is poured a glass of light wine, and I have a glass of Sapporo beer. Takanori brings out some photo albums.

The Seyamas are world travelers. Michiyo is an ardent scuba diving enthusiast, and has pursued this hobby in tropical oceans and seas the world over. We are astonished at the beauty of the underwater scenes this remarkable lady has photographed, and her husband and son are justifiably proud of her accomplishments. "These photos are breathtaking," Carolyn remarks.

Then, as planned, Carolyn and I bring up the subject of our granddaughter, Monica, and her mother Miyoko. Mr. Seyama hadn't met them, but his son had, in 1990, when we drove him to San Diego for a visit just prior to his return home to Japan. "Those were memorable times," noted Carolyn. "We celebrated Monica's fifth birthday and Takanori's seventeenth that summer."

Mr. Seyama listened with interest as we begin to recount the bizarre behavior exhibited by Miyoko in the later months of her marriage to David and, with the culmination of that marriage, her virtual kidnapping of Monica and flight to Japan, where she has been ever since.

"We would very much like to count on your acting as a go-between and contact Miyoko on the phone," Carolyn says.

We think Mr. Seyama is declining this request when he doesn't reply, except to say, "Excuse me one moment," then stands up and leaves the room.

When he returns with a pen and a pad of note paper, he begins to jot down what we have just related, and asks that we continue while he makes notes. Carolyn and I both take turns to describe our familiarity with Miyoko's disturbed mindset and unstable behavior (which I won't recap here, having dealt with those difficult times in previous pages of this narrative). But it is time now to familiarize our dear friend and confidantes with some facts.

"David has paid the sum of $1000 monthly to Miyoko for child support," I relate, "but she is so profoundly spiteful that Monica is not permitted even to write her dad."

"In fact," Carolyn adds, "the letters and gifts mailed her have not been acknowledged by even one letter."

Mr. Seyama listens attentively, interjecting his own thoughts, such as, "Can this be happening? Can anyone be so mean-spirited? You mean to say Monica isn't allowed to write thank you notes or respond to the letters you and her father write? This is very un-Japanese! "These people are not right," etc.

We are so grateful to this dear friend, who now says, "Come, let us eat. And afterwards, I will telephone for you." We join in a sumptuous feast of dishes too numerous to describe, all of them prepared authentically Japanese, and served on beautiful lacquerware plates and side dishes. The *itadakimasu* (I eat thankfully) was said by my wife and me, not just for this splendid meal, but also for the splendid acceptance of our request of help in fulfilling our quest to see our granddaughter in Japan.

Just as we finish dinner, Satoko returns from her work as a swimming and gymnastic instructor. This is Takanori's younger sister, who visited us with her family two years ago. We tease her about the dress-up party she and Takanori attended when they visited us in California. Neighbors their age, Kenny and Gigi, invited our guests from Japan to accompany them to a prom-dance affair. "You looked so cute in that gown borrowed from Carolyn, Satoko," I remember.

"You mailed us photos of that evening," recalls Carolyn. "I think Takanori wore a dark suit coat of Tom's that matched a lighter shade of trousers Takanori had. He looked spiffy."

Satoko was tired and famished. Her mother had prepared such an abundance that she wasted no time partaking of the ample quantities of that delicious repast remaining on the table.

Carolyn and I hold our breath as Mr. Seyama proceeds to

dial the telephone number our son has written in an address book under our granddaughter's town — *Suzuka-Shi.* "I am not familiar with that area," he has just told us. "It is somewhere in *Mie Prefecture.*"

We sit close enough to our 'go-between' to hear the phone ring in response to his dialing: once, twice, three times — a fourth. Carolyn and I exchange worried glances . . . "Please let there be someone at home to answer," is these grandparent's prayer.

CHAPTER XV

arolyn and I waited with bated breath for someone to pick up the phone as the necessary first step in our quest to see our granddaughter. "Perhaps she might even be the answering party and we will get to talk with her," Carolyn and I were thinking aloud.

On the fifth ring Miyoko answered. A brisk exchange of Japanese conversation ensued, and Mr. Seyama referred to his notes. The quality of the language our benefactor employed was so rapid and advanced (to us) that it was very difficult for these Americans to follow the conversation taking place. We could gather enough of its substance, however, to realize that Miyoko was declining us a visit to see Monica. The conversation was lengthy, with Mr. Seyama doing his level best to arrange a visit to see our grandkid soon.

"At least Miyoko isn't hanging up the phone," I whisper.

"Hush, Tom. I want to listen," Carolyn admonishes, as Mr. Seyama continues to articulate politely on our behalf.

Finally, he succeeds in a request to have Monica come on the phone to talk with her grandparents. Mr. Seyama talks with Monica while we wait our turn expectantly. It is obvious that Monica can understand and converse well in Japanese. In fact, as Mr. Seyama passes the phone to Carolyn, he comments: "Monica has learned Japanese and speaks well."

Our granddaughter feigns all past knowledge of the English language, just as her dad predicted she'd do. The calls David made to Monica went awry when she giggled to her dad, "Uh, no understand you. Speak Japanese." Her dad is ill-equipped to handle Japanese, and his daughter now speaks it fluently, so David is ready to throw in the towel. "It becomes sort of a game she plays with me," our son related about the few times he has had Monica on the phone. "It's a useless waste of money when she doesn't answer me in English."

Monica knows more English than the average person over here, I reflect. This is curiously amusing, for when Carolyn and I would ask her to use her Japanese words in the U.S., she would scold us, saying, 'Don't talk Japanese, Grandpa. I know only American.'"

Well, she is performing thus now, either to be cute or, probably, with mother listening in she is apprehensive now to speak any English to us on the telephone. Nonetheless, I trick her by calling her by a pet name, *flibber-gibbet*, and speak only English to tell how much we miss her, and how we have missed having any word from her all these months. When I ask, "Did you receive the photograph of the dollhouse Grandpa built for you?" Monica forgets herself and responds in English, "I don't know. Did you bring it to give me for a present, Grandpa?"

I could hear Miyoko say something in the background in apparent chastisement for those last words, and Monica obediently fills the phone line with strings of Japanese sentences, spoken with such rapidity that her grandpa pleads, "*Doozo, yukkuri hanashite chodai, Monica-chan* (please speak more slowly little Monica)." She giggles in response to this, and Miyoko comes back on the line to talk briefly with Carolyn, asserting in plain English: "*You not welcome to come see Monica. I not mind you talk with her on phone, okay.*"

Hearing this, my wife tearfully hands the phone back to Mr. Seyama, who signs off to say that he would call again at a later date. I thank our good friend profusely for having done this good deed, even though his appeals were rebuffed.

Yes, an ardently-expressed request for Carolyn and me to visit this child is flatly denied. This woman is obsessed with guilt perhaps. Her mind filled with hate and jealousy. Knowing this, our son should have sequestered Monica elsewhere to thwart the subterfuge and deceit of this woman. Then Miyoko might have failed at taking his daughter off to Japan to exact punishment for divorcing her. This malevolent act of retribution directly affects the lives of the many American relatives who see Monica no more.

My wife cries tears of disbelief into a ream of Kleenex tissue. But at least some headway has been made this evening, thanks to Mr. Seyama's intercession. Otherwise, I believe Miyoko would have undoubtedly hung up the phone on Carolyn or me. In her sick, mental condition she wrongfully conjectures that we seek to re-abduct Monica. This is pure hogwash! And forbidding us to see the child is outrageous to the extreme!

Carolyn and I are devastated, and also somewhat embarrassed that our sadness affects our dear friends. "I'm sorry," Carolyn apologizes, "Tom and I should be expressing enjoyment of this evening in your company and the wonderful meal we've just eaten. And here I am crying."

My wife's apology set off another round of tears, but perhaps tears express better than words one's emotional bewilderment when anger runs so deep. These were feelings incomprehensibly difficult to record in my diary later. When I attempted to explain them to American friends upon returning home, they inspired an arousal of their emotions also. These tearful feelings are hung out to dry from diary to manuscript to publisher. (Several friends encouraged me to make a book of this diary, so overwrought were they to learn of trials such as we experienced this evening.)

And surely this circle of friends encompasses the delightful family with whom Carolyn and I have fellowshipped this evening. Mr. Seyama tells us, "I know how you must feel." His wife, son and daughter convey their sentiments with sympathetic facial expressions, shaking their heads in disbelief as he explains the substance of what has just transpired on a telephone line connecting Yokohama with Suzuka-Shi.

"*Shitsuboo shimashita*" (we're disappointed), and, "*Okashi*" (strange), were all I could think to say to these friends.

On a lighter note, our considerate host, Mr. Seyama, tells us, "I will telephone Mrs. Sudo to see if we might stop there for a visit before my son and I escort you back home to your son's house at Atsugi. The Sudos live not far from my house."

That phone call accomplished, we bid fond farewells to Mrs. Seyama and her daughter, Satoko-chan, with the hope we will see them again before returning to America. This is not likely, however, as we are told they aren't taking part in the vacation to the hot-springs resort of Hakone. There isn't space in the Seyama's BMW and, besides, the Seyama ladies are taking an alternate vacation to the seashore to do some scuba diving and underwater photography. Satoko, like her mother, is an excellent swimmer, and a swim about a hot-springs spa is not challenging enough for them.

It is a treat for us to have this impromptu reunion with Tomomi-chan and her gracious mother, Mrs. Sudo. We are introduced to Chiyumi, the third member of this family, who is eighteen and still in school. This respite spent now in a small home built for them fifteen years ago, was only shared by Mr. Sudo for one year. He then, was to suffer a fatal heart attack while still a young man. We see photographs on the wall of that handsome father, and a shrine to his memory in a room off the hallway. I reflect that Carolyn's and my estrangement from a granddaughter doesn't compare with the loss of a husband and father. At least Monica is alive.

Our minds are no longer troubled by that vexing phone conversation, as we drink tea and eat sweet cakes in company with the Sudo ladies and the Seyama menfolk. What wonderful and supportive families these Sudos and Seyamas are!

It is fun to do a little mild teasing with young Takanori and Tomomi, joking that these young people should date and marry, or else Takanori will end up at our home in Paradise, California, and run off with our cute blonde neighbor, Gigi. Actually, all teasing aside, Takanori and Tomomi would make a great couple. He is a bit shy, and she's gregarious, so the vibes are good for a happy contrast of natures. People who are too alike sometimes see the worst in each other — a sort of reflected mirror image of themselves.

Wouldn't it be coincidental if these matchmaking suggestions of mine (with Carolyn joining in), result in a future together for these two neat young people of marriageable age? It would be a fitting payback to Tom Seyama for his go-between role on our behalf earlier this evening.

After a pleasant but short visit, it is getting late, and we are transported back to the comfortable and familiar surroundings of Dave's and Izzie's apartment. Mr. Seyama drives this peppy BMW skillfully down an unfamiliar route with Takanori, map in hand, serving as his able navigator. It is midnight when we reach the Atsugi main gate, and the sentry is kind to phone David, to say he will direct his parent's host vehicle on through (after assuring that David *is* our #1 son).

CHAPTER XVI

unday, May 22, Atsugi Base:

By the time Carolyn and I checked in from Yokohama and bathed, the clock showed 1:00 a.m., and we talked softly in bed before sleep overtook us. Therefore, we both slept in unusually late and had no idea when Dave and Izzie got up. Fortunately, Kirby was a good girl and didn't interrupt her grandparents' slumber.

I hear my family stirring about as I awaken close to nine o'clock and come into the kitchen yawning as if I hadn't slept at all. Kirby was sitting up in her highchair looking bright eyed and bushytailed. She held out a morsel of dry cereal to share with this funny grandpa who kneels on the floor at her feet to beg like Dixie Dog downstairs. David and Isabel have foregone breakfast until their parents are up and around, and suggest that this Sunday morning is a good one to breakfast out at the *Nineteenth Hole.*

We are able to make it up to our son and his wife for having canceled out of baby-sitting last night by looking after Kirby this afternoon, when they will travel to Zama to meet David's friends. It would be fun to see Mr. Sagami and Kiyomi again, whom we met in the early '80's. But we are duty bound to ride herd on the little rascal so her parents can go out for a quiet time alone together.

Monday, May 23:

David's vacation ends today and he returns to work full time. I volunteer an hour's worth of time to assist Ms. Ruby at Kirby's nursery school, and discover that Kirby has learned a new trick. There are pictures of animals cut from magazines and affixed by scotch tape to the door, and when grandpa barks, in imitation of Dixie the dog, Kirby trots over to the picture of the dog and points to it. The other tots think this little game is the best invention since sliced bread, and quickly join in the merriment. Even pouty-boy Joe participates.

After those fun and games, it was the old folks turn, and Carolyn and I have the tennis courts to ourselves for an hour and a half. It is so warm and sultry that, when our ice water runs out, Carolyn takes a breather on the bench while chewing on ice cubes from the cooler jug.

This evening we baby-sit Kirby again while Dave and Izzie have some togetherness of their own on the tennis court. I retire on the couch with the television generating such pap that Kirby, followed by her grandma, are both soon asleep. Grandpa sits in melancholy, thinking thoughts of journeys that lie ahead — journeys by train that will take us from these comfortable American-like confines to the hinterlands of this interesting country we have only begun to explore.

This reverie is brief. Dave and Isabel's footsteps are heard coming up the stairwell and I open the door to caution, "Shhh. Kirby and Grandma are asleep."

These two have had an active time of it on the court this warm and humid evening, and both look ready for a shower. Izzie looks particularly wilted, and Dad suggests they flip a coin to see who goes first in the shower, but then second-thoughts that notion with, "Why don't you two shower together and save water?"

"We don't get billed for water usage, Dad, or gas or electric; all utilities here come with the basic rental package. You go ahead first, honey. I'll have a beer with Dad."

"Party pooper," Isabel slyly rebukes her husband while making a face at him.

All this commotion has awakened Carolyn from her nap on the couch. She sits up, stretches, and joins the men in her life for a chat. "It's warm this evening. Is there something cold you can bring me from the refrigerator, David, like maybe a Coke?"

"No Coke, Mom," comes a call from the kitchen. "There's some root beer, but it's not too cold. Isabel must have just put it in. I'll bring you a glass with ice."

David returns with a root beer for his mom and an unopened can of regular beer for me. "Well, you guys will be off on a long trip tomorrow, and I'd sure like to be joining you two for a second visit to the Mori's. It would also be nice to see Carolyn's aunt and cousins down south near Hiroshima; the last time was back in '83."

"What!" says his dad sarcastically. "And leave your wife and daughter behind, the way your ex-wife was when you were assigned for two weeks in Norfolk back in 1989? Heaven forbid a rerun of that monumental disaster and tumultuous saga in your life and ours, Son!"

"Tom's half joking, David. He talks like this after a few beers. But that period preceding your divorce with Miyoko was a terrible episode for us. We love Isabel, but can't help wishing, for Monica's sake, that Miyoko's mental health had been restored and your marriage salvaged."

"We were never so happy to see anyone as much as you, David, when you arrived at our door to greet a wife gone berserk," I comment. "Miyoko was overjoyed to see you, too, but that joy was too brief — like one night only. Remember the very next morning when Miyoko accompanied us to Chico, where you were to shop at the mall while I looked at a truck for sale?"

David is uncomfortable to be reminded of that period in our lives, but his mother continues. "I was delighted to stay home and grandmother Monica that day. Miyoko had certainly put us all through the wringer, and I urged you to seek medical help for her immediately."

"And she sure put David through the wringer that morning in Chico," his dad continues. "We should have turned around and come right back home when, once again, Miyoko attempted to open the car door while it was moving — more hallucinations apparently."

David finally joins this conversation to say, "Yeah. That guy at the car dealer's called the police when I tried to restrain Miyoko from running out into a busy street because he thought she was in danger."

"When it was just the opposite! You and I were the victims, not that woman. I observed from a distance as a squad car pulled up on East Avenue with two officers. One of them interviewed you while the other talked with Miyoko. After they were assured that no harm or spousal abuse was intended her, they finally took their leave."

Isabel rejoins us, towelling off her wet hair, and she has obviously heard the tail end of our conversation. "Would you have bailed your son out of jail, Dad, if the cops thought he was being mean to Miyoko instead of letting her run out in the street?"

"Are you kidding, Izzie? I would have told those cops to lock the both of them up for at least the three days his wife had subjected Carolyn and me to so much grief! No. All joking aside — while we drove back home, I told David that as soon as he returned to San Diego, to seek medical help for his wife. This was an untenable situation."

Truly, those were sad times. Carolyn and I were deeply concerned for all their sakes, particularly Monica. That poor dear was an innocent party to Miyoko's utterly bizarre behavior.

We managed to journey home back then without further incident. Miyoko became less sullen, made small talk with David and said she was hungry. David looked relieved. "What say we stop off at Burger King?" he smiled at his wife. "We'll return with a takeout order to include Monica and Mom."

Miyoko acted pleased (but Carolyn and I weren't merely *acting* pleased when, after the first decent night's sleep for all concerned, our guests departed early the next morning for their home in San Diego).

Medical help was ultimately available soon after their return. David asked for some leave from his job to pursue this, and the physician consulted for Miyoko's physical quickly placed her in the hospital and recommended specialists for an ongoing work up there.

Miyoko was to spend two weeks in the San Diego Naval Hospital, but, unhappily, the treatment didn't result in a cure. "I'm okay. Don't need medicine," Miyoko insisted. And her mood swings continued unabated,

The aberrations of mind persisted with repeated incidences of unstable behavior. For example, one time, a guy who once worked with David came to visit, and Miyoko, right out of the blue, cracked her husband over the head with a plastic toy of Monica's! Scarcely a dish was left unbroken in their kitchen when unhappy Miyoko decided to fling them asunder. While visiting them, Carolyn and I heard the noise of dishes being thrown and broken in the kitchen sink. We merely shook our heads in dismay, and slipped outdoors to take a walk in the condominium garden area.

It became difficult to take Miyoko anywhere with us. She pouted about God-knows-what, and often refused to leave the car. So violent were her tantrums that David became fearful of sleeping under the same roof. He related an incident to us involving a rude awakening from a nap on the couch. Miyoko swatted him with a metal tennis racquet as he slept! "That was it — finished!" David told us. "I'm filing for a divorce and will ask for custody of Monica."

During their marriage, Miyoko had been able to spend vacations of a month or two with parents in Japan, with Monica accompanying her. As her parents were reputedly wealthy, they generously subsidized these expensive trips. And now, with divorce on the agenda, Miyoko telephoned them to ask that her mother come to San Diego for a short while. She would then go back to Japan with her and find her own attorney. David knew nothing of that plan, except to realize the phone bill was excessive, which reflected that Miyoko had made a goodly number of contacts with Japan.

This was in April of 1992. David phoned us to ask that his mother come to visit him once his wife and her mother left. Monica was still in school, and considering the demands of his job, David needed his mom's help. Since Carolyn and I were fully retired at that time, this request was forthwith affirmed. She packed a bag to await our son's call.

With Carolyn in San Diego to stay with our son and granddaughter for a week, David took a week's leave, checked Monica out of kindergarten a month early, and the three of them drove northward to rescue me from a sentence or 'bachelorhood.'

With Monica's schooling interrupted, the grandparents fell heir to tutoring her from the first of May through mid-June. Grandmother was relegated most of these tasks, and she fortuitously had met with Monica's teacher at school, receiving materials to better accomplish this. That packet of booklets and papers, when completed, was mailed to her teacher in

San Diego. We wanted this child to be prepared for first grade come fall.

Etched in our memories are those untroubled days, from May first until Labor Day in September of 1992, spent with a granddaughter we thought would continue to live with her dad, and possibly have a new 'mother.' David had begun seeing a lovely woman, named Isabel, and they were already making plans to marry.

Her grandparents enrolled Monica that summer in a swimming class, an art class, and gymnastics — all sponsored by the Paradise Parks and Recreation District. Gram and Gramps became thus involved in a post-retirement 'taxi service,' and this child was so tired by the end of her busy day that bedtime stories often went unfinished.

On Labor Day weekend we drove the six hundred miles south to San Diego to help out. David was busy at work, so it was convenient for us to enroll Monica in first grade. The services of a good nursery school were also undertaken.

As our son left early for work in the morning, he was able to take Monica to her preschool until regular school began. Then she was transported with other children to their respective private or public schools in a van provided by the preschool. After Monica's public school class ended, the van driver picked her up to return her to a private day care center.

As grandparents who must soon return to look after their own home, we were comforted by an arrangement that was convenient for working, single parents like our son. We knew that father and daughter would be managing well, as Monica was a bright, reliable child, who had reached an age to be self sufficient in many ways. We also knew this household would soon include David's new bride, and this relieved even more concern for Monica's welfare. Carolyn and I couldn't but think, that Isabel, although a stepmother, was a significant improvement. Having met her, we saw someone who could bring love and care to Monica. Every child deserves a good, stable "Mom!"

The divorce proceedings of the past year were reaching the final phase, and would officially conclude in two month's time. Then, Miyoko, accompanied by her mother, was to return from Japan to sign the final papers and pack her belongings and personal effects for shipment to her home in Japan.

Little did we realize that, once packed, Miyoko would furtively — with her mother's aid and abettance — alter their return flight schedule, check Monica out of her class at Sundance School, then spirit her away to a place in Japan, *where her dad, grandparents, and the rest of her American relatives have not heard from her since!*

This deceitful abduction was consummated while her father was at work, and a note was left behind for David to pick up his car deposited at the airport parking lot (in spite of Miyoko's lapses and relapses, she was nevertheless competent to drive in San Diego).

Upon returning home and reading the note informing of this unexpected departure, David enlisted the aid of a friend to drive him to the airport to find his car, which he located and retrieved. He phoned us that evening to tell us of the day's events and the bizarre twists that had been Miyoko's trademark for some time. "I should deduct the airport parking fee from the thousand dollars I send her in monthly alimony," he intoned sarcastically.

David was tired and crestfallen, conjecturing that, "Monica must have been in a terribly agitated state during the drive to the airport. I discovered that she had torn her school papers into pieces, leaving them on the floor of the back seat." Since littering was not one of this child's vices, we could only assume that Monica — just as with the breadcrumbs of Hansel and Gretel, familiar to her — had left behind some telltale signs *that she also hoped to be found!*

Carolyn and I strongly advised our son to seek the immediate help of an attorney to explore every avenue that might get his daughter returned.

"I'm reconciled, Mom and Dad, but I know how you feel. I know how *I feel!* Monica will be in the care of wealthy grandparents in Japan, whose financial assistance will more than match my alimony. And, as you know, Isabel and I will be married soon, so I have to get on with my life."

We hung up the phone, a saddened pair of grandparents. This revelation had reduced Carolyn to tears, and I walked back and forth, talking to her, to myself, to the *world!* "This is damnable — the utter futility of it all. Is there no justice in this world?!"

And now, in the aftermath of this forced separation from a grandchild we know and love, can we, as grandparents, get on with our lives?' Indeed, will we ever see this precious child again?

The trip we set out on tomorrow will hopefully result in finding and seeing a child unheard from in two years. Circled on a small calendar I carry is the date of May 31st, my dear wife's 61st birthday, and it is time to look at the positive side of our lives. We have just spent ten splendid days with our son and his wife, where we have gotten to know another granddaughter who soundly sleeps in the next room. Dave, Izzie, Carolyn and I are tired and will soon join baby Kirby.

Before turning in, I share a final thought for this evening. "Your mom and I watched an episode of *Unsolved Mysteries* on TV awhile back, where the narrator, Robert Stack, portrayed a number of children abducted from their parents. At least we know Monica's address and phone number, so I'm optimistic we will manage to find her."

David squelched this reasoning by saying: "Good luck, Dad. I wish I could share your optimism but, like I told you, as soon as you and Mom get near the place where Monica resides with Miyoko and her parents, she'll probably be shuffled off to her aunt's home nearby — and I don't have that address."

"This is helpful to know, Son, and for that very reason I do not intend to announce our arrival time. But believe me, I've picked a date, and even an alternate date."

Carolyn and I stay up awhile, both too awake for sleep to dispel the anticipation of our coming journey. "You know, honey," she tells me, "should we fail in our quest to see Monica, at least we have many photos to remember her by."

"Sure, and we have videotapes, Carolyn. But, like I've said before, these are no substitute for the real McCoy."

"Well, I just wish Miyoko and her parents would have the decency to have her write to us and send some recent photographs."

"It's criminal that this hasn't occurred, honey. That's all the more reason why I remain determined to see her! I know it won't be easy — for we've been told to stay away — yet, somehow, we must! You and I have got to learn if Monica is healthy and happy, and how she's doing at school with classmates who have been immersed in the Japanese language since birth."

"I understand, Tom. This trip has provided us memorable moments to share with our son and his family. Even so, it will fall short if we don't get to see Monica."

"That is our mission, dear — a grandparents' quest. I'm finally getting sleepy. Shall we hit the hay?"

CHAPTER XVII

Tuesday, May 24:

The past two days have been uneventful, but we have rested up for the long journey we will make today. David reported to work early and is now home to see his parents off. He tells me, "Since you must go to the JR terminal at Shin-Yokohama to get your passes, I will take you to the Ebina Station, Dad."

David is surprised at the weight of our two carry-on bags when he puts them in the car trunk. "You're gonna miss me, Mom," he says. "Remember how I hauled your bags *and* mine when we took the bullet train south back in 1983?"

How well we do recall the memorable events of those days before David embarked upon the responsibilities of marriage and fatherhood. Now we are to retrace that same path leading to reunions with dear friends in Shizuoka, dear relatives near Hiroshima and — if luck will have it — with a dear grand-daughter living somewhere in *Mie Prefecture*.

Our first stop is at Isabel's bank, to give her a last good-bye and exchange some more traveler's checks for a bunch of large Japanese yen bills. We are well apprised of the yen money expenditure for this travel about the Japanese countryside. The cost of living is expensive in this nation compared with the past. Yet, we are glad to see these hard working people prosper, and are not too put out by the realization that our lodging and meal expenses during the days to come will weigh heavy on our purse. We give our bank-teller 'daughter' a hug, and I tell her, "Well, this is good-bye until around the third of June, unless we go broke sooner, Izzie."

She laughs, and replies, "Well, Dad, you always know where to find us."

Number-one son delivers us to Ebina Station and our eyes are moist at this parting. We puzzle over the right amount of coins to feed the ticket machine, and are helped by a man in a dark blue business suit. I speak the first of much Japanese required in the days ahead, and receive instructions for the correct sum. This trip from Ebina requires one transfer before we reach the large and bustling Shin-Yokohama Station.

Carolyn is dressed stylishly in a print dress, and I wear a light blue, cotton seersucker suit with inside jacket pockets that shelter our passports on one side and a map on the other. Then, once we exchange our prepaid vouchers for Japan Rail Passes, these will also find a place inside my suit coat.

We report to a JP Station room to exact the voucher for pass exchange, and find that these cardboard passes are of a size which just manage to squeeze into my inside pocket, so my observant and helpful wife says, "Your jacket looks too bulky, Tom. I'll carry those passes in my purse."

This is agreeable until I read the list of eleven *Conditions* printed in English on the back. Number seven clearly stipulates: *This pass cannot be reissued if lost or stolen.* "Whoops," I tell Carolyn, "Bulky or not, I will keep these passes in my inside pocket. Your purse might get lost or stolen, but no one will likely steal *me*, and I dare not lose these expensive and important documents so essential to our travel."

Our luggage is made heavy by a number of gifts we carry and the set of eleven books we are taking to the Mori family in Shizuoka. Carolyn struggles with her heavy carry- on bag on one arm and a bulky purse on the other, so I suggest, "Here, honey, let me take your bag. It will balance my load.'

"Maybe later. I'm not tired yet," this intrepid lady replies as we traipse down long corridors and up escalators leading to the *shinkansen* (bullet train) platform.

By the time we get on board our sleek Bullet, we are huffing and puffing. Unfortunately for us, the car where we now sit has many 'puffers.' From now on, I will follow *Condition Number Four* on my pass, which states: *Seat reservations may be made in advance without additional payment. To do this the holder should apply at a travel service center or a Midori-no-madoguchi (Green Window) in a JR Station.* This will be the last time we will be stuck on a car full of smokers. From now on, our car will be identified by one of the universal 'no-no' signs (see figure 1):

At any rate, these *shinkansen* cars are spacious, with ample luggage storage racks above large outside windows. The win-dows have curtains one can pull to cut off the glare of the sun or, as with the passenger across the aisle, to catnap if so de-sired. One business-man has removed his suit jacket and hung it between windows to doze contentedly.

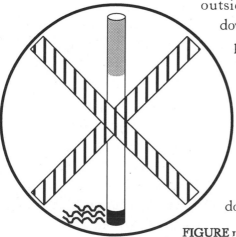

FIGURE 1

Other passengers have their pull-down tablettes in view, and I observe them partaking of a variety of snacks and liquid refreshment. About this time, a young lady enters our car from the front entrance and passes slowly down an aisle just wide enough for her to wheel a cart laden with all kinds of edible goodies. She softly repeats the same phrase in the melodious, almost child-like manner affected by the female of the species here: "*Oh-bento ni, oh-cha eekahgah deskah* (would you care for some snacks and/or drinks)?"

I remark to Carolyn how much like commercial airplanes these bullet trains are, both in speed and food service. Some of the dishes made available are meat or fish, vegetable and rice lunches, dispensed with disposable wooden *hashi* (chopsticks). Carolyn suggests, "Let's split one of those, Tom and order some soft drinks to go with it."

Since I am on the aisle side, I select a box lunch whose main feature, along with rice and pickled vegetables, is *unagi*. *Unagi* is eel, and your average American would yell "EEK" at the sight of it (but we are not average Americans). I, for one, enjoy *unagi* so much that at home we keep expensive tins of that oriental delicacy stocked in the cupboard.

We take turns sharing bites of our *bento* lunch as the countryside whisks by in a blur outside our window. We finish, then sit back in air-conditioned comfort, in contemplation of the upcoming reunion with our dear friends in Shizuoka. Our pace is so rapid that we will be there by noon.

"This is the only way to fly," I remark to Carolyn, while struggling to retrieve our cumbersome luggage and disembark to a platform leading to an ultramodern station. I can see that much remodeling has been undertaken here since our visit eleven years ago.

We drop our bags on the clean and shiny floor next a wall of telephones. Japanese are meticulous about keeping things clean, so litter is not a problem here. Numerous waste bins abound with the Japanese word character for *Refuse,* and English words *Dust Bin* imprinted thereon. There are designated smoking areas, but this telephone area is fortunately not one of them.

From my wallet I take out the telephone calling card that our dear Tomomi-chan mailed us to use when phoning her or any of our other friends while we are in this country. Mrs. Mori answers the phone to say she was expecting our call and will be here to pick us up in twenty minutes.

In less time than that the Moris arrive, and it is not difficult to single out the presence of this writer's American face, and not only because we have met before, but it is the only one in the station. Our 'son,' Hirokazu, does not accompany them, as his holiday from work is not until tomorrow.

Mr. Mori places our *neemotsu* (luggage) on the rear seat of his car. Carolyn and I momentarily wonder precisely where we were to fit on the seat beside these bulky bags, when we make the discovery that Mrs. Mori has commandeered a taxi in the meantime. Mr. Mori departs — we assume homeward — while the three of us are driven by the white-gloved cabbie a short distance to a large multi-storied department store, called *Shizuoka Isetan.* We are greeted here by Mr. Mori, who has arrived ahead of us.

This is an upscale department store which is now the workplace of Hirokazu, whom we adopted as our own during a summer's visit to America with a classmate from Shizuoka's *Tachibana* High School. That visit was eleven years ago. Now, Hirokazu is the manager of the *nee-kahee* (2nd floor), and it is there that we greet again this personable and gregarious fellow. He was the first of our Japanese friends to call on us at Dave and Isabel's apartment, and we thought him very brave to have driven all that way.

With his parents, Hirokazu shows us around his sector of influence. It is always a mystery for Carolyn and me to see that the mannikin displays have Caucasian faces. *Can it be that these figures are imported from America?* I wonder, then dismiss that idea as utter nonsense, yet continue to puzzle over the use of these 'fake foreigners' for this purpose.

Mr. and Mrs. Mori silently look on, justifiably proud of a son who remembers sufficient English to converse with these visitors from abroad. We reminisce about a reunion we had, along with David, in 1983, when this family first introduced us to their fair city. After a wonderful tour to see the sights of Shizuoka, we were taken to City Hall to meet the Mayor, who bestowed us with gifts.

With Hirokazu attending university in Tokyo, and his father occupied in business, it was Mrs. Mori who steered us to the Isetan Department Store, when we thought our destination was the train station. Generous and kind person that she is (indeed, this lady's face radiates kindness) Mrs. Mori was insistent that Carolyn, David and I each select a good-bye gift before going to the train station. When we got there, she told the ticket taker she wished to enter the turnstiles with her guests and stay with them until they departed. From our train window, we said good-bye to this demure and gracious friend who waved a delicate hanky until our train was out of sight.

One cannot forget these acts of kindness and now, after an interval of eleven years, Carolyn and I see that this hospitality is unchanged. Hirokazu explains on behalf of his parents, whose ability to use English is limited, "My father and mother like you to find present they want buy you."

I try to find words in Japanese to politely decline the generosity of this couple and their son, explaining that it is more than enough of an *omiyage* (gift) for them to be sharing their home and company with us; they need not go to this expense; our travel luggage is already full, etc.

That same tactic hadn't worked in 1983 any better than it was working today; so Carolyn — noting that her husband's protestations again fell on deaf ears — picked out a lovely blouse. It was apparent that we weren't going anywhere until I followed suit, so I pointed to a necktie. These two items, small as they were for us to pack, bore price tags that were anything but small. Yet, we just managed to escape this store without them buying us two or three of each; such is the extent of this family's determination to bestow one kindness after another.

Mr. Mori is a distinguished looking and successful businessman, and closely resembles his son, Hirokazu. His attractive wife is elegant in the choice of apparel she wears, usually beautiful dresses in subdued colors. When people foreign to the Japanese culture observes the manner of dress in this country, they are inclined to speculate that these folks must all be uniformly wealthy, or else spend an inordinate amount of family income on their wardrobe. Carolyn and I are impressed by the expensive-looking clothing and accessories worn by the Japanese women we encounter everywhere.

By way of contrast, average, middle class women in the U.S. dress in quite modest and simple attire when out and about. On one of our early outings by train while here in July of '83, Carolyn wore Bermuda shorts in a colorful floral print with a matching halter top. The poor dear received so many shocked expressions from the locals that she chucked the idea of wearing that outfit again, saving it for use back in casual, carefree America.

There is a distinction drawn in Japan as to what is suitable attire for the young and what is proper wear for the middle-aged or older. It is all right for the former to wear bright, colorful dress. The latter, however, must wear subdued colors of tan, dark blue or grey.

American choices in both men's as well as women's clothing — the young, as well as elderly — run the gamut in terms of style and color. Personally, I draw the line at emulating my male counterparts over here who wear dark suits of gabardine, sharkskin, or silk material, neckties with white shirts — and heavy leather shoes to boot (unintended pun)! No way, Jose; this fellow will keep to comfortable cottons and casual shoes (and, where neckties are concerned — only if threatened that a jail cell awaits one bereft of that accessory)!

CHAPTER XVIII

fter bidding good-bye until later to Hirokazu-kun, we exit this building, which is a Shi-zuoka landmark in terms of size. Mr. Mori has some business to attend to, so he departs as I tell him, *"Mata atodeh aeemashow* (we will see you later)." Mrs. Mori walks us across a busy street and flags another taxi to transport us to her home. We remember this lovely place for its uniqueness and beauty......

The Mori home was built in 1937, and escaped the ravages of war which razed many like it to the ground in the larger and more strategic areas of this land.

It is a totally Japanese-style house, unlike so many built post-war, with kitchens, baths and living areas along western lines. Yet, even in these, there is generally a 'Japanese' room or two, enclosed by sliding *shoji* panels and a *tatami* mat floor, and most will have the traditional Japanese entry, where one sheds outdoor shoes for slippers.

The Mori home bears *no* western influence. All doors, inside and out, are *shoji* panels. The floors are 'carpeted' with woven reeds called *tatami*. The bath is a *furobath*, with an area for one to cleanse the body before dipping into a deep and soothing hot tub. A sweeping, traditional tiled roof covers this quaint, old-style home that is more spacious of rooms and indoor area than most houses one now sees in Japan.

A wide veranda permits the occupants to view the natural charm of a small Japanese garden. It strikes me that this garden of ornamental shrubs, trees and plants, is much lovelier than the European-influenced gardens of America, where a plain expanse of grass becomes the centerpiece of their design. Carolyn and I are particularly impressed with the characteristic placement of stones and rocks. Indeed, these gardens are naked without these inanimate objects to set off the animate plant life. Stone lanterns complement this picture to create a special air of tranquility. These gardens, small as they are, serve as a buffer to the tumult of the outside world (a land where people live so crowded together it can feel stifling at times).

Little has changed since we visited eleven years ago, except, of course, the flower arrangements in small alcoves, accented by a lovely old vase, large dish, or wooden stand. The furniture is sparse, but rich in select woods, and beautiful paneling adorns the walls and ceilings. Everything we see is understated — no bric-a-brac here. All shoes are placed inside a spacious, slate-floored entry, where comfortable and clean slippers await the occupants and guests. Indeed, there are even separate slippers placed just outside the two toilet areas for one to wear therein.

When Carolyn and I enter, we feel as though we have been transported in time to a much older, more refined Japan. The reader knows, as well as we, that the refinement of these settings failed to rub off on certain of the military and political spheres of influence in those bygone days (the dichotomy of which a true scholar might explain, but is beyond the scope of this diarist, and remains an inexplicable mystery).

It is enough that Carolyn and I enjoy this setting now, for we learn that its days are numbered. We see an architectural scale model of a two-story house with an attached apartment, and learn that this is a model of what will be erected on this very site later this year, once the present older home is demolished.

Such is the price of 'progress' in Japan as elsewhere in the world — that such monuments as this unique home must keep a date with the wrecking ball. Carolyn and I are astonished. Yet, in consideration of a woman's role in the scheme of things, my wife says, "Dear Mrs. Mori will now have a modern kitchen and bathrooms of easy-to-clean tile."

"Yes, that's true honey," I respond, "and there will be many other modern enhancements, such as built-in appliances, contemporary lighting and new electrical wiring and plumbing — all salubrious changes."

Still, I can't help but reflect what a darn shame it is that this lovely, older home of exquisite workmanship must give way to modernity. This thought leads to further reflection, that so many of the 'monuments' to my own country's history have been abandoned, if not to the wrecking ball surely, in a similar way, to the crippling effect of neglect and decay. So many of those sturdily built homes and buildings in our older American cities — many with the charm and skilled workmanship of the Victorian era — have been written off and forsaken by former owners who have moved to newer 'havens' in the suburban areas of those cities. Most of the newer homes are so look-alike in their sameness —in tract after tract, ad nauseam — that for one to call this *progress*, borders upon absurdity.

Mrs. Mori, ever the cordial hostess, is vigilant to our every perceived need, filling our tea and soft drink vessels, worried about our comfort while seated Japanese style on the floor. She thinks I may be uncomfortable at the low table, and scurries to bring a chair with back and arm rests, so I can sit with legs stretched out and extending underneath the table. It is a more ornate version of the stubby, aluminum lawn chairs used at home in America.

We are introduced to Hirokazu's cousin, Yumi, a slender, early-twentyish lady with a beguiling smile. Also present is Hirokzau's elder sister, Junko, with her six-year-old daughter, Haru-chan. Junko's husband, Mr. Kawai, is to come for dinner later this evening when Hirokazu and his dad return from work. I have found that Japanese families are generally more closely knit than American ones. Older and younger members 'break rice' together whenever possible, and share in one another's conversations. American families, however — with the exception of the Thanksgiving holiday tradition and perhaps Christmas or birthday celebrations — generally prefer to stay with their own age group where company is concerned.

While Mrs. Mori prepares the evening meal, her daughter and niece are pressed into a different service — taking Carolyn and me on a fascinating nature hike. A walk of a few minutes brings us to a block-long city park. The park is ordinary — just an expanse of lawn and a bit of shrubbery here and there — but it serves as a transition to our first destination, a small neighborhood shrine. This is the final resting place for many of our guide's ancestors, and we pause for a photograph session in this serene place of beauty so near the noises and activities of the boulevard it adjoins.

We follow the lead of our guides to take part in a ceremonial hand-washing from a long-handled dipper. The water, which Yumi says comes from a mountain stream, runs continuously into a concrete tub and feels cool and looks sparkling clean.

My heathen hands are thus sufficiently 'purified' to engage in the next ritual. Next to us is a rectangular vessel, several yards long and about a yard wide, covered with bamboo latticework. We each take turns clapping our hands in front of it, in the respectful hope that the deity who looks with favor upon this spot will be awakened by our noise and grant future health and happiness.

Junko offers us some yen coins from her purse to pitch into this vessel. I think this a bit of a bribery to the deity, and tell her, "No thank you. I have some coins for Carolyn and me to use for..." and stop just short of the heresy of calling this offering a bribe.

I hand Carolyn a ten yen coin and we each perform the ritual toss into the ceremonial vessel. "In a way, this is not unlike our American custom of tossing coins into a fountain while making a wish," Carolyn remarks.

Our business here finished, we are led along the busy boulevard with shops of every description. During our walk through this profusion of people and shops, we come upon yet another shrine in a lovely and secluded park-like setting.

Unlike our imposing church steeples back home, these areas of consecrated ground do not stand out. Indeed, one unacquainted with this place might easily have passed by, singularly unaware that, just off this busy street, a space has been provided for quiet meditation and enjoyment of nature.

But our energetic young guides, Junko and Yumi, don't permit time for reflection, and lead us to gaze up at a verdant green hillside. Carolyn and I look in awe upon the wide, chiseled stone steps leading upwards. "Why, there must be a million steps here," I exclaim.

"There are exactly *hyaku* (one hundred)," Junko points out, then asks, "Want to go up?"

"Yes. Let's go!" says my energetic wife, before I am able to state my preference, which would be to find an escalator like the one in Hirokazu's store for this ascent.

But up these hundred stone steps we climb, and about half way, pause to listen to some interesting bird calls. The raucous cry of ravens are typical of the lower elevations here, but these are the pleasant melodies of songbirds flitting about this forested hillside.

The air is redolent with the scent of flowers, once I catch my breath enough to notice. On both sides of our stonework path, it is so forested with pines and tall bamboo groves, one cannot view the valley below. We see a large number of tunnel-like steps leading upward, and the thick foliage embraces both sides of our steep ascent.

Once atop the hundred steps we catch another breath, then follow a winding trail through a *torii* gate. This trail is enhanced by concrete steps made to look like the logs Abe Lincoln used to build his home. So naturally log-like are they that Carolyn and I make the test of rubbing our fingers over the 'bark' to confirm these are indeed man-made.

After a journey of perhaps ten minutes we come to a fork, with one trail continuing higher, the other descending. Our ever-solicitous guides want to know if we care to go further. Junko is a robust, athletic-type lady, and obviously wouldn't mind hiking on. Yumi, however, is more fragile of form, and looks relieved to hear Carolyn say, "I think we've had enough. Will this path take us a different way back to the hundred stone steps?"

Assured that it will, my wife starts her descent ahead of us, exercising caution lest she slip and fall on these peculiar concrete-log and gravel steps. We are startled when we hear Carolyn scream and, thinking she's taken a tumble, we hurry to catch up. I breathe easier to find my wife hasn't toppled into the thick underbrush. "Tom!" she exclaims, "a large snake just slithered across my path and went that way."

"In that case, I'll go *this* way, honey." Our guides still don't understand the cause of Carolyn's fright. Apparently, they don't comprehend the word 'snake,' — so I proceed to translate the name for this creature.

When they learn the source of Carolyn's scare was only a mere *hehbee*, their concerned expressions change into grins. "It is a sign of good luck to see *hehbee* when one is on a *sampo* (hike)," informs Yumi-chan. And it must be so, for neither did we have another encounter with a snake, nor did any of us slip and fall during the steep return to level ground.

As we retrace our steps past throngs of pedestrians and bicyclists, Carolyn remarks, "You know, Tom, I haven't seen another Caucasian face since we left the Yokohama Station this morning."

"That's true, dear. For some reason, this area is just overrun with *foreigners*."

Our hike has been a success and a treat, but nothing like the treat spread before us when we return to the home of our gracious hosts. Mrs. Mori has been busy, and is setting out dish after tempting dish of food to share with their American visitors.

I'm sure Mrs. Mori is a whiz of a cook, yet I think it impossible that all these dishes could have been prepared by one woman alone. Her son later shared with me a secret of Japanese housewives: When expecting a large group at her dining table — or a husband whose return from the workplace is of uncertain time — it is common practice for a Japanese housewife to select ready-to-eat food from the countless variety sold in the basement level of large department stores.

Unlike America — where home-cooked food is the order of the day for company — the Japanese think anything made from scratch is unsuitable for the palates of guests. They rely, instead, on pre-prepared culinary masterpieces, turned out by professional chefs, such as we see here on our table this evening. It was reassuring to hear this, mostly because I dreaded the thought of our dear hostess slaving away in the kitchen while we were off on a lark in the park.

The evening meal is delicious, and so bountiful that it must have cost a fortune. Rascally Haru-chan, the only child present, trots about in imitation of a pony, then glomps onto her dad's back while he's eating, attempting to convert this patient man into a horse.

Grandmother, Mrs. Mori, issues a mild reproach to see the child acting thus. Unused to the sight of heathen Caucasian faces, Haru-chan distances herself from me, until Junko carries her over for a good-bye hug. She explains that she and her husband must take Haru-chan home now, or this little lass will be difficult to awaken for school tomorrow.

Before we go to bed, Carolyn and I are given towels, and I enter the *furo* bath behind a sliding *shoji* screen. Once my kimono is hung up, I soap my tired body, then rinse with warm water while surrounded by steam issuing from the hot bath.

Carolyn also emerges to disrobe and wash up, while I gingerly place one foot inside the two-foot-deep cauldron, and just manage to squelch a yelp similar to her earlier encounter with the snake. "Yikes, Carolyn! I don't think I can tolerate that hot water. People will hear me yelp from here to Yokohama if subjected to any more of my body than a scalded foot!"

"Listen, you silly," says my unsympathetic spouse. "Top it off with some cold water if you must. Not everyone's a sissy like you. "

"Sissy, hell!" I grumble. "I notice you haven't tried to enter this lava crater yet."

"Just let the cold water cool it down while you scrub my back," Carolyn admonishes her *sissy*.

I have to admit that, although nearly scalded alive in water that took my breath away, it made for a sound sleep; after reading only two or three pages in my book, I drifted off, and no snakes or scalding water encroached upon my dreams to startle me awake.

CHAPTER XIX

ednesday, May 25:

During our thirty-nine years of wedded life, Carolyn invariably falls to sleep later than I. Conversely, I generally awaken earlier, as is the case now. I'm up, treading softly down a corridor to brush my teeth and hoping the electric razor won't disturb the peace and tranquility of this domain. But I needn't have worried; the sound of a television and some activity in the kitchen next to our room can be heard.

I enter the kitchen where Mrs. Mori is busy while her husband, a newspaper in hand, sits and watches TV in an adjoining room, convenient to talk with his wife about what's what on TV and in the paper. I attempt to explain how my wife and he are alike, in that both have a knack for being able to do two or three things at once. Carolyn, for example, seldom watches TV without doing something else, such as reading, bookkeeping or playing solitaire.

The Moris speak almost no English, and I feel it rude to have interrupted their little togetherness before Mr. Mori must leave for work. If that is so, it's too late for me to exit back to our room, for hot green tea has been offered, and Mr. Mori asks me to join him in front of the TV. He tells me his son is still sleeping and asks if my wife is awake.

"Hirokazu, your number-one son, worked long hours yesterday, and since this is his holiday, that fellow can enjoy the privilege of sleeping in. Unlike my dear wife, who played all day yesterday. I will check on her now."

Returning to our room, I see Carolyn is up and applying makeup in front of a hand mirror — not an easy task in the absence of a dressing table. You'll note, however, I clearly stated, 'returning to our room,' with no reference to a 'bedroom.' In a true Japanese home there is no such thing as a bedroom per se; one beds on the tatami floor once the futon bedding is taken from behind a sliding *shoji* closet area, and unrolled in the center of the room. Only then can this room be construed as a bedroom; during the day, it can serve any purpose. It can be a parlor, dining room, den, anything actually, except a kitchen or bath. Aside from a built-in alcove where some lovely vases and plates are displayed, the only other furniture here is a table turned on its side to make bedding space.

That last paragraph became a lengthy explanation for why my wife now uses a hand mirror instead of a dressing table. Yet, I hope the reader will gain some knowledge of how different are the American and Japanese cultures.

I wish Carolyn a good morning and ask, "Are you ready for breakfast? I think Mr. and Mrs. Mori are. He just asked about you."

Well, I was half right; Mr. Mori is ready. Japanese wives typically serve their husband and guests without joining them at the table, which is the case this morning.

Mrs. Mori pours hot coffee and Carolyn is delighted. "I

haven't tasted coffee since we left David's yesterday." She sighs, then sleepily reflects, "Was that only yesterday, Tom? It seems we have been away longer than that."

"No coffee for me, thank you. I'll continue with more hot green tea." This surprises Mrs. Mori, then Carolyn and I are both surprised by a western-style breakfast of sausage and scrambled eggs with sweet breads, concluding with a dish of large, sweet strawberries and cream;

As we finish, a sleepy-eyed Hirokazu makes his entrance and tells us good morning, his voice still raspy from a sound sleep. He stretches and tries to gain a more wakeful state of mind, eager to explain what lies in store this day, once Cousin Yumi comes over to accompany.

Hirokazu's large Toyota Landcruiser becomes our bus for a grand tour to see the highlights of his hometown. Our first stop takes us up a winding road to the Shizuoka Museum of Art, a fairly large and assuredly beautiful building that features paintings and sculptures of European and American artists from very old to modern.

We enjoy walking from room to room to view these many works of art, and then enter a magnificent, high-domed architectural wonder of a building, newly annexed to this museum for one reason — to display a treasure of Rodin's stone and metal sculptures.

Mere words are insufficient to describe the statuary we see of *Mercury, Ugolino and his Children, Centaur, The Creator* — and on and on of these life-sized and larger sculptures created by Auguste Rodin (who lived from 1840 to 1917).

Even New Guinea tribesmen are familiar by now with Rodin's world-renowned *The Thinker*. But here, the most impressive work is given a place of prominence under the canopy of this beautiful building — Rodin's gigantic masterpiece *The Gates of Hell*. Frankly, I fail to savvy American's trifling apology of *excuse my French*, when a profane word tumbles forth. Anyone with half a brain can't help but note that the French words for this majestic sculpture — *La Porte de l'Enfer* — are much less profane-sounding than their English rendering — *Gates of Hell.*

After a walk about the museum grounds, where myriads of azaleas in bloom are a feast for the eye and a target for the camera, we leave this museum overlooking Shizuoka, and drive to a *soba* and *udon* noodle cafe.

We dine on this delicious fare, amused at how such a demure and quiet lady as Cousin Yumi can slurp her noodle dish with such gusto (slurping is common practice in Japan, and not considered unrefined). *What better way to show one's appreciation while dining on soup*, I think, and proceed to adopt the slurping custom of my friends as the polite thing to do.

Our gregarious host is in a joking mood as we finish up lunch. Hirokazu teases that the museum trip was a first for him, the cafe a first — and where we are about to go next, a first, but he grins while speaking thus. "You are not being truthful, Hirokazu-kun. Your face can't tell a lie, and look how Yumi-chan stares at her cousin when he attempts to fool us with untruths," I chide this fellow, as Carolyn and Yumi-chan laugh, caught up in the amusement of the moment....

We journey next to a famous Shizuoka landmark on a mountain top which translates as *The Table Plateau*. Its claim to fame is not a table, but what they refer to as *roppu car*, (rope car), whereas I prefer to think it a *cable* car, as even the stoutest of ropes would be unsafe for transporting a group of about twenty down a steep incline in slow motion.

A steep descent along forested hillsides of evergreens and broad-leafed, deciduous trees takes us to a shrine, notable for its oriental architecture, in shades of deep red and gilt accents. This type of *pagoda* is usually what the western mind conjures up when thinking of the Orient.

This Shizuoka landmark is a special place to take guests,

and I hope Hirokazu has asked for atonement for trying to hoodwink us into thinking this shrine — as well as the museum and popular cafe — were first-time visits. We take numerous photographs to remember this special day spent with our Shizuoka 'son' and his cousin.

"Are you tired now," Hirokazu-kun queries, "or you like see teahouse before we go home?"

Before her husband is able to get a word in edgewise to vote in favor of returning home, his wife outbids him. "Yes, " Carolyn exclaims excitedly, "I'd love to experience a Japanese tearoom ceremony. "

"But this is not an 'August Moon,' Hirokazu, " I tease. "You mean to tell me your city has a 'Teahouse of the May Sun?'" My quip requires a little explaining, as we set out toward the outskirts of town, and see honorable teahouse sitting prettily off the highway next to a small convenience store and plant nursery.

No other parties are waiting at the house, which looks remarkably like that of Hirokazu's own home, so Carolyn and Yumi readily secure admission tickets. Hirokazu is not surprised that I abstain from this particular adventure, and he joins me on the banks of a lotus pond to watch a number of *koi* (carp) swimming lazily about in the warm afternoon sun. "I think you like watch fish here, better than sit on knees inside and hold teacup," this cheerful fellow grins.

The lotus pond and Japanese garden are worth the trip. If this were America, we 'd almost certainly see an area set off with grass, but growing and mowing lawns are not obsessions here. The purveyor of lawn mowers and fertilizer better have a second income or starve.

This meditation ends, now that our ladies have been ritualized in how to comport oneself in a teahouse, and we head home. It is good to see the cheerful and kind face of Mrs. Mori, who listens to her son tell her about the busy day the four of us have had. She suggests a brief *yasumi* (rest) before we go out for dinner.

Words fall short of telling the reader how truly grand this family is. Everyone here is so considerate to make Carolyn and I feel welcome (even if this Japan Diary doesn't find its way into print, having set these sentiments into the innards of this word-processor machine, they are easily extractable for me to print out and send as thank-you letters).

On this sunny day turning into early evening, we are taken to a popular Chinese restaurant in downtown Shizuoka near the rail station. Mr. and Mrs. Mori collaborate on the menu selections, and their son offers some ideas, then turns to me and asks, "My mother wants know anything you cannot eat."

"We eat everything," Carolyn beams. "We enjoy all types of dishes." That is true, and I nod in agreement.

The food is delicious, but quite unlike the tastes my wife and I have encountered in American Chinese restaurants during so many visits in quest of a favored food.

Our evening does not end with dinner, as there are other songs to be sung and other attractions to see. We drive to visit where the Mori's daughter, Junko, and her family live. It will be good to see Junko, Mr. Kawai, and little Haru-chan once more before departing early tomorrow.

Their home has a number of stories and resembles a small hotel. The bell is rung, but with no response, and Hirokazu tells us, "My sister family not home so we come back. "

These folks reside in a hotel, I think, as we meander just around the corner, intrigued by the sight of a wide plaza where an engineering marvel enchants us. A huge cement-lined pond with high circular walls of concrete on the far side has been built here for the citizens of Shizuoka to enjoy. And now at dusk, the fun begins. Dozens of lighted sprays begin shooting both from the water below and from the walls above, dancing rhythmically to the strains of European classical music. The effect is utterly stunning when viewed as we do at dusk. These geysers of water are silhouetted by colored lights, and computerized to alternately start and stop, again and again to the rhythm of the musical background emanating from the speakers situated high atop tall concrete and stainless steel columns.

Our hosts have obviously witnessed this spectacle before, but for Carolyn and me this is a wonderful added attraction on this day of many attractions. She tells me, "These fountains, lights, and the music have an almost Olympic-swimmer dance effect, Tom."

"How true, hon. We are seeing Shizuoka's aptly-named *Rainbow Fountain.* And it's so close to where the Kawai family live that little Haru-chan must be delighted to come and see this often with her parents. "

"And with their windows open, they can hear the strains of a Mozart concerto," returns a wife who has forgotten more about classical music than this husband ever learned.

After twenty minutes, Mrs. Junko Kawai is here to invite us to her home just a stone's throw away. Upon entering the large double doors, a wall switch is pressed to summon a small elevator, we think to transport us up to the Kawai's apartment on the fourth floor. Carolyn and I are taken aback to learn that this is no apartment elevator; in fact, only a family of three reside here, and this is *their* elevator.

Mr. Kawai is an architect and, although it appears he has designed a hotel instead of a house, we are terribly wrong in that assessment. It is truly unique. The first two floors comprise the office and reception space for this husband and wife architectural team. The third floor is a tea room designed in the quaint, old style, befitting that ancient ceremony. The fourth and fifth floors are the family's living area.

The elevator goes only to the fourth floor, where we are greeted by Mr. Kawai and little Haru-chan. Upon entering the living room, we are made welcome by this affluent family. The room is beautifully furnished with modern western couches and lounge chairs. A well designed kitchen is to the left and, heading right, we take a tour up a stairway leading to the fifth floor, where Haru-chan's penthouse playroom is located, lined with all manner of stuffed animals and toys.

While the Moris sit comfortably on the couch, and Junko readies some snacks and drinks, her husband leads us back to the elevator to go one story down for a tour of the tea room. I see no stairs one can use instead of the elevator. In fact, inside space doesn't permit a stairway to the ground floor, so it is located on the outside of the building. "Well, babe, this is your second tea room visit of the day," I tell Carolyn.

"But the first for you, Tom. You and Hirokazu passed up the chance after lunch today, to sit and chat while Yumi and I toured that place for the price of a ticket."

Junko follows us now into this quaint, almost mystical setting, and explains aspects of the age-old tea ceremony performed here on the straw *tatami* floor. Everything about this tea room is uniquely Japanese, and a shiver runs down my spine in this setting as I whisper to Carolyn, "It's so restful — like being alone in a quiet village church."

"You know, Tom, I'm surprised Hirokazu went out of his way earlier today to take us to a commercial tea room. I'm learning more about the aesthetics of this in his sister's very own home than I did there."

We leave the third floor to return to the living area for snacks and drinks with the family. I play a few numbers on their piano, then ask Junko to play something. "Sorry," she declines, and inserts a tape into this Yamaha Clavichord to transform it, *voila*, into a self-paying piano, so adroit of chords and style it humbles this self-taught musician into thinking, someday, to take up proper lessons.

Junko has a vocal music background and a good voice. We sing a duet which seems to elicit a favorable response. But that's undoubtedly an erroneous assumption on my part, for Mr.

Mori announces in Japanese, *Kaerenakareba narimasen* (it's time to go home).

We've had a truly splendid and full day in company with our super 'son's' family, but now, since he and his father must begin work early, we don't linger for any more conviviality, except for Hirokazu to grin and say: "I hope the water in *furo* bath not too hot: I hear somebody almost got cooked last night." I bared my teeth in dog-fashion at this rascal 'son,' whose teasing mannerisms are so like my own son's.

We have been too preoccupied today and yesterday to think much about the days just spent with David and his family. But after a soothing, much less scalding dip in the furo bath, his mother and I lie on our pillows wondering how Dave, Izzie and Kirby are doing. We already miss our family, and anxiously await a time to tell them how the Moris have made these two days spent with them in Shizuoka so wonderful.

It has been too eventful and wondrous for these grandparents even to think about a granddaughter living somewhere south of here - in a town called Suzuka.

"Wouldn't it have been neat if Monica had been here with us today?" Carolyn sighs while turning out the light.

"Sure, babe, but this is Shizuoka — not Suzuka. Close, but no cigar."

CHAPTER XX

Thursday, May 26:

This is the morning of our departure from the Mori family in Shizuoka. Our intention today is to reach Nagoya (a city our travel booklet highlights as having much of sightseeing interest), or travel to the more distant city of Hiroshima to look up Carolyn's aunt and cousins.

Mrs. Mori is fretful during breakfast, as this genteel lady is very concerned that Carolyn and I have not booked our lodging ahead, and the uncertainty of our itinerary troubles her. I try to console this dear lady by seeming upbeat and optimistic, although I confess to having some doubts myself, since Carolyn's mother has lost contact with her deceased husband's side of the family.

The breakfast Mrs. Mori prepares is grand in the Japanese manner. A whole barbecued fish — head, eyes and all — is served with rice, salad and vegetables (cooked and pickled) and accompanied by numerous cups of hot green tea. It's a veritable feast for the Emperor himself! This peasant from abroad, however; is so full he can only nibble at the assortment of tea cakes presented for dessert. What a deliciously different breakfast send-off!

We bid sorrowful adieus to Hirokazu and his dad as they leave early for work. "You simply must come to America to visit us," Carolyn and I stress in concert.

"My father, mother think their English not good travel."

Carolyn insists, "Then you will come and interpret, Hirokazu!"

A light rain falls as, together with dear Mrs. Mori, we board the cab and wend our way to the train station. We decide that, owing to the rain in the Nagoya-Mie area, we will put off a sightsee there. We were to inquire about the location of our granddaughter's house, which we know is somewhere in this prefecture. Instead, we elect to journey onward to the Hiroshima area to visit Carolyn's aunt and cousins.

Mrs. Mori continues to be *shimpai* (perturbed), as we bid a last good-bye. It is a genuinely worrisome thing for her that we have no particular travel plans with hotel reservations pinned down in advance — something obviously unheard of in the Mori's own travel planning.

We experience no difficulty booking a non-smoking compartment for Hiroshima. In no time, an efficient rail employee checks our passes and punches us tickets from his computer for the next train to Hiroshima, which requires a transfer at Osaka.

Rain falls alternately on and off as we skim along on a bullet train even more comfortable than the last. In addition to airplane-style, fold-down tables from the seat ahead, these also have a small table that can be extracted from the arm rests (a real convenience for this diarist to begin filling pages of Mori family remembrances).

Exiting this train at Osaka, we brave hordes of folks scurrying to meet their trains, and I comfortably elicit directions by speaking Japanese to a man in a designated smoking area.

We only have a twenty-minute layover before catching the Hiroshma *shinkansen*. Incidentally, these *shinkansen* are called 'bullet trains' only by foreigners. The word *shinkansen* actually translates as 'New Fast Rail Line.' Yet 'bullet' is an apt description to use for the streamlined bullet shape of the engine, and obviously by the speed these trains manage between stations

This Hiroshima-bound train now travels through our granddaughter's prefecture of *Mie* (pronounced 'me-ay'). "Were it not for a downpour of rain," I tell my wife when we slow for a stop at the Kyoto Station, "we could get off here at this city we enjoyed so much during our '83 trip, have a second look, and make inquiry to lead us to Monica's town. I remember David mentioning that his ex-wife made frequent visits to Kyoto from the place where she lives with her parents, so it can't be too far."

"Yes, I recall that, Tom. But we'll go on. My throat is bothering me, and this rain won't help that. I hope it eases up as we travel farther south."

"You hope what eases up — your throat, or this rain?"

"Both, silly," Carolyn quickly and correctly informs me while reaching for another Japanese cough drop, purchased from a kiosk when changing trains at Osaka.

"Well, a must on this itinerary is to find our little pumpkin once we visit other sights to the south." (Carolyn doesn't know it, but I secretly calendar her birthday in six more days, as befitting a special day for this long-awaited reunion.)

Our train arrives precisely on time at the large Hiroshima Station. It is 2:30 p.m. as we tote our heavy bags to the front of the station, following a sign in familiar use at all train stations: *Basu Noriba* (Bus Stop).

When we arrived here eleven years ago we hailed a cab and showed the driver Aunt Maki 's address. After a short ride, that driver paused away from traffic to use a taxi telephone station, requesting specific instructions to this address in the outlying suburban reaches of *Gyon,* where Aunt Maki resides. That taxi fare of July 1983 was expensive, and in consideration of 1994 prices, we now seek a bus for a trip of considerable distance from this station.

Complicating matters is that Carolyn's aunt, while still residing in Gyon, no longer lives at that previous address alone. She shares a house with a daughter or son now — we're not sure which. Carolyn's mom in Los Angeles was uncertain of the precise location, having gleaned information secondhand from Aunt Maki's brother in Hawaii.

Our main concern now, is to find a bus marked *Gyon* or *Gyon-Machi* (Gyon Town) — again, we 're not sure which. And now, watching one bus after another arriving and departing, and unable to read the *kanji* symbols denoting their destinations, it baffles us as to which one to take. "Those symbols are as clear as mud, babe. I'll seek help from the next driver. " That man is much agitated at this interruption and signals for me to look elsewhere for directions.

Japanese are not always polite when confronted by the unexpected; I have even heard that Tokyo cab drivers assiduously avoid stopping for foreigners. Although the foreigner may be fluent in Japanese, these drivers take no chance, and avoid the possibility that precious time will be wasted by an encounter involving communication difficulties.

And now, *I* get a taste of this, and withdraw from the bus to remark to Carolyn, "That surly driver must have arisen on the wrong side of the floor this morning."

Seeing that we were having difficulty, a young lady approaches. "I know little English. Where you looking?"

"We need a bus to Gyon," I answer in Japanese.

She then takes a sheet of notepaper from her purse, and uses a ballpoint pen to write down two Japanese kanji-character symbols. "Look for this, front of bus. But please, while you wait, close your eyes two minutes and make hands this way." She clasps her hands in an attitude of prayer, and Carolyn and I think, *how strange*. This very same thing occurred during our fifteen-minute wait at the Shizuoka Station for Mr. and Mrs. Mori.

During that wait, I stopped in a Baskin-Robbins Ice Cream Parlor to buy Carolyn a cone. Upon bringing the ice cream to her, I found that she had her eyes closed and hands clasped prayerfully, while a young man stood in front of her, chanting something incomprehensible. Both that young man — and now this young lady — were of neat appearance, but God only knows what their mission is. In any event, Carolyn and I cheerfully complied on the first occasion, but she refuses this woman's instructions to close her eyes this second time around.

Grateful to be helped by her to gain information about the bus to take, I go along and, whatever this person chanted must have worked, for our bus pulls up and I thank her. What religion these two young people espouse — or if they were seeking a monetary contribution — we were not to learn. Both occasions of this were followed by the arrival of our transportation, and left these American sojourners in a perplexed state of wonderment.

After a half-hour journey on the bus some distance away from the Hiroshima metropolis our bus pulls up to a stop in the town of Gyon on the outskirts of Hiroshima (a beneficent distance for our Aunt Maki and her family, away from the epicenter where the first atomic bomb was unleashed upon the unfortunate populous on an August day in 1945). We thank the driver as we step off the bus. Carolyn and I have journeyed far to achieve a second reunion with her father's relatives — a father whose memory we both revere, and we can do no less.

CHAPTER XXI

Our bus has deposited us in a commercial area of small shops. As light rain is falling, Carolyn thinks to dig into one of our bags to find a small umbrella, but discards that idea; it's an inopportune time to ransack two pieces of bulky luggage. I am quick to inquire of the whereabouts of the *yuubin kyoku* (post office) from an elderly lady wearing wooden *geta* as footwear. She carries an oval, wicker basket of vegetables under one arm, an umbrella in the other, and nods her head to the right. We follow the clomp-clomping percussion sound of her *geta* down a narrow lane of commercial enterprises.

Walking as briskly as the heavy luggage permits, we reach what I think is the post office, and Carolyn waits outside under an awning while I seek information here. A chubby lady with a winning smile looks me over quizzically. "Do you know where the Mizote family lives? We are looking for my wife's elderly aunt. I thought this post office a good place to ask." My Japanese is understood but, unfortunately, this place is not the post office!

"*Chotto matte* (just a moment). Next door post office. I show you."

We trot next door to the small post office, where a friendly group of three workers return my salutation of good afternoon in their language. One of them listens to our benefactress from next door, and produces a thick book of names and addresses, plus a telephone directory. "Ah so. Not very far," these kindred spirits beam.

The rest of the postal workers hear this and seem delighted to have helped these travelers from abroad. I guess that these folks, in an area so remote from the city, seldom see a Caucasian face. Anyway, they seem genuinely glad of this interruption. I return their bows with a hearty, "*Sayonara,*" and set forth with Carolyn to follow our gregarious lady back to her shop.

While this effervescent woman reports back to her boss or co-worker (I'm not sure which) of the happy finding of the Mizote's address, I see that this shop is some sort of packing and wrapping enterprise. The gentleman telephones and then signals to us everything is *daijobu* (okay). "I take you now," the lady says, and we thank her co-worker who seems equally happy to assist.

Our jolly guide wishes to share her umbrella, but since there are three of us and the rain is light, I ask that she please proceed ahead of us. Where umbrellas are concerned, the old adage: 'Two is company — three's a crowd,' certainly fits.

"Your wife, Japanese, ne? Strange that I not hear her speak." Our helpful guide thinks perhaps Carolyn is hard of hearing. Carolyn has been characteristically unresponsive but is merely reluctant to attempt the tedious struggle of speaking Japanese to strangers. She is content that I be the go-between in this undertaking.

"Well, she was born in America, so is somewhat embarrassed to talk. But she understands much," I explain in Japanese.

This good Samaritan has led us four blocks to greet Chizuko Mizote, a daughter-in-law of Aunt Maki, who has been alerted by phone that we are on the way. We know this friendly woman of our age from a visit in 1983, and she seems delighted to see us again.

Chizuko and I both thank the shop lady for her kindness, and we exchange bows before she returns. I tell Chizuko that I want to buy that lady a gift to thank her for her assistance. She understands, and tells me *ato deh* (later).

This familiar home is not where Chizuko and her husband, Toshio, Carolyn's first cousin reside. We learn later that this couple lives behind a small machine shop they own. This place, rather, is the home of Fujie, Aunt Maki's widowed daughter, and shared now with Aunt Maki.

Cousin Fujie welcomes us at the door, then escorts us to Aunt Maki, who is resting in bed. We are in the company of senior citizens who attended school when English was not taught in this country. So, unlike the younger generation, it is difficult to speak and comprehend our language. They compliment me for the ability to carry on a conversation in Japanese, and fully understand that, due to World War II, Carolyn was prevented from going to Japanese language school as a youth growing up in Hawaii.

Carolyn's elder auntie is mentally alert, and looks spry for her ninety-five years. "Gosh, she looks like Daddy, Tom. There's no doubt about them being sister and brother, is there?" My wife smiles as we sit for tea and rice cookies.

We enjoy a chat with these three ladies, and Carolyn understands much of what they say. She 'wings it' in broken Japanese, comfortable in the presence of family visited once before. She hands each fifty dollars in yen, apologizing that it would have been difficult to pack gifts, so they should please buy something with this gift of money.

I inquire of the cute white dog who shared this home with Cousin Fujie when we visited here in 1983. "She lived a long life and died. I remember how you enjoyed taking her for a walk," Fujie relates in comprehensible Japanese.

That the dog is no longer here is probably just as well, for now that Aunt Maki has come to live with her daughter, such pets spoiled by room and board, bode ill with her. This lady has undergone severe wartime and post-war hardship and deprivation, so it is understandable when auntie makes disparaging remarks about grandson Motoaki's household. "He and his wife keep not just one dog, *Iya* — *four* dogs live there," this lady chafes, in disdain of the ways of the younger generation's affinity for acquisitive gain. "Can you imagine how silly to keep such a zoo of animals?" the family matriarch adds.

Interestingly enough, we don't linger long before being taken to this grandson's home where we can see firsthand these pooches of whom Aunt Maki speaks. Auntie's son, Toshio, arrives to drive us to his son's house. Excuse me, did I say 'house?' A better synonym for that palatial residence would be *oshiro* (castle) — for indeed, *that's what it is.*

Second cousin Motoaki and his wife Asako dwell in this castle I will soon describe, reached by a winding ascent through a Hollywood Hills-type setting of expensive homes overlooking an urban valley below. It is a mansion, built of sturdy bricks surrounded on three sides by retaining walls of chiseled stone, varying from perhaps fifteen to thirty feet in height. Atop this vertical wall is a forest of young evergreen trees and shrubs that serve to provide seclusion.

It astonishes me to see a large western style home of two stories and four bedrooms, expensively furnished with western imports. "I imported this furniture from 'Pennsylvania House' in America," Motoaki asserts in English as he shows Carolyn and me around. His dad sits at a large, Queen Anne-style dining table drinking a beer with some slices of ham and rye bread set out for him.

And yes, the objects of Aunt Maki's scorn dwell here in the form of four dogs; two long-haired Chihuahuas are kept in an indoor enclosure, each with their own small doggie house. Outside dwell the other two — a large, friendly Golden Labrador and, pointing out the fourth dog, our proud host apologizes, "That last one you see is abandoned dog."

Carolyn and I are startled to view the stylish quarters the two dogs outside have. There is a large picnic table made especially for their dining, and (would you believe?) a doghouse built of bricks to match these mutt's owner's home! "Honey, these dogs aren't *that* wealthy," I jest. "Their home may be upscale, but it has no garage attached."

"But you can bet if there were it would have a dog-sized, Rolls-Royce inside," asserts my spouse.

Incidentally, we learn later the garage here accommodates three vehicles, and is situated at basement-level beneath the home.

Our hosts are cordial and generous to a fault, even though I tease Cousin Motoaki with an English word he's familiar with. "You folks are *Yuppies*, I kid this serious man in his mid-forties. He grins, and doesn't mind the appellation to designate young, upwardly-mobile folks of his generation.

Motoaki is quite fluent in English, and tells me he has a real affection for American movies and music, as he bids Carolyn and me to join his father at a platter of ham and cheese slices. Carolyn nibbles at this and I accept a glass of beer poured from a large bottle on the table. After snacking on pretzels, a glass of 'suds' is satisfying.

Our host is gregarious, and speaks English that I think his wife, Asako, and father, Toshio, barely comprehend. "This home cost over one-million dollars, and is all paid for in seven more years. I like to retire early. Too much stress."

Carolyn and I are impressed, if not downright amazed, by the prosperity of this fellow we first met in July of '83, when his only child, a son, was nine years old."

"By the way," I inquire, "what business has made you so *kanemochi* (wealthy)?"

Motoaki laughs, "My company makes glass windshields and rubber gaskets to fit all cars, and has contracts with Honda, Mazda, Nissan and Toyota."

"What about Subaru? I drive one of those in California."

"Yes, Subaru also. All Japanese cars and trucks. My company very busy."

So busy, that I see this genial host carries a portable telephone in his luxury vehicle when Carolyn and I are transported down from this hillside view for an evening out.

It seems only these two Americans are invited. As explained in an earlier chapter, Japanese wives aren't generally included when business associates or guests are entertained outside the home. And when Carolyn naively inquires why Asako hasn't accompanied us, her cousin strokes his chin awhile in thought before explaining, "My wife and I reach good understanding. She knows my business requires that I go out evening alone with guests, the Japanese way. She used to pout sometimes. But now — I think our marriage good. She loves looking after dogs at home, and anything she needs, I buy."

"What is your son doing now that he is grown?" I ask.

"Oh, we see him once in awhile. He is playboy who doesn't like work, so we get along so-so. He only like to hang out with the crowd and go surfing. Right now, he is going out with Australian girl who is go-go dancer. He not like school much, so now that he is twenty, he want his father support."

We are taken to a friend's *sushi* bar where we sit at the counter and are introduced to one of Cousin's buddies, the owner, nicknamed *Mastah* (Master), who jokes with us and his other clientele, while he performs the skillful tasks attendant with *sushi* making.

"This is not unlike other *sushi* bars we have encountered

in California," I conjecture. "But truly, Mastah, your *sushi* is *ichiban* (number-one)!"

Our plates are constantly replenished with all varieties of this fresh and delicious seafood, prepared with cones of vinegared rice or tubes wrapped in thinly sliced seaweed. Carolyn sips one glass of wine, and I lose count of the glasses of good Kiirin beer Motoaki pours for me. As soon as my glass is half empty, he reaches around and refills it.

Since our host is driving, I hope that not too much beer flows his way. It is somewhat more potent than American beer, so I reach the point of having to turn down more of that beverage, in case I get silly and challenge this generous host to a singing contest ala *karaoke* (which was to happen our second night out on the town, but more about that later).

Stuffed with some of Japan's most cherished contributions to the palates of the world, we thank Mastah for his culinary wizardry in the production of *sushi* and our host for treating us. Motoaki picks us up at the entrance, and drives us back to his house.

As we view the twinkling lights of the valley from our bedroom window, my wife sighs, "This cousin reminds me so much of my brother, Ben; both have made it big in the business world — one in America, one in Japan. What a grand evening, Tom."

"It was, babe. I only wish Monica were here with us to see how well her grandmother's relatives are doing. Someday, perhaps, she will have that chance."

CHAPTER XXII

Friday, May 27:

Arose late and breakfasted American-style on ham, eggs, toast and coffee. The dogs are jealous, and peer in hungrily through the sliding glass doors. Even though her husband has departed earlier for work, Asako conforms to the Japanese custom of serving her guests without joining them at the table. And now that they are dining, she gives the pet dogs their breakfast, which they wolf down at their private table just outside.

"Uncle Toshio will be here at ten o'clock to take you to visit Aunt Maki," Asako explains in her soft voice.

"That gives us time to walk around this lovely neighborhood, honey," my wife suggests as we finish eating.

"A small *koen* (park) is over there," points out Asako at the entry door where we slip into our shoes. A short walk around a hairpin turn in the road takes us there, and we sit on a bench to admire the panoramic valley below.

We then backtrack past the front of our host's brick home and wave at the 'abandoned dog,' luckily adopted to live an upper-class life. We have yet to hear the Golden Lab bark, but the 'orphan' has learned some bad manners somewhere in his past, and growls at us with gusto.

We ascend a steep hillside road, admiring the custom homes built on large lots — certainly rare, I think, in a nation so densely populated as this. "David and Isabel won't believe this when we tell them," comments Carolyn.

Toshio is as punctual as the train system, but these Americans, like the mongrel dog just described, have learned some bad habits somewhere in *their* past, and can see Toshio and his wife, hands shading their eyes, looking right and left for us. We quicken our pace and apologize for being tardy, dart inside to change into different shoes, and say good-bye to Asako.

We journey downward from the affluent heights of one cousin to the modest residence of another who shares it with her mother, Carolyn's Aunt Maki.

While taking tea and rice cookies, Carolyn asks, "Are there some old family photographs I can look at?"

Perplexed by this question, asked in English supplemented by pointing to Fujie's deceased husband's photo, I clarify, by 'quarterbacking' a signal in Japanese, using *furui* for 'old' and *shashin* for 'photograph.'

Chizuko smiles and responds in her language, "There is a box of old pictures I will bring you from my home."

This was a home, incidentally, we were not to see at any time. I think Toshio and Chizuko have never invited us because of the Japanese predilection for thinking that what is newer is always infinitely better, and I assume that they think their home unworthy for our eyes.

But that is only to hazard a guess, based largely on the fact that one seldom sees an older model vehicle on the road here.

Our son has told us that there is virtually no used car market in Japan. "Temporary workers like Isabel and me generally must buy the used cars sold by other Americans who are returning to the U.S. The Japanese ship *their* used cars out to the Philippines or to various Pacific-Islander buyers."

Also, I recall a visit to see an old friend during our 1983 trip to Japan. I was never invited to either her house or her cousin's, another close friend. And when I suggested it would be nice to visit her home rather than meet in a restaurant, she replied, "No, no — you would not like see the rabbit hutch where my husband and I live."

My guess is that a certain cultural pretentiousness stands in the way of welcoming visitors into the privacy of just any home here. Japanese people have a strong desire to show only their best side — whether in dress, automobiles, houses, or other material possessions.

And these of my wife's relatives have never been to the U.S., where one finds the customs significantly less formal. When Carolyn and I — as do other Americans — visit in the homes of friends or ride in their cars, little notice is given to whether these are new or old, small or large, expensive or modestly priced.

Old photographs, fortunately, don't fit into this category, and Chizuko returns with a box of them. Carolyn and I enjoy sharing these old black and white and sepia-toned photos preserved from the past. She is delighted to discover several photos of her father, two of which are duplicates, and Carolyn is happy to receive these to take home.

Toshio returns and places an electric hot plate in the center of the table. Then he and Chizuko begin chopping vegetables in sister Fujie's modern kitchen.

At one time this couple were restauranteurs — and the *sukiyaki* they prepare is proof they were good ones: The thinly-sliced beef, cooked with sliced green and white onions, mushrooms, tofu, and translucent rice noodles in a broth of *sake* and soy sauce is delicious!

We dine family-style, directly from the sizzling metal *wok* on the hot plate, placing in our bowls as much or as little of each ingredient on top of a raw egg before eating.

And, eat we did — from Master Chef Toshio's *sukiyaki-grande!* Carolyn and I overdo it, I think (forgetting that our chef's son intends to take us out for dinner later this evening). When all have eaten heartily, although there is ample left, I push away from a seat on the tatami-matted floor. Chizuko won't permit my help in clearing the table, so I lean against the wall for back support.

With the table cleared, we chat some more. The subject of Aunt Maki's brother comes up, and she tells Carolyn, "It must have been hard on your mother to have lived with a man who drank and smoked so much." We have an idea about the source of that secondhand information, and Carolyn rises to her dad's defense.

"On the contrary, your brother was not a difficult man to live with; while Dad did like strong drink and tobacco, he was a good and responsible man. Tom, and others who knew Dad in Hawaii and California, feel as I do — that he had a kind and considerate personality. You should see what he accomplished with carpentry and building tools. It's sad that you live so far apart from your brother, Aunt Maki. You never really got to know him. To know Dad was to love him." Carolyn was passionate and eloquent, but spoke mostly in English, so I searched for the proper words in Japanese to reinforce sentiments shared about the memory of Pop Matsuda. Cousins Chizuko and Fujie nod in agreement. They act pleased with the kind words spoken about their deceased uncle, who became an American citizen and led a productive life.

Before giving this fond subject a rest, I recalled how much Pop Matsuda enjoyed playing cards. "Poker and rummy were favorite card games of Carolyn's dad," I tell them, "and even the Japanese card game of *hana fuda* was good fun."

That caused Aunt Maki's old eyes to light up. This lady has much in common with a brother she's hardly known since they were young children, except via letters and one brief visit here, in 1956, when brother and sister were reunited.

The cards are spread out to check that they are all there. That passes inspection, so Aunt Maki shuffles and deals to Carolyn, who eagerly looks to see what the gods of fortune have dealt her this hand. Cousin Fujie plays to make it a threesome.

"This is a good time for me to buy a present for the kind lady who brought us to you yesterday," I tell Chizuko.

"Yes, I will go with you."

A walk of two blocks on this warm but dry afternoon brings us to a shop where I find a thousand yen ($10) box of assorted, fancy cookies. Japanese merchants are true artists at the business of wrapping packages, and their wrapping paper, a mixture of vivid and subdued colors and artistry of design, seems almost too lovely to throw away. It's all a part of the spectrum of a culture, where *omiyage* (gift-giving) is almost a religion.

Chizuko leads me to the shop next to the post office, and I place the package on the counter. The cordial lady there smiles in recognition of our rainy-day introduction yesterday. "This is a present to thank you for befriending my wife and me upon our arrival."

She bows several times and thanks me while exclaiming, "This is not necessary at all."

Chizuko and she exchange some rapid conversation I fail to understand, and we depart, bowing our way out the door.

"*Tada ima*" (We've just returned), salutes Chizuko as she opens the front door and we slip out of our shoes.

Aunt Maki, Cousin Fujie and Carolyn, are still at it, with a focus of such intense concentration on their cards they scarcely notice our return. Fujie gets up from the table, saying she feels tired. Chizuko takes her place, and the game resumes with a brisk, sideways shuffling of the deck (so different from the manner of American cards, these are thick and stiff, so can't be bent to shuffle as easily).

"Would you like to watch *terubi* (television)?" Cousin Fujie asks. When I reply in the affirmative, she points out the TV on the far side of the kitchen, where I find a comfortable floor chair with the remote control beside it. Dear Fujie says she will go upstairs to rest. This lady must be in her mid-seventies, and has not appeared well this visit; indeed, her mother of ninety-five seems more vigorous.

Turning to channel 12, I view some explicit sex scenes, showing a medical doctor taking liberties with a female patient. The doctor is examining the lady's large, exposed breasts with some sort of spatula-like instrument.

Scenes of nude young women bathing in hot spring baths, or diving for pearls in oyster beds, are common fare here, and apparently so are 'lewdies like this startling episode. In America, one pays extra to subscribe to an X-rated station, but this is regularly programmed daytime fare(!), and my eyes open wide to observe the unscrupulous doctor do more than *bow* to an uncomplaining and, I think, even *cooperative* patient.

The card game in the next room breaks up with Aunt Maki very animated over besting Carolyn and Chizuko this afternoon. She grins and calls Carolyn *kawaiso* (poor thing). "Auntie Maki *ichiban* (number one) today."

At five o'clock, we bid good-bye to Aunty and Cousin Fujie with the expectation of seeing them again before traveling away from their hospitable home (but this was not to be).

Toshio and wife drive us to their son's hillside 'castle' again, and we are surprised to see Emi Matsuda, visiting here from America. She is the wife of Carolyn's first cousin, Yoshio, and has just returned from Hopkinsville, Kentucky, where he is employed as an engineer. Emi is fluent in English and tells us, "Yoshio is in good health, but due to his work commitment in Kentucky, couldn't join me on this vacation to see relatives and friends."

As soon as Carolyn and I freshen up, the entire family goes in two cars to dine at an Italian restaurant. According to Cousin Motoaki: "This place famous, Hiroshima. It been in business twenty years same location."

The food is exceedingly delicious, and is accompanied by rounds of draught beer ('fresh beer,' as Motoaki describes it), served in chilled, copper mugs.

Motoaki is dressed in a sporty, double-breasted suit and a loud, flowery tie. Carolyn affectionately refers to him as her 'Yuppie Cousin' in conversation with Emi and Asako. He steadfastly refuses my offer to pick up the check. With arms extended wide, Cousin Motoaki insists, "You my guests this evening. Now, how about we go sing *karaoke?*"

I envision a trip to a *karaoke* and food establishment, such as we experienced with Carolyn's family in Los Angeles. This *karaoke* system, however, is located upstairs. It is in a soundproofed cubicle, just spacious enough to accomodate Motoaki and Asako, and their guests from America — Emi, Carolyn and me.

Motoaki leads off with a robust rendition of the old American standard, *Smoke Gets In Your Eyes.* The fellow obviously has sung this a number of times, probably in the company of other Japanese businessmen out for a *karaoke* lark after work. He belts out this tune while chain-smoking cigarettes and, in this small karaoke booth, the rest of us reflect how apropos are its lyrics.

Motoaki and I trade off microphones and each sing a half-dozen numbers backed up by the *karaoke* big-band accompaniments. Emi takes the mike at one point to sing a popular song in Japanese, so we give this delightful lady a round of applause. All in all, it is a great party to cap an evening as splendid as the previous one hosted by affable Motoaki.

Upon returning, Emiko is taken to the home of a friend. "You must come visit us in Northern California," urges Carolyn with a good-bye hug.

Continuing on a short distance, we reach our host's home for a nightcap. We sit on a comfortable, wide couch imported from the U.S., and host cousin invites us to watch a videotape of the classic American movie, *The Magnificent Seven*. As the film unfolds on his huge screen, Motoaki comments, "This American film adapted from Japanese Film maker Kurosawa's masterpiece, *The Seven Samurai*."

Our eyelids begin to flicker but, before we start snoring, Motoaki ejects the tape and turns off the TV, which has the effect of fully awakening us.

Both this family and ours have a strong passion for antiques, as one could readily discern here (or by a visit to our home in the U.S.). I give our hosts an old (1936) Japanese magazine full of beautiful color prints, and a 1920 picture postcard of a Tokyo street scene; both were bought in an antique shop in California. "Carolyn and I are grateful for all your cordial hospitality, and want you to have these."

Motoaki takes these items to an antique *Pennsylvania House* secretary desk, turns on a green-shaded, antique lamp, and begins to leaf through the pages. Asako looks over her husband's shoulder momentarily, then leaves the room. She returns with a blue and white batik jacket of faded cotton material, crafted from other garments. "From fifty years old. Looks like fit Carolyn. Please try on," she says.

I'm afraid I've set in motion a chain reaction of gift exchange and realize, too late, that my tokens of appreciation should have been withheld until our departure.

My wife dearly loves the jacket. It fits perfectly, and I think,

Oh, no! What do we have in our luggage besides some gifts for Monica? Then I remember the expensive silk tie I bought here (at the time I thought that, if it were absolutely necessary, I would tie that 'noose' around my neck to look dignified for a change). It's still in the original box, so I let dear Asako give Carolyn the jacket she admires so much she will probably wear it to bed tonight, and present her husband with the accessory item coveted by Japanese businessmen. Motoaki strokes the material of this tie, comments on its exclusive brand name, and thanks me. "I will wear this proudly," he says.

Before retiring, Carolyn tells Asako, "When I return home to America I will send you some things, because I know now what you like."

"And take some time off from your busy work schedule to visit us in California," I stress to this energetic cousin of Carolyn's, so like her brothers of the same age in California.

I remain awake another hour to write feverishly in this diary, recounting two days of unique and marvelous experiences. I would give the world to have had Monica here to participate in these doings with her grandma's dear relatives; she would have enjoyed every moment. Jeez, I hope to visit the little rascal before another week goes by!

CHAPTER XXIII

Saturday, May 28, Near Hiroshima:

Junko certainly knew my wife's taste; Carolyn has worn the cute and stylish batik jacket to complement her skirt and blouse today. It's her traveling ensemble as we journey away from her Aunt Maki (whom we thought we would see again, but didn't) and all these other cordial relatives. Our destination is Kyushu.

As we clip along on another comfortable bullet train, I recap the final moments spent with relatives near Hiroshima. As I write in this diary, our train shoots under a body of ocean called the *Shimonseki Straits* — an underwater tunnel connecting the main Island of Honshu with its southern neighbor, Kyushu. Our coach darkens — a good time to pop the seat back and reminisce....

It is Saturday, so Cousin Motoaki slept in late. While we

enjoyed a super breakfast of grilled salmon steaks, his wife went upstairs to announce that our departure time was approaching.

With a cigarette hanging from his lips, Motoaki trots down the stairs from the master-bedroom suite. He notices our luggage in the hallway off our bedroom door and carts the two bags to the entry area.

"No praburum," he tells me without dislodging the cigarette from his lips, a mannerism that reminds me of Humphrey Bogart. "I ready take you station when you want go. All I want is cup coffee first."

So, this two-day saga of events at the birthplace of my wife's father draws to an end, and we bid good-bye to our gentle hostess, Asako. Toshio and Chizuko have come here early to see us off. All have been so kind, and our every wish has been met by our considerate hosts.

Our luggage is loaded in one of cousin's three cars (this one a VW convertible), and, with its top down, we take off for the Hiroshima Station. "This VW convertible cost me forty thousand dollars, but I like it for weekend and holiday drive. Next time you come, we go fishing in it. My friend has ocean boat."

"What a likeable and unforgettable character," I reminisce aloud. Our journey now will take us to the terminus of the *shinkansen* bullet train line at Okura. Carolyn provides a pleasant interlude from these diary entries to read aloud from a guidebook that highlights places to visit in Syushu.

"Oh, let's go to Beppu, Tom. It's a famous resort city."

"Sounds good, babe. We reach Okura in fifteen minutes, and we can check there to learn what train goes to Beppu. But are you sure that place is really a city? It sounds more like some kind of Japanese soft drink."

The Beppu Line train from Okura turns out to be a Toonerville Trolley-like affair called the *Red Express*. Although a flashy red in color, it's minuscule and plain compared to its 'bullet' cousin.

Traveling due south along narrow train tracks skirting the Pacific Ocean, we go from *Kitakyushu* (North Kyushu) to *Minamikyushu* (South Kyushu). We pass through scenic countryside of verdant mountainous terrain of mixed evergreen and deciduous forests. The tile roofs (mostly blue and red, with a few yellow) glisten from the reflected light of the afternoon sun.

Carolyn and I enjoy the view. There are a number of boat harbors for small craft, protected by concrete sea walls or curious cement 'stones piled high. We see fishermen on the hunt, and a few swimmers in the rivers and streams. Where the water meets the ocean, there are networks of man-made canals to handle boat traffic. It is altogether pleasing and interesting to observe. But my dear wife didn't get enough sleep last night, and the rhythmic clatter of this small train is sufficient to mesmerize her to sleep now.

When we pause at one town, I am taken aback at the sign outside the window. Although I hesitate to awaken Carolyn from her nap, but this is a 'must-see' for another American. I nudge her awake and say, "Wow, you're gonna think I'm joking babe, but please take a gander outside our window before this train makes Sacramento. While you napped, we covered so much ground we're back home in America, U.S.A!"

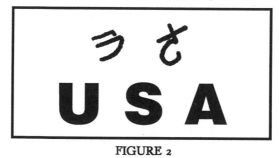

FIGURE 2

Carolyn knew better, but was amused to observe the name

of a city in Japan named *USA*, and grins at me (it was one of many fascinating names of cities and hamlets that the Red Express passes through in rural Kyushu).

While my wife remains awake, I kid, "If *shinkansens* are called 'bullets,' baby, then this Red Express is a *BB*." Somehow, Carolyn is not amused. I assume she's anxious to see what's 'bopping in Beppu.'

Reaching Beppu took four hours on a train whose progress is impeded by stops along the way. It is also rather slow-moving for one spoiled by the mighty Bullets, although it's a nice change to see things in slow motion.

Beppu is one of the largest, if not *the* largest city on this southerly island. The station is ultramodern, with a number of small shops along a wide corridor, and we see a very large (perhaps two blocks long) department store beyond these. I request directions to the luggage storage area, and judge my accent to be improving in Japanese; this fellow listened, promptly instructed us, and we had no trouble finding the wall of lockers.

By using arms and feet to compress our luggage, we finally make them fit a space which requires five 100 yen coins before the key is given over. "For the equivalent of five dollars, it's worth it not to haul these bags around, honey. Every time I do, my ears grow longer," says I. My wife ignores an often-heard complaint, and proceeds to look about the shops.

It's growing late, so I decide to walk from the station in search of a hotel. A wide boulevard of business establishments lies straight ahead, and just to the left I discover a hotel whose rates are posted outside. "Is there a room available for two?" I inquire of a desk clerk who looks up from a book.

"*Hai, gozaimashita - doozo* (yes, your honor - please)," as he slides a sheet of paper across the counter for me to register. "I surprise just now. You speaking Japanese."

"Please permit me to take a look at the room first," I ask in his language, and am quickly provided a key attached to a hunk of three-sided plastic as long as an umbrella. The clerk bows and points me in the direction of the elevator, and the key and I squeeze in, to be taken to the sixth floor.

I find the room clean, but smelling of tobacco; there are enough ashtrays here for one to play checkers with on the squares of the tatami-matted floor. There are two chairs, a table and a TV. It has a small private bath, but I see no bed. *Aha,* I think, *Old Sherlock is wise to this. The prior occupant has stolen the bed! What think you Watson, my astute companion?* Even *Watson* wasn't needed to observe that there were futon beds and pillows stored behind closeted shoji doors. Further inspection turns up starched, blue and white kimonos with lettering on them: *BEPPU INN - Finest Hotel Near Train Depot.*

Finding these quarters acceptable (although Carolyn later discovered her 'inspectors,' Sherlock and Watson, hadn't even noticed that the TV wouldn't work without 100 yen coins to motivate it), I returned to the desk to register my wife and me.

Meanwhile, Carolyn is joyfully browsing the shops inside the station, thrilled that our hotel is literally littered by miles of shops in every direction. "You look tired, Tom. Why not rest while I look about? There's a supermarket in the basement-level of our hotel next door that offers a variety of goodies to take out if you're hungry."

I am quick to remind her, "Honey, go easy on the shopping. If we try to shovel much more in our luggage, it's apt to burst its seams and spill all over the sidewalks of downtown Beppu when we leave!" (As the reader has perhaps gleaned from this journal, I take the remotest pleasure in a sightsee of a sea of shops. Recently, while I was foolishly following my wife about as she shopped, she perceived her husband's interest to be flagging, and cited me for 'Moping with Intent to Creep').

So far, the most alluring thing about this trip has been the view from the train windows as we wind along scenic seashore through hills and valleys made green by abundant rainfall. It is spectacular and refreshingly rural, compared with previous train excursions. Rice fields predominate this landscape, and they are actually beautiful in their geometrical precision, each plant carefully placed equidistant from its partner plant. Fields of rice are often interspersed with rows of other vegetables — cabbage, corn, tomatoes, and the like. But I think it strange that, during the course of all these travels, I have yet to view a single grazing animal — not a cow, horse, sheep or goat — just *Kubota* brand tractors.

Throngs of Beppu vacationers are being bused to and from the outlying hot spring areas this city is famous for. Many have arrived using canes, crutches and wheelchairs, as the baths here are reputed to be medicinal. But not this Yankee! Overheated mineral baths may be just the thing for physical ailments, but my mental health has already suffered from previous experience in Japanese hot baths!

My wife raps at the door. "This has been a fun place to look around, honey, but I'm starving!"

We find a nice dinner spot featuring tempura dishes. Carolyn has never been overly fond of Japanese food but, as one who never tasted it until my early twenties, I feel as though I've missed the boat for a lot of years, and there's much catching up to do to compensate that.

"Tom, there's so much sameness in meals of fish and miso soup," my wife asserts while passing me half her fish and soup to polish off. This practice works out well for me, yet, while Carolyn claims to be losing weight here, I'm in training for the next sumo tournament! (I try to picture myself squaring off against one of those fatsos in loincloth after a 'cleansing' ringside shower of pure rock salt. What mighty mountains of meat are we!) *Nah - my legs are too skinny*, I muse, while listening to the sounds of late Saturday night revelers drifting upwards to our window from the streets below. In only two more days, we will be calling on a granddaughter.

Carolyn is ready to turn in. She smells of face cream and reaches over for a goodnight smooch. "Honey, do you suppose any of your mom's ancestors heard of Lafcadio Hearn?" I ask.

"Laf-mafio who?"

"Lafcadio Hearn — an author from America who made this area of Japan his home over a hundred years ago. He was a contemporary of Edgar Alan Poe, and wrote exceedingly well. I first heard about him from my Japanese professor at U.S.C. He took a Japanese wife, too, Carolyn, but I hope she pronounced his name better than you did just now."

"I'm sorry, Tom, but with a name like that....where are we headed tomorrow — Kumamoto?"

"No dear. I'm homesick, so if possible, I will persuade the train conductor to let us exit at *USA*. I bet ol' Lafcadio got a kick out of that Japanese town's name, if it was around way back then, but I don't remember reading of it in any of his narrations."

And indeed, if these Americans weren't so determined to fulfill their grandparents' quest in a town called Suzuka, it would have been of interest to investigate more of Kyushu as it related to author, Lafcadio Hearn.

"I'm kinda homesick too, Tom, homesick to see our granddaughter, Monica. Let's keep our fingers crossed, dear."

"And our rabbit's foot flossed, too. Goodnight, baby."

CHAPTER XXIV

Sunday, May 29, Beppu, Kyushu, Japan:

The sun is high on the horizon as I awaken; Carolyn and I have slept in later than usual. The activity and noise of Saturday night celebrants postponed and disturbed our sleep in this tourist mecca. "Was there a full moon last night or what?" I ask my wife, who rouses but looks as if she could do with a few more hours in bed.

"Such excitement in the middle of the night," she recalls. "I wonder what the police were involved with down below in the parking lot. Any idea, Tom?"

"Who knows, honey, but whoever it was must have sampled something a mite stronger than Beppu Brand Mineral Water, I reckon. The gendarmes were obviously sweeping the streets of various and assorted drunks."

The city is stirring now at 9:45 a.m., and I see some sweeping of another sort taking place below. These sweepers have

manned their brooms, sloshing water about to make the sidewalks habitable for this day's slate of activity. After some magical
daubs of cosmetic lotions and creams, Carolyn looks fresh and
silky-smooth. "What's on the agenda today, Tom?"

"I thought it might be fun for us to jump on that
Toonerville Trolley, go south, and catch some more glimpses of
that breathtakingly lovely seacoast. I hear tell it is almost tropical at the southern tip of Kyushu, and we can catch the city of
Kagoshima."

"You've forgotten that I spent my first seventeen years in
tropical Hawaii, Tom. Can't we see something different? Yesterday, we talked of visiting Kumamoto, where my mom's ancestors
hailed from."

"Okay, babe — Kumamoto it is. 'Man proposes — woman
disposes,' my father used to say."

But a perusal of an area map discloses that unless we
mountain climb over Mt. Aso, the world's largest active volcano,
it will be necessary to entrain farther south to the city of
Miyazaki, then connect to a Kumamoto-bound train there.

Had Carolyn and I not been armed with Japan Rail passes,
valid on this Kyushu line, these budget-minded Americans
would have been more discreet with their travel plans. (I am reminded of the streetcar passes that money-strapped youths of
my 1930's generation used to take long rides to the end of various streetcar lines in St. Louis, Missouri. Those squeaky-
wheeled, old fashioned carriages carted a younger brother and
me, with neighborhood pals, on many an urban sightsee in
those days of yore.)

This Red Express crawls, almost streetcar-like, in its slow
progress to Miyazaki. It requires approximately three hours to
cover a distance its 'bullet' cousin would have made in an hour
or less.

Once there, we again check our luggage into a large locker,
and after unloading this weight we do some considerable walk-

ing and window-shopping. This exercise whetted our appetites, so we find a soba noodle restaurant and make a convenient rest stop.

Carolyn daintily spoons her bowl of steaming noodles, which are topped with various vegetable and seafood ingredients only the locals could identify properly. Her Caucasian husband slurps his with reckless abandon, enjoying both the dish and the approving side glances of the waitresses.

"We're the odd couple in the eyes of the other diners and waitresses, honey," Carolyn smiles.

"Not quite, babe. Your hubby is the oddball here. We haven't encountered one Caucasian face during these escapades about Kyushu, and I look about as inconspicuous as a horsefly cooling himself on the crest of a vanilla ice cream cone."

That remark sparks some uncontrolled giggles from Carolyn, who looks about for a napkin to stem a flow of soup resulting from this. "Why other foreigners avoid this area is a mystery," I continue, "Perhaps they know something we don't — like Mt. Aso is due to blow its top."

"I don't know about Mt. Aso, Tom. But, if you make me giggle again while I'm trying to eat, I will blow mine. And, by the way, will you stop slurping that bowl of noodles through your 'tea strainer' moustache, you fake Japanese man!"

That last remark reminded me of what our daughter said about her dad: "Mom is of true Japanese ancestry; Dad only *thinks* he's Japanese."

As the hotels were remote from this train station, we think it prudent to continue by train rather than enlist the service of an expensive taxicab. And no way am I going to be harnessed to our heavy luggage to hike about searching for lodging!

"We can continue on a westerly loop to the city of Kumamoto, honey," I suggest. "We'll send your mom a card from there."

"Goody. You'll find me browsing in that jewelry store

across the way while you book seats for us, Tom. I'll meet you there in fifteen minutes."

Alas, the information I received at the ticket window was that, since it was a Sunday, no more trains would travel south until *manana* (excuse, please — *ashita*). Overhearing this, and sensing my consternation, an effeminate, rosy-cheeked guy steps to the counter and asks in passable English: "May I-ah hep you find-ah sumpsing? Pureese sit obah der. You speak rittle Japanese, no?"

With a sweep of his arms and hands, maitré d' style, this stranger bade me sit down on a comfortable bench, and introduces himself as Shigeru. "My age thirty-four, but no married yet, so eef you not-ah stay hotehru (hotel), I eenbite you stay my house."

"Thank you, *arigato*, but my *kanai*, will meet me at *san ji goro* (about 3 o'clock) at the shopping area."

At the mention of a *kanai* (one's wife), this chap gets up, shakes my hand and announces, "Ah soo, *okusan* (another's wife) wesah you...habba nice day. Goodabye."

Methinks this dude was out to polish up on something other than English conversation practice, and having just shaken his hand, I make sure to wash mine before rejoining my wife.

Carolyn laughs merrily when told of this 'gay' encounter, then exclaims, "Let's get out of here, Tom. Did you get our train reservations to Kumamoto?"

"There's big trouble, pard," I respond in my best cowboy accent. "The train's been derailed down the line by a thievin' gang of robbers, and they're gettin' a posse together now."

"You kidder. C'mon let's get our luggage. I'm ready for a rest, and I bought some snacks we can eat on the train."

"Seriously, honey, would you believe we can't go on to Kumamoto?! The last train left already. But maybe we can retrace our path back north as far as Okura, where the bullet train can speed us on to someplace like Kyoto tomorrow."

"I hope so, Tom. Please try. I'll stand over there and pretend to be looking in that shop window while keeping an eye out for you, partner."

As luck would have it, there was a Red Express arriving in ten minutes, heading north to the city of Okura. I managed to secure tickets for a non-smoking car, scurry to tell Carolyn the good news, and scramble some more to retrieve our luggage. With no time to spare, we make it aboard, huffing and a puffing (us, not the train — it's electric).

We're pleased our car is almost empty of other passengers. Our seat numbers are in the middle on the right side — perfect for another look at the scenic coastline traversed two days ago. I wrestle our bags into an overhead rack, then catch my breath and join Carolyn, who eagerly digs into her rattan tote bag to fetch several bags of goodies bought in Miyazaki.

From my aisle seat I observe a conductor escorting an elderly Caucasian couple down the aisle to the rear. The lady grimaces unhappily while struggling with a bulky suitcase. It is obviously heavy also, so this old Boy Scout seeks to offer her help. The conductor, however, is quick to intervene, and totes this lady's luggage down the aisle to a seat at the rear of the coach where her partner waits.

The lady spoke to me in an American accent, expressing annoyance that she and her husband weren't allowed to sit in the other car near the rear entrance/exit door. "Look at all these empty seats, would you? Yet we must adhere to the specific seat numbers printed on our tickets! Does that make sense?"

Carolyn and I had already discovered this on a previous trip. When comfortably ensconced in a train seat, enjoying a soft drink, a grey-haired lady approached to glare at the two of us for monopolizing her seat assignment! Only my abject apologies prevented this angry woman from a hostile reprisal, and our offending butts were quick to move to assigned seats before she could swat us with her purse (no ifs, ands, or 'butts' about this seating business)!

And for good reason; this train, though nearly empty now, was to take on more passengers at depots for many miles along this line, and would be almost at capacity before reaching the end of the line at the major hub of Okura.

Our American neighbors to the rear evidently didn't anticipate this, for when I looked back there they had turned around the empty seat in front of them, and were using it as an ottoman on which to rest tired feet.

Seeing this, a light bulb suddenly clicked on in my head, and I said to my beloved wife, "I have an intelligent idea for once, babe. See this lever on the seat in front? Watch." Standing in the aisle, I pressed the lever with my foot and swung the seat around for us to rest our feet in comfort, after taking off our shoes. Carolyn waxes ecstatic and pats me on the back while praising, "What a smart idea, Tom! This is so comfortable." And so it was until reaching Beppu, where so many passengers boarded that it spelled finish to this makeshift arrangement, and I hastily redid the seat properly.

The deep, resonant tones of the American man can be heard from behind us, and my wife speculates: "I bet you he's some kind of college professor, Tom."

"Perhaps, but not a nature professor, honey. His eyes have been constantly focused on some printed matter while ignoring this luxuriantly green countryside and stunningly beautiful shoreline. Nevertheless, I will seek to be neighborly and make pleasantries with this couple. Do you realize, these are the first Americans we've had a chance to speak to since taking leave of dear Dave and Izzie one week ago?"

I learn that they live to the north of us in Washington state. "I retired from the Department of Education some years ago. We have lived near Kyoto since January, and are to return home on the sixth of June. My wife and I spent mornings teaching English conversation to Japanese adults of various ages, then joined with other foreigners to work at conversational Japanese during the afternoons," the man explains.

"It's been slow going, learning so much Japanese. We're in our early seventies, and can't assimilate at the rate we did when younger," adds his wife.

"It was suggested that we watch Japanese TV during our spare time to facilitate our comprehension," continued the gentleman, "but the rapidity of the Japanese spoken on television shows made it an impossible undertaking."

Without going into detail, I said good-bye and good luck with the parting comment, "My wife and I hope to see our granddaughter in two days. We hope that is not an 'impossible undertaking."

Nestled at Carolyn's side, I tell her, "The man is not a professor, honey. But you were close; he's retired in the state of Washington from the State Education Department. Since January, both he and his wife have been engaged teaching English a half day and learning Japanese the other half. They said that, at their age, all the sightseeing by train before returning home, has been arduous and tiring for them."

"Tell me about it, Tom — *I'm* exhausted! It was so comfortable in Shizuoka with the Moris, and our visit with Dad's relatives was equally super. We were spoiled rotten in those havens. How much longer 'til we reach our destination?"

"You may as well nap some, babe. It will take about two hours to reach Okura. Frankly, I don't like the idea of getting there this late and looking for lodging. Do you suppose honorable conductor will let us turn the front seat back to permit us an overnight sleep on the train when everyone gets off?"

"You just try that, silly grandpa, and the next thing you know you'll be cartwheeling through the air."

"Hmmm — that's right. There must be a seat-eject button hidden somewhere on this oriental express," I tease, while pretending to read from the list of regulations on my rail pass. "Hmmm... Maxwell Smart will check Condition # 86...let's see here...'Refusal to disembark a JR train at the end of the line, signifies that one must forfeit passing GO and head directly to JAIL, and will not be paid Two Hundred Dollars!'"

We reach the city of Okura in 9:30 p.m. darkness, and step out into coolish evening air, our nostrils filling with exotic scents from nearby food stalls combined with strong charcoal-odor messages. "Honey, if you'll bird-dog our luggage, I'll trot across the street to see what awaits in terms of lodging."

On the corner I spot a sign announcing: *Yukata Hotel*. Upon entering this multi-storied building, I happily learn that a room for two with *beddos* (beds) is available and affordable. "I'll draw to that without looking at my hand," I tell the clerk in poker-playing jargon.

Carolyn is elated, for she has also learned that a large store will be open until 11 p.m. "I must have gotten my second wind, Tom. Do you mind if I stop there awhile before turning in?"

Some yen coins dropped in a vending machine yields a can of beer, and I have enough change for a second to leisurely consume while watching TV in our room. It's nice to note that this machine, unlike the previous night's stay, does not have a yen coin appetite to make it function.

An interesting documentary, filmed by a Japanese crew on location with Eskimos in Alaska, is just concluding when a rap at the door signals that a certain lady first met forty-one years ago wants in. And it was lucky for me that the solitary figure I embrace in the dimly-lit hallway is that special person instead of a bellhop!

"Tom, you silly grandpa. Why are we rubbing noses? Have you forgotten where we are?" She then crosses the threshold and teases, "Now, how about a proper Japanese bow if you will, sir — or better yet — how about a proper American kiss?"

"Nope — not until we hit the proper American *beddos*," I

tease in return, while pointing to the large double bed, a rarity in a land where portable *futons* are usually employed to undergird one's sleep. "With this monstrosity of a bed, be careful walking, babe. It takes up most of the space in this room, and what's left over is taken up by the TV. You've probably guessed that I've just watched a program about life in Eskimo land."

Carolyn inspects the tiny bath and says she's ready to scrub up. While listening to the swish-swish of teeth being brushed, I reflect that, if it were left up to me, I prefer the Japanese way of bedding. Why does anyone need a bed permanently fixed in place anyway? Americans, like their European cousins, have the extravagant notion of this necessity, until traveling to a country with other customs; where folks can tip bowls of soup to their lips rather than using a spoon to transport that liquid; where all kinds of outdoor filth and dirt stop short of one's front door; and where people don't gorge themselves with such quantities of calories as to become 'fatsos.' The paradoxical exceptions to this last are the *Sumos*, who become grotesquely elephantine, parading themselves, circus fashion, in the wrestling ring. At least, their motivation for weight gain is monetary; I read where Sumos pile in as much dough as they pile on pounds. (One wrestler married an attractive airline stewardess recently, and when viewing the nuptials on TV with my son, he commented, "Sure hope for your sake, little lady, that the 'missionary position' isn't used on your honeymoon.")

The last thing I remember before drifting off to sleep is attending a side show at a County Fair in rural Missouri with my dad. I recalled gaping at a large canvas picture of an overstuffed woman with a Mona Lisa smile. "Come, now folks. Don't pass up this chance to enter here and look upon the world-renowned figure of 'Two-Ton Tessie!' Where else can you see so much for the price of a twenty-five cent ticket? Come on, folks....right this way...Come now folks -right this way . . . Come now — right thi...."
Z-z-z-z-z-

CHAPTER XXV

onday, May 30, Okura, Kyushu, Japan:

Apparently, the switch to a regular bed for the first time during this week of travel was not beneficial to Carolyn. She awakened this morning with an acute soreness on the right side of her slender neck, and begs, "Massage my neck awhile, honey. I must have slept wrong last night."

"It's that cotton-picking bed, Carolyn. The mattress is too soft and thick. There really *is* something to be said for sleeping on *futons*."

"Don't get any ideas, Tom. I love a bed, and you're not going to sell ours when we return home. The reason for my sore neck is…"

"Me," I interject, in anticipation of my spouse's statement.

"Not you, silly. You didn't let me finish. I was about to say that I went to bed with damp hair, and remained too long in one position in bed while watching television."

"Whatever, honey. But I know it hurts. Here - take one of these Advil tablets."

"Thanks, I'll save it for after breakfast. I'm ready for coffee."

We have until 11 a.m. to check out of the Yutaka Hotel, so leave the luggage in the room while we go for breakfast.

Outside, under a canopy of soft, fluffy clouds, we find a corner store with large windows framed by buffed aluminum. There are no plastic menu samples in the window, and we are about to continue on when we look inside and see five empty stools at a counter, behind which, two ladies attired in white dresses and aprons preside.

The door stands open, as the morning air is still cool, so we enter and sit down. A pleasant, smiling lady pours us coffee from a quart-sized thermos, then returns to the business at hand.

While sipping from tiny cups, we watch the two women deftly slice off bread crusts into a bin placed on the floor. This is apparently a precision assembly line for making tea sandwiches — and these two workers have it down pat. They layer slices of bread, top and bottom, with egg salad, tuna salad, and what looks to be some type of diced meat salad. They then cut these into approximately two-inch-square pieces, and squeeze them into clear plastic cartons, to be sold (we are told) to the numerous kiosks at the Okura Train Station, as well as other stations down the line.

"Let's try some, Tom. I'm starved."

"Well, hon, I don't see any menus — and this is not exactly what one would call breakfast — but we need something in our tummies besides coffee. I'll order the works."

I then address these busy ladies in Japanese, "Excuse me, but my wife and I would like to order all three types of your small sandwiches," then add, "My, but you certainly perform your work with amazing quickness."

These workers seem delighted for a break from their 'assembly line,' and a platter of tea sandwiches is proffered by the smiling lady, who inquires where we live.

"My wife is *nisei* (second generation Japanese) on her father's side, and *sansei* (third generation) on her mother's side. We live in a rural mountain town in the northern part of California. We're Americans."

Carolyn hungrily wolfs down several of the tiny morsels. "These are delicious, Tom. Please tell them so."

"*Anatatachi no sandoichi wa taihen oishii - Honto ni.*"

This compliment delights both ladies, who bow in an acknowledgement of thanks, then return to their work with renewed vigor.

Carolyn uses a warm, moist cloth napkin (furnished in most restaurants here); and thinks this a convenient time to debate today's destination. "Are we going to Kyoto, Tom?"

"If you like, babe, but we visited there in 1983. What say we travel to another K-city — Kobe? It's a huge seaport on the Inland Sea."

"Yes, but Kyoto was so pretty, I'd like to return. But anyway, I want to look around here first before we check out of the hotel."

For some reason, the shops are not big on sales with percentage discounts — a common marketing device back home. And it is unheard of to ask a merchant to take less for an item, as is the accepted practice in many Third World countries.

No haggling here, folks. Sorry. So just imagine how my sales-happy wife's eyes light up to see this sign in a Kokura clothing store:

FIGURE 3

Carolyn was so excited she didn't take notice that this

shop's glass doors were self-opening, and the eager dear almost crash landed on a rack of skirts and blouses!

With her sore neck, and this incident, the day has not gone well for my wife — and there was yet another mishap to follow...

I returned ahead of her to our hotel to read a travel guide-book, and the poor dear returned later and mistook our hotel for another. When Carolyn entered and the desk lady inquired of her business there (in Japanese), Carolyn struggled to explain that she was merely going upstairs to join her husband in Room 316. The desk clerk rose up and frantically waved this stranger off like an L.S.O. (Landing Signal Officer) on an aircraft carrier, gesticulating wildly that Carolyn's landing at this particular hotel was 'faulty,' and shooed her away in no uncertain terms!

Hearing of this encounter, I told Carolyn, "It sounds as though her combination of arm signals to you would have done justice to the best L.S.O.'s efforts on the *U.S.S. Midway.*"

"I don't understand what you're saying, Tom. That hotel lobby looked just like ours — not a navy ship — and I was very embarrassed by the entire encounter!"

For all that, we managed to leave the city of Okura behind as the swift bullet train dashes on to other destinations; this day ours is Kobe, and the ride thus far is uneventful. Large, sprawling metropolises sweep by outside the window, interspersed with rice fields. The farmers try to utilize as much land as possible, so these fields are terraced from the lowlands upwards along rolling hills, gaining a prohibitive steepness.

"I miss the scenic Kyushu countryside of the past two days," says my wife, while she massages the pain still stiffening her neck. "When do we reach Kobe, Tom?"

"In early afternoon. Why don't you press your seat back and rest, honeybun. I'm going back to find the restroom."

I exit the rear door of our coach and enter the next, nodding to two uniformed employees who sit with a large ledger of some kind in their laps. As I reach the rear door and seek to go on, a trainman approaches to warn me that this is the last car on this train, and I must walk forward. *Yikes,* I reflect, *I'm having problems just as mixed up as Carolyn's in entering the wrong door.*

It turns out that a restroom is located two cars forward, and the door signs indicate one has a choice between Japanese or western toilets (when all this one needs is a *vacant* one — like *now!*). Luckily, I find one and, returning to my seat, I find Carolyn in a peaceful slumber on this fast but surprisingly quiet train taking us to Kobe.

We have been on many types of trains — small, medium and wide-bodied, like this one, but, regardless of size, several things about Japanese trains are uniformly true:

1) They are clean and free of graffiti.

2) They are punctual to the minute; if your timetable calls for your train to arrive at 10:27, you can bet it will not reach that station at 10:26 or 10:28.

3) They are quiet; all passenger trains are electric.

Truly, the Japanese train system is the envy of the world where mass transport is concerned — and I don't use the word *mass* loosely. In urban areas, during peak use time, there are *masses* of people milling about, boarding and departing trains, or leaving and entering the station. All seem to know precisely where they're headed, and if you are unsure of yourself or hesitate at all, you will most certainly feel overwhelmed. The maze of people is amazing and, particularly at major train stations, they seem always to be sober, serious and unsmiling as they swiftly march along — usually in overdrive.

There are many escalators at the larger stations, and it is not uncommon for people to override those mechanical steps to scurry right around you. With our heavy luggage, Carolyn and I try to remember to stay sharply to the right when using escalators, so that those behind can stomp on by.

Paradoxically, the determined mobility of the masses to reach their destinations in these stations undergoes an almost magical transformation once there! The same guy who just shot by you while running up the escalator now appears of calm and collected countenance while awaiting his train. And if this foreigner sought information from him, he undoubtedly would respond in a kind and courteous manner. In fact, every time I've asked for help by first saying, *Chotto sumimasen, ga* (kindly excuse the interruption, but), I have yet to be refused an answer. The brusque demeanor exhibited by the same man who just sailed around you to this platform changes drastically once he's standing still, to become one of the most polite extensions of helpfulness one can expect to find anywhere on the face of this multicultural planet!

One young lady, pointing out our intended route, did so with such care that the poor dear missed her train departing on the opposite side of the platform!

Admittedly, I've digressed in this diary while Carolyn naps, but now Kobe awaits. The size of this station and the multitude of people in it on this cloudy, Monday afternoon is reflective of Kobe being the sixth largest city in Japan, and a seaport since the 13th Century. Today, it is this country's busiest port, handling 31 percent of its foreign trade.

My wife and I have managed to shift, feint and dodge our way to an information room. She waits outside with our luggage while I enter and await my turn to express the wish: "*Ryo-kan no sutairu no heya wa futari de onegai shimasu* (we'd like a Japanese-style inn for two, please)."

Usually, the *ryokan* (inn) is less expensive than a western-style hotel with beds. And when quoted the sum of 90,000 yen, I thought, *Fine — this is only a little more than I paid in the rural Kyushu countryside. And this is a thriving city.*

The man in dark suit and tie could pass for an undertaker

back home, but this fellow takes hotel reservations, and he's now on the phone to make sure that a room is available to accommodate my wife and me. Assured that we have a room at the inn, I fill out the requisite information, which doesn't go as far as to asking my rank and serial number, but comes close. It surprises me that there is always a space to state one's age on these forms. I lie, as usual (so as not to embarrass my wife, who looks much younger than the sixty-one years she turns on her birthday tomorrow), and fork over a large yen bill.

There are no paper money bills smaller than 1000 yen (about 10 dollars); all denominations smaller than that are coins. And now, I politely stash the change of bills and coins returned me into my pocket, so as not to offend my reservation man by counting it, thus implying that he may be less than a gentleman, and would seek to cheat me in this transaction.

With receipt in hand, I return to Carolyn to report our good fortune in finding a reasonable room rate. Imagine my chagrin when Carolyn looks at the receipt and gasps, "Tom, this states you've paid 90,000 yen apiece, or a total of 180,000 yen!"

"Good grief," says I, dumbfounded. "The 90,000 yen quote was for only *one* person. It's obviously double for the *two* of us - which works out to about 180 dollars!"

"Wait here just awhile more babe, while I hurry back to see my 'benefactor' about finding us something less pricey."

After awaiting my turn for the 'mortician' who's just 'embalmed' the old wallet, I complain, "This room is very expensive. I understood the price was 90,000 yen," then added for good measure, "This price is more than *double* what we paid for a room with a bed in Okura last night."

'Benefactor-san' was quick to assure me that what I paid is reasonable for Kobe at this time of year, and that we will find this hotel and our room very much to our liking.

Wearing a look ill-concealing my chagrin, I nodded with a shrug of the shoulders, and rejoined Carolyn to conclude, "Well, dear, it's downright *mucho expensivo*. But, after all, it *is* your birthday tomorrow, so we'll splurge this time."

I then look my fretful 'Ingrid Bergman' directly in the eye, lift her chin and, in rakish Humphrey Bogart persona, emphasize, "But this joint better meet our strict standards for lodging, sweetheart!"

"By that — do you mean 'indoor plumbing?'"

CHAPTER XXVI

onday, May 30 (p.m.), Kobe:

As there were no empty seats in this particular station waiting area, Carolyn has been standing all this time while leaning against a columned pillar, our luggage at her feet. A young couple have been feeding their baby and rise soon after I return, saddling the tot in its dad's backpack carrier. While my wife strokes the babe's chin with a, "Cootchie- cootchie-coo," impressing bystanders with her impeccable Mandarin Chinese dialect, her husband, meanwhile, captures the two seats vacated by the baby's parents.

When we sit, I unfold the receipt on our laps. I read it and sigh, "Why, the two of us could have stayed a *week* in a motel for this price back home. And guess what, my dear?" I continue, "this isn't even the Japanese-style *ryokan* inn we requested!".

"Yes, Tom, I see that we are booked into The Kobe Hotel. I wonder what floor we'll be assigned? I hope, for the price we're paying, it doesn't overlook a department store parking lot."

"Rats, honey!" I respond, envisioning a typical city hotel.

"Don't fret, dear. But how do we get there?"

"A good question. I asked about that and was told, "a few minutes by taxi, and perhaps a ten minute walk.' Now, shall we go, Madame? I'm prepared to show you to your suite at the Waldorf; your suitor is done and finished sleeping at the Walmart."

"And how to you propose to get to the Waldorf, Sir, by chariot or limousine? Please do not even consider such peasant transport as a taxi - and perish the thought of what the peasants in our kingdom call a 'walk' or 'hike!'"

"Oh non, non, non, non, ma cherie! Please do not eevahn conseedaire — what you zay — zee *walk*! I now sznap mon feengairs to right away zummon ze reek-shaw chariot, Madame!"

"Honey, you're an absolute nut! Don't you remember reading to me that man-powered rickshaws are a thing of the past in modern Japan?"

"Well, eenzat kaze, I peek you up and carry you forth, Madame."

"Oh, but you will not find your Madame as light as a Butterfly, you chivalrous but phony Frenchman. And what about Madame's luggage?"

A line of spotlessly immaculate cabs await outside the station's street entrance, and we take the first one in line and tell the driver our destination. After a short weave through congested traffic, we turn uphill and soon reach a quiet, peaceful scene of tranquility.

The Kobe Hotel is modeled along the lines of the best of ancient Japan's architecture. It is about as hotel-like as the Emperor's Palace, and Carolyn and I are delighted. The entry, lobby, verandas and floral displays express a beauty of surroundings difficult to describe in the space this small diary permits. Suffice it to say, this building is not gaudy in the sense of the old Victorian-style edifices erected as monuments to posterity. But I don't intend here to demean the skill of those Victorian crafts-man, which is significant, and which Carolyn and I have long found most interesting in artistry of design (although the ten-dency to praise *man's* accomplishments and dwarf *nature's*).

Yet, what focuses our attention now seems to express a de-sire to put Mother Nature first, and rid one of the constraints put upon us by humankind. All here is simply but exquisitely stated, from floor to lofty ceiling. Dear Carolyn gapes, as I do, at the incredibly exotic vista.

These two Americans must now awaken from their en-chantment and formalize their reservations at this 'castle.' They report to a spacious L-shaped front desk, executed in natural woods in contrasting colors of light and dark. We are asked what time we desire breakfast in the morning and, although the desk clerk looks squarely at me to appoint a time, Carolyn speaks up to assert that 8:30 will be just fine.

(In this way, we subtly teach that, in America, womankind goes first. This, of course, is a myth in many cases. In truth, American men are as capably *macho* as any dude who pride-fully wears that insensitive insignia.)

A kimonoed maid comes forth and bids us follow her. She reaches for our two suitcases, and I tell her, "*Iie, omoi da kara* (no, because they're heavy)." She is reluctant to let me be the beast of burden, but acquiesces when I steadfastly grip our two bags and tell her to lead the way.

Carolyn and I are led some distance down a wide, high-ceilinged corridor to our room. We enter to look about as the maid prepares tea, and we are too awestruck to speak for awhile. The room is spacious, with a bath three to four times larger than the tiny cubicles of previous nights in more modest accom-modations. But forget the bath! Our room opens to a magnifi-

cent garden of shrubs and small trees, set off by tall stone lanterns and interesting rocks of varying size. With azaleas in full
bloom, for some color contrast to the grey and green tones, the
entire setting is exquisite!

My breath is still too taken for any conversation. I step out
into the adjoining veranda and collapse into a comfortable armchair to admire the view from outside, fetching my diary to
make notes, while Carolyn reclines in a matching armchair, and
we are served tea and rice crackers. Before the elderly maid
takes leave, I arise to politely exchange a succession of bows,
which manifested a crick in this elderly grandpa's neck for days
afterwards.

After tea, Carolyn is so rejuvenated that she immediately
wants to take off to see the sights of Kobe, disdaining her
husband's suggestion of a photo session in these lovely garden
surroundings. "The stone-lined walkways, lanterns and water-
fall should be captured on film with you in the forefront,
baby."

"We can take pictures later," opines the birthday gal.
"Time's a'wasting. Let's go."

"Whassa mattah, sweetheart?" her 'Bogie-man' responds,
"I don't hear your stomach growling, so you can't be hungry yet.
Sit awhile in this heavenly setting, baby. These are some 'digs' -
even bettah than the Hotel Casbah."

"To answer your question, *Humphrey* — no, I'm not hungry. And when I am, we better be somewhere else. You can't af-
ford to order here in *this* joint, Mister Bogart.

"Whaddaya mean, sweetheart? That we ain't got the
dough to set the tables here? Why, just you remember, we're
takin' breakfast here in this dive tomorra, right?"

"Only because breakfast is included in our room price,
silly grandpa. C'mon, let's get ready. I'm anxious to go."

Before venturing out, we freshen up in a bath with a
double sink, commodious for both to share. To the right is a

separate room with a door to the commode, and on the left a large spa tub with a shower and bathing implements awaiting one to employ a "wash and rinse cycle" before soaking.

Our lesser-priced baths featured a small prefabricated plastic sink basin butting up against a plastic bathtub; both of which are served by one faucet — a tall, long one, easily swung to direct water to tub or bath. Albeit a practical and utilitarian bath arrangement, it is nonetheless too frugal of engineering to interest and serve the needs of the wealthy Yankees the two of us have become in *these* plush surroundings.

So, freshened up in the bath, it is now time to enter the luxurious, marble-floored reception room and lobby, where numerous Japanese businessmen in expensive suits and ties, discuss how the stocks are doing on the Nikkei Exchange.

Exiting two huge, curved glass doors, I remark to Carolyn, "Except for their size, those curved doors remind me of a china cabinet my mother treasured back in the early 30's until younger brother, Bob, ran his head through one side."

"How terrible, Tom. Was he hurt?"

"Can't rightly say, hon. Everyone was too concerned about the china cabinet, which I recall went glassless on the right side from then on. We were depression-era poor."

But things are looking up in the 90's, as I take Carolyn's arm and lead her down a short flight of broad, slate steps to a circular drive. After a steep downhill walk of two blocks, Carolyn and I encounter three schoolboys swinging their customary schoolbags at their sides. "*Kaimono miseya no tokoro wa doko* (where is the shopping area)?" I ask them.

These three are very animated while interjecting English words learned at school. "Heroo (giggle), How-ah-you (giggle)?" etc. It seems to be fun for young kids to see and talk with foreigners, although shy by nature. This strange Caucasian face delights them in a manner I remember when I was their age (while peering intently at an orangutan and pondering what he was

thinking that moment in time when our eyes fixed upon one another at the St. Louis Zoo).

These lads, who looked to be fifth or sixth-graders, gleefully pointed us in the direction of a bus stop. As one was approaching, we exchanged hurried *sayonaras* and *good-a-byes*,
and squeezed aboard behind a line of waiting passengers to find
it is 'standing room only' time. Enough passengers exit to permit
my wife and I room to sandwich in together (it's fortunate we're
slender-type Americans).

When we pass a sign denoting *YMCA* on this busy boulevard, I point it out to Carolyn and grin, "Wow, hon. Too bad we
didn't find lodging there. You could have enjoyed a decent
lunch instead of splitting half a sandwich with me when we get
off this vehicle." No reply is forthcoming from my wife's lips,
and understandably so, when considering that tomorrow is her
birthday. "That was an untimely remark, dear. I was just kidding, of course. I will buy you a *whole* sandwich."

As we step off on the sidewalk, Carolyn finally speaks to
say, "I'm not hungry enough to eat even the half-sandwich you so
generously offer, honey. There are a few snacks in my purse to
munch on. Then let's eat an early dinner."

We discover that this is the terminus of the bus line, and
we are at Kobe's other large train station called *Sannomiya*. "Try
your best not to get trampled on, babe. The multitudes only
look like they're united against us; in reality, they merely wish to
catch the next train."

We are on the threshold of Port Island, our destination this
afternoon. A traffic light signals okay for Presbyterians — excuse — *pedestrians* to cross. (Actually, this suspect pun, *Presby-
terian*, is an apt description of a race that exhibits every nuance
of the Protestant work ethic, irrespective of the fact that few attend church services.)

There is a bridge walkway thoroughfare to Port Island, but
we think it fun to board a monorail to cross the ocean inlet to

the Kobe landmark. This island is an engineering marvel, constructed by moving millions of tons of earth to form a land area that was once seawater. It is one of several standing as a tribute to the technical abilities of mankind in the 20th century. We also learn that Port Island has been developed over the space of a decade into numerous hotel, convention and shopping buildings.

We exit the monorail from its circuitous path about the island at a stop called *Minami* Station (South Station), and traverse a rampway leading to an amusement park, where we pause and I say, "Let's leave this kid area, honey."

"Kids or not, Tom. Let me pose you with that huge rollercoaster in the background. The folks back home will be impressed, and I won't let on that you were too chicken to try it out."

"That's ridiculous, Carolyn. I went on the *Comet* at Forest Park Highlands when I was barely ten years old."

"Yes — and you've been dizzy ever since. Now stand up straight and tall and say 'cheese.'"

We follow a sign to *Exotic Land*, but that spot is anything but exotic, we see, when we enter a warehouse (very much like a Home Club), organized into various departments that feature such un-exotic items as plumbing fixtures, hardware, furniture, and other mundane objects.

The only exotic attraction here, perhaps, is a pretty lass in the piano sales department. She's not only attractive but helpful, and steers us out of this maze by pointing out the way to a jewelry museum and sales building.

Carolyn's attention is riveted upon heading there — the faster the better. Along that route, some boys were playing catch, and when I affected a catcher stance one threw me the ball and I lofted it back. My return sadly misfired but, thanks to a bank of shrubbery, failed to keep on rolling down the street.

By this time I could see that Carolyn had 'rolled' down the

street, and I hurried to catch up before that devotee of jewelry got into that store *Alone! With A Visa Card!*

The shop girls all wear summery white bonnets and serenade us with the customary *Irrashaimases* (Welcome, welcome). We meander around a large room displaying merchandise for sale. Carolyn finds nothing she *has to have* at prices intended for princes and oil sheiks, so we enter an adjacent pearl museum room.

There are some fabulous pearl jewelry displays in glass cases, each with a tumbler of water. I nudge Carolyn, "How about that, honey. They stick a glass of water in these cases, with the idea these pearls yearn to return to their underwater oyster wombs."

"What an imagination, Thomas Drake. The water glasses are only there to prevent dryness."

Anyway, we are fascinated to see crowns of pearls, tiaras of pearls, and striking pearl necklaces. Each exhibit case has explanations in Japanese and English. One wall of cases describes how pearls are formed, and Carolyn reads aloud while I clean my eyeglasses. "Each pearl is formed by accident, as it were, on the..."

"*Bed*...but aren't we all?" I interrupt.

The next foray takes us to a series of walkways lined with shrubs and trees, each bearing an attached sign to identify that specimen in Japanese *hiragana*. I've learned that alphabet, so it's my turn to read to Carolyn. "*Kuroi Matsu no Ki* (Black Pine)," etc.

Carolyn looks as though she could do with a rest, and I know I could, so we park on a bench underneath a broad-leafed *momiji no ki* (maple tree). "Does this make you feel at home, honey?" my wife asks. "The place of origin states: 'California, U.S.A.'"

With my nose in a pamphlet describing the wonders of Port Island, I have only half heard her. "It says here that this island's periphery is lined with sophisticated port facilities, babe. Let's continue on to there and watch some of the large steamers coming and going."

One thing's for sure: This particular island, formed by the hand of man, is bereft of hills and valleys. It is as flat as Kansas, and very similar in size to Treasure Island in San Francisco Bay (which is also as flat as a pancake). We are disappointed in our quest to see any ships at dock or at sea. In fact, the monorail afforded a better view than we managed on this walkabout.

"Shall we skip back to the main streets and look for a restaurant, Tom? I'm ready for that half a sandwich you promised me in a fit of generosity."

We examine various restaurant windows, most of which display exceedingly realistic plastic models of the dishes offered within. "Perhaps my eyeglasses need cleaning again, honey. None of this plastic looks very appealing."

Carolyn agrees. "Let's board the monorail to the mainland and search out a restaurant in that busy street of shops we saw before coming here."

"Good idea. By then, we'll be suitably famished to eat the plastic models," I reason — and this turns out to be a splendid decision.

Departing the monorail, we enter a humongous department store at bridge level, then descend three escalator levels down to the belly of 'restaurant row.' We circumnavigate a dozen or more while eyeing the menus. An Italian restaurant looks promising, but we finally decide on Chinese food, and what a feast ensued there (fortunately, only the chop-sticks were plastic)! It is a fitting end to our afternoon travels.

"Our beautiful hotel suite and garden await at the other end of town, babe. Shall we go?"

"Providing we can find a bus, Tom. And I hope it's not too crowded."

But crowded it was. Thank goodness we weren't carting

any luggage, or we'd have created a panic (if not a riot), by block-ing the bus aisle thoroughfare leading to the front exit. The folks here board the bus from the rear, and don't pay until exit-ing up front. We're generally in the dark as to how much fare to pay, and now, to the driver's dismay, I hold out a fistfull of coins for him to make the requisite selection.

"Darn, honey," I tell my spouse as we quickly round the corner from the bus stop. "I swear that driver threw in one of my American coins intermixed with the yen. And what a marriage! That poor fellow is probably still trying to unjam his fare box machine."

In any event, we did not give him any chance to fix the blame if that were so. The two of us turn the corner and climb the sidewalk up the steep hill leading to the door of our en-chanting castle — better known as the Kobe Hotel.

It is evening, and Carolyn and I notice kimono-clad ladies scurrying about in cloth *tabi* slippers. It seems a gala geisha party is winding down in the cavernous ballroom off the lobby. (Westerners have the misconception that *geisha* and *prostitute* are synonymous, which is not so. Geishas act as hostesses only, to serve the meal and pour tea or sake.) "You know, honey," I re-mark, "those colorful 'bathrobes' these ladies wear have all the sex appeal of horse blankets. Why, Las Vegas cocktail hostesses have it all over these maidens. How in the world do you suppose *geisha* acquired the reputation of being prostitutes? Any idea?"

"Nope. But some *geisha* are quite musically talented, Tom."

"Not to my ears, babe. Some of those stringed instruments appear to be missing a string or two. And they sound like they haven't been tuned in a year."

"Silly grandpa, you jest. That's Japanese folk music."

"Why, I've heard better folk music performed back in Mis-souri on a woodsaw, Carolyn. Whaddaya mean jesting?"

Anyway, through these open doors we have seen a crowd of

wealthy Japanese businessmen being entertained with singing and dancing. Now the party ends, and a grandma-aged chaperone (not a madam), escorts her troupe of charges to several vans waiting at the door for transport to whatever type of quarters *geishas* occupy these days.

"Having gotten through this day without too much strenuous bowing, my neck is straightening out and feels better, Carolyn."

"The way you gawked at the *geisha* party in progress, I don't understand how, Thomas."

"Can I help it, honey? Our tennis buddy, Chuck Wood, told me to check out the *geishas* in Japan, remember? And this undoubtedly was my first and last opportunity! I frankly wouldn't give a nickel's worth of yen to be entertained in that fashion. *But don't tell Chuck!* When we meet on the tennis courts back home, I intend to fake a long story (just to tantalize that lecherous so-and-so) about seeing the most expensive *geisha* strip-tease show in all of Kobe!"

CHAPTER XXVII

onday, May 30, Kobe Hotel:

It is nearly midnight as I sit on a veranda overlooking a lovely Japanese garden and make journal entries with a pen that is giving out.

I slip in the room quietly, hoping the swishing sound of my starched, cotton *yukata* robe won't awaken a sleeping wife. Our robes have been provided by this splendid, Japanese-style inn, and Carolyn thought I looked funny enough in mine to take a photo an hour or so ago when she caught me reclining on the floor, my nose in a book.

The photo session contemplated in the garden, however, has been postponed until daylight. Although a few lantern-like lamps are lit there, we thought the light insufficient for the camera. But now, I borrow a pen from Carolyn's purse, give it a test swipe in the diary, and continue: *By the time I exited the hot tub bath, this neck of mine feels restored to normal, I* write. *Likewise, Carolyn no longer complains of neck sore-ness....*

Normally, a hot tub would be a precursor to a restful sleep, but I'm both concerned and excited about what is to transpire when we depart this plush hotel tomorrow. I'm concerned be-cause, other than a mailing address, Carolyn and I have no knowledge of the place where our granddaughter is living. Our good friend in Yokohoma, Mr. Seyama, had no acquaintance with that location either, except, as he noted to his friends from America, "It is a remote village in *Mie Prefecture.*"

It's of interest to note that, subsequent to the initial phone call to Miyoko and Monica when Carolyn and I were guests in his home, Mr. Seyama systematically made several follow-up phone calls to state our case for visiting this grandchild as being reasonable and just. "These American grandparents have not seen the child in two years," he asserted to Monica's Japanese grandmother, who told him that Miyoko was visiting relatives in Kyushu, and she and her husband were in charge of Monica's welfare. Pressing home a salient point, Mr. Seyama continued, "You must take into consideration that the child's father has been paying $1000 monthly for her support since the consum-mation of his divorce with your daughter. Mr. Thomas and Mrs. Carolyn have rights as grandparents," etc., etc.

This good friend's appeal on Carolyn's and my behalf fell on deaf ears. Miyoko's mother reiterated with each appeal that it was all right to telephone Monica, but we should make no at-tempt to visit her. These American grandparents were *persona non grata* — at the end of the line — no dice — struck out — done with!

Perhaps David's prediction will come to pass, I think this evening, and his words return to haunt my thoughts: "There's little likelihood that you will see Monica. Her bitter mother will yank her out of the Japanese school just as she did with her American school, and take her elsewhere — probably to an aunt's residence. Miyoko's lawyer was better than mine," etc., etc.

Confound the injustice! I almost cry aloud. I want to shatter the stillness of this night by pounding on the table, but I check my impulses, as I don't wish to awaken and disturb Carolyn. These random thoughts, however, are just too uncomfortable for me to join her in a restful sleep.

With address book in hand, I slip quietly out the door and along the corridor leading to the lobby and main desk. Things are so quiet and uncrowded at this late hour that I am able to buttonhole the distinguished looking man who presides there. He understands English and listens with interest to my problem. "I wonder if you might aid a grandfather with directions to a grandchild's home. I don't know how to go there by train."

The desk attendant studies the address, and notices the phone number. "I don't know this area, but since you have phone number, why not call to get directions there."

No way, Jose, I think to myself, *not only would directions be denied, the party would likely hang up fast and spirit Monica elsewhere.* "Yes, we could phone for directions (a lie), but tomorrow is my wife's birthday (a truth), and we want this to be a *surprise* visit."

"*Ah soo,*" grins the clerk. "I see . . . just one moment. I look rail line book." He enters a large office to the left of the main desk and consults with a man I think to be his senior (or at least, senior in age).

Both return to the counter and produce a large atlas to search for the Japanese three-character word for *Suzuka-Shi.* After some extensive scanning, aided by a magnifying glass, they locate and circle a spot with a pencil. "This quite far from Kobe, and I think difficult by train."

That 'difficult by train' was the understatement of the year. Their job of figuring out a way to route me to this town in the 'boonies' was a demanding one, but these helpful gentlemen were equal to the task. Jotted down on notepaper is the route we must take, painstakingly written in English on one side, Japanese on the reverse. I am astonished to see that Carolyn and I must make *four* train transfers from Kobe. This schedule calls for a switch at Osaka, Tsruhashi, Shiroko and Ise Wakamatsu before we arrive at Monica's village of Suzuka.

"Thank you so much for your kindness," I bow to these two gentlemen. "My wife will be relieved to see this paper."

Stealing as silently as possible into our room, I watch my wife turn over in her sleep, yet not awaken. While exceedingly anxious to tell her of tomorrow's travel plan and how it was obtained, it would assuredly be criminal to rouse this dear so early on the very day she was 'roused' to take a first breath some sixty one years ago.

At any rate, I think, while slipping under the sheet, *a birthday reunion with our granddaughter will be significantly more ceremonious than the geisha party conducted to amuse the guests earlier.*

I breathe a silent prayer that the events in store for this grandmother sleeping soundly now will eclipse anything she has experienced in Japan to this point. Only by the fulfillment of a certain 'quest' will that goal be attainable.

CHAPTER XXVIII

Tuesday, May 31, Kobe:
"The train schedule on the horizon today is a bear, Carolyn — but what's a little difficulty? I'm ready to move heaven and earth to find our precious grandchild on this your special day. Happy Birthday, dear!"

My wife looks rested. She's excited to see our route and learn how it was mapped out at midnight — thanks to the two hotel staff employees. "We must start early, Tom, honey."

"Yeah. Too bad we signed on for an eight-thirty breakfast. Had we known earlier - that this journey of ours requires four train transfers (yes, *FOUR*, baby,) we might have requested the earliest breakfast possible on this morning of mornings."

"Anyway, it's almost eight-thirty now, Tom. Do you have any idea where the dining room is?"

There is a light rap at the door leaving the question un-answered. "Wow, babe, that must be our signal for breakfast.

It's not just the trains that run precisely on time. The meals do, too!"

Carolyn and I were ready to exit to the dining room but, upon opening the door, I greet our tea-server from yesterday. This morning she's accompanied by a pushcart bearing dishes, some covered by shiny stainless steel lids, others with elegant lacquerware tops.

"We should have stacked our futons and bedding materials, Tom. It looks like we are to eat in our room."

But the maid has other ideas. She ushers us into the room next door, which is accommodated in like manner to ours, except that a large table has been placed in the center. Like our own room, this has a sweeping panoramic view of the lovely Japanese garden, offering a delightful and private spot in which to breakfast. The dishes before us are artfully presented. "How grand, birthday gal! This is impressive enough to sum up in capital letters — first chance I get to log it in the diary. Shall we start out with a bowl of miso soup?"

"You can have mine, too, honey. I'm too excited to eat."

"Ah, but you must. We have a long series of train rides ahead, and that task calls for some healthy nourishment."

The maid fills our teacups, then exits. Upon returning to our room to fetch the luggage for a hasty retreat, we observe that our bedding is replaced inside the *oshiire* (closet).

I drop off the room key at the front desk, preparing to leave, when the clerk produces a paper that indicates a surcharge tax of three percent is due. I think this odd for we paid in advance at the train station. "Oh, well, honey," I sigh, while reaching for the billfold, "the night clerk and manager were extremely kind to spend so much time routing us with this complicated train schedule, I'll gladly pay up." And while the wallet is handy, I extract the paper with that very schedule and place it in a shirt pocket next to my heart. Then, laden with heavy luggage, we head for the bus stop of yesterday and return to the Shin-Kobe Train Station.

The first of our good adventures (as well as misadventures) were about to unravel. A young lady approached as we scanned a sign displaying a network of rail lines servicing this large station. "Where you want go?" she asks in halting English.

I produce the paper with the complicated series of train changes we hope will ultimately lead to our granddaughter's door. Our volunteer inspects it and says, "Two these stations, same me. I show you, no trouble."

Carolyn and I follow her up a stairwell to what is called the *Kintetsu* Line. Since this is a non-Japan Rail Line, our pass is not valid, so I stand in line and pay the yen equivalent of $64 for the two of us. In fact, our expensive JR passes would not serve us for the balance of this day's rides, and the cost is substantial. "My guess is that if David were to travel from Atsugi base to where his daughter lives now, the price of tickets would cost him three to four hundred dollars," I remark to Carolyn upon returning from the ticket window. "Number-one son was right in his assessment of travel expense, honey."

"And lodging, too. Don't forget what we paid out to stay at the Kobe Hotel, Tom."

"Ah, yes m'love but tis only money. And forsooth, one's birthday but comes once a year. 'Twas but fitting, lass."

Our helpful young lady has been asking questions for us at the information counter, and now returns to lead us up another flight of stairs from a series of subterranean rooms and passageways. Straining with heavy luggage, I am gratified to reach a platform with yet another ticket window and drop my bag for a brief respite. Carolyn's luggage, at least, has a handle that telescopes it into a pull-along, but it is still inconvenient to negotiate stairwells like these. (I learned, from a near mishap earlier, to maintain a safe distance from this gal when she's in the process of leading that pull-along luggage. Once, while disembarking a train, Carolyn halted abruptly in front of me to telescope the handle of the blamed thing, and I ran smack dab into that luggage of hers and was almost catapulted into oblivion!)

Our kind informant has some type of weekly pass which she uses on this Kintetsu Line, as she explained, "to go college and study art." She now informs us that the tickets we have will take us only part of the way, so we must purchase additional tickets here in order to continue beyond the vicinity of her art school.

"Is there no end to this yen drain?" I remark to Carolyn as the large express train arrives for the three of us to board. When we reach the next transfer point, I understand the need for a second ticket. The first was picked up by the train conductor; the second is handed over to a conductor on the platform we now alight upon to accommodate a transfer to a train at the opposite side of the platform, obviating the need for turnstile exit and entry — a new experience

We now bid good-bye to the young lady who so graciously volunteered her service, and thank her for assisting us. She must continue on from this junction on yet another line before reaching her art college. This commute involves a round trip of three hours daily, Monday through Saturday, we learned.

The expensive train we now board is a very streamlined, fast express. It zooms past many small stations and travels long distances, stopping only at large cities. It is wide enough for the food service people to ply their wares up and down the aisles in the manner of the Japanese Rail Line bullet trains.

Carolyn and I are too tired for conversation, and we notice many Japanese workers and students who are also fatigued enough to be dozing. They are obviously dead tired from their long commutes to work or school, fraught with hectic and arduous train connections.

"You know, Carolyn. Without the help of that young lady who came part of our way to her school destination, this trip may well have taken us much longer by the time we figured out how and which train to catch. She was indeed an angel of mercy."

My wife nods her head without responding; her gaze is fixed on the window looking out, and her thoughts or dreams are all her own. I noticed a few foreign faces at the Osaka Station transfer to this express train, but now I find that I must certainly be an oddity, as my Japanese neighbors are sneaking quick glances in my direction. And I do mean quick; when I glance back in return, they abruptly look away in pretense of never having made this foreigner an object of scrutiny. It's quite possible these folks are familiar with the time-worn adage, *Curiosity killed the cat*, for these ebony-haired *cats* aren't about to be caught in the act of seeming curious! Occasionally, I give them a break and close my eyes to feign sleep, which affords my neighbors an opportune and leisurely 'size-up.'

But I dare not risk falling asleep and missing the *Shiroku* station! So, although sufficiently fatigued to conk right out in my comfortable seat on this quiet train, I open my eyes wide and adjust the spectacles to watch for any pertinent sign, my ears attuned to every announcement periodically percolating from the train loudspeaker.

Carolyn's head slips forward by degrees as she naps. Her chin dips to a certain level, then snaps back with a jerk. At these times, she half-opens her eyes before resuming an attitude of sleep. Bless her heart; this gal has every right to enjoy a bit of repose on her birthday. Today's travel has been taxing!

It's an observation, based on experience, that one will never see a group of people better dressed than the Japanese. As noted before, businessmen wear expensive suits and ties; women are smartly attired in finely made dresses; and students always look immaculately clean in starched uniforms. Expensive leather handbags and briefcases are much in evidence, and most women can be seen wearing what appear to be costly accessories in the way of necklaces, rings and brace-lets.

Aside from catnapping, the next favored avocation of Japa-nese train passengers is reading. These folks are avid fans of the print medium. There are times when I look about in the belief that I have happened into a library — such is the preponder-ance of books, magazines and newspapers commanding the at-tention of most passengers.

Some of this reading is obviously not for pleasure; I see many businessmen studying highlighted pages of material in preparation for their workaday world. During an earlier train excursion, I spotted one college student boning up on the Rus-sian language, studying from a book with explanatory Japanese script, while making marginal notes with her felt-tipped pen.

Truly, the Japanese achievements of the past decades have not arrived by accident. It pains me to reflect that our American young people are far less motivated. Theirs, perhaps, is a *gravy* train. These trains in Japan are work/study/rest-trains, and not an unsuitable place for any of those undertakings, either. The seats are neatly upholstered and spotlessly clean; there is no graffiti; there is no rubbish strewn about. Nice! The Japanese are a proud people and, although our Western Bible teaches that "Pride goeth before a fall," at least these folks *goeth* will not accrue to a stumbling *fall* over a litter heap!

This journey to the next connection will take almost two hours, so I must make use of the *otearai* (honorable hand-wash place). A trek forward takes me through several smoke-filled cars to the *otearai*. Each car has an automated glass door that opens when one steps on a mat in front of the door, where a switch mechanism is located. The door remains open, until one steps forward into a small passageway between cars. Then, a switch under the mat there closes the door. Once, while waiting to depart a train, I absentmindedly left my luggage on the mat;

the door thus remained open to engender some genuine stares (no 'furtive glances' that time)!

Returning to my seat now, I see that my wife, is wide awake. She smiles and says, "Look what I've got, hon — snacks!" "That raffia bag of yours is magical, Carolyn. What ya got?" We then snack contentedly while the train progresses in pursuit of our next destination. A check of my watch indicates we will reach there in a matter of ten minutes. I stress again, *will* reach, not *should* reach. The latter expression is reserved for our dear, unpredictably-oriented Amtrack trains doing service in the U.S.

Shiroku is a medium-sized rural station, where we secure tickets for the next passage, leading to the exotic-sounding destination of *Ise-Wakamatsu.* "Will we ever see our eight-year-old grandkid, Tom?" Carolyn sighs, as we come to a platform uncharacteristically empty of other passengers.

"And if we do, honey, will she appreciate the difficulties involved in this day's travel to find and see her?" I add.

There is only one other person waiting here. Since I'm nervous about boarding a train in the right direction, I seek verification with that solitary figure, who is decked out in rather sporty attire — checkered trousers and a short-sleeved Hawaiian Aloha shirt(!). It's warm, so this fellow's tan sportcoat is folded over his arm. "What a contrast with the conventional male attire, Carolyn. No dark suit and tie here," I opine quietly. "This fellow has *got* to be an American. Dare I speak English?" It's well I don't; he answers in Japanese to assure me this spot is *daijobu* (okay), and the next train will arrive in fifteen minutes.

Carolyn thinks that we must really be nearing the rural reaches of Japan to see a man dressed thusly. "I thought for a minute that fellow hailed from Hawaii, Tom."

We both take some deep breaths before latching on to our luggage and boarding a small, trolley-like train, similar to the 'Red Express' models that carried us about Kyushu this past weekend. We are now sitting bench-style along the wall of this

car, where one cannot see out of the window except by execut-
ing a difficult, over-the-shoulder maneuver, which I strain to do
at every little station. "Help me keep a lookout for *Icy-
whatchamacallit*, babe — *Ise-Wakamatsu*, that is. Missing that
stop after what we've endured would spell *hara-kiri* time for this
traveler."

"Don't use that word for 'suicide,' you silly grandpa. See
how you've startled some neighbors who overheard you? It's
downright embarrassing."

Indeed, the seating arrangement on this train offers a feast
of viewing for our fellow passengers, as we sit facing one another.
It is unfortunately less convenient for a gander at the outdoor
scenery. I fight the idea of dozing off while the train clacks along
narrow-gauged tracks, stopping occasionally at rural hamlets.
"The other passengers must know we're tourists, babe," I whisper softly. "Aren't you getting excited? One of these little burgs
will be Monica's hometown. *Banzai!*"

"There you go again, Tom. These passengers will think
you've gone balmy. Couldn't you have merely said *hooray*, or
something? We've been stared at enough without you using
words like *hara-kiri* and *banzai*. Oops, excuse me! *Darn* — see
what I mean?"

Well, at least Carolyn's slip of the tongue just now, has
turned those stares her way, giving this *gaijin* (foreign) face of
mine a rest. Carolyn, poor dear, looks nearly exhausted; so with
her almond eyes closed like pulled blinds, she is oblivious to any
surveillance from neighbors now.

Since viewing the outside is not easy, I scan the advertising
signs present on these smaller trains, and chat with Carolyn
about those we can decipher. Although comprehending both
Japanese syllabic scripts, my knowledge of the *kanji* word characters is meager, and seldom affords full understanding (yet it
passes the time when there's no space to write in this journal).

The day looms cloudy, and I'm troubled that rain may

spoil our passage on this auspicious day. Thinking the Japanese catch-phrase for 'what will be will be' (*shikata ga nai*), I close tired eyes to catch a few winks. In a twinkling, however, I am startled wide awake by a microphone that clicks on with a fingernails-on-the-blackboard screech, and announces in understandable Japanese: "We will soon be making a brief stop at *Ise-Wakamatsu*. Please do not forget your bags."

I take Carolyn's hand with a gentle squeeze and say, "Well, here we go again, birthday bride — up and at 'em. This little town is the last transfer junction before reaching our long lost granddaughter's home port." And now I'm cautiously prudent not to punctuate that last remark with a *Banzai!*

CHAPTER XXIX

Tuesday, May 31 — Suzuka-Shi, Japan:
Arriving at Suzuka City after a short trip via another small train, Carolyn and I depart with a sense of elation, knowing we've finally made it to our grandchild's home town. We see various poster bills indicating that this area is the home of what is called *The Suzuka Circuit.*

"Check this out, babe. The 94/CIK FIA World-Cup-Formula-Shell-Kart-Race has just been held this past weekend of May 27th; that particular time must have been selected to coincide with the Memorial Day weekend race called the 'Indianapolis' back home."

"I see that, Tom. But we should breathe a sigh of relief that the event is recent history, or we would likely be hard-pressed to find lodging hereabouts."

Yes, thank heavens — this is the 31st, it's my dear wife's birthday, and soon we will be setting eyes on our grandkid. All is glorious! This is 'cloud-nine-time' for us as we prepare to exit this small station with only two turnstiles. "There must be some other way for spectators to reach the Suzuka Circuit Racetrack, honey. With but two turnstiles, there would be an impossible logjam of folks trying to make it out of here," I speculate to Carolyn, envisioning a throng of fans congregating here on race day. In any event, there are no throngs this moment. A mere handful of passengers exit here with us as we place our tickets on the station-master's window.

At larger stations, this is done by an automated process, whereby the placement of one's ticket into a slot in front of a turnstile gobbles it up — providing the ticket bar code shows a correct fare. If the coding reflects that one has paid through for a transfer, then the ticket pops up from the machine's innards at the opposite end of a yard-long turnstile for retrieval. What could be more functional? But watch out! Woe be it to one with an incorrect ticket or, worse, no ticket! A loud horn sounds immediately, and the exit turnstile slams shut to prohibit one's exit!

That latter matter didn't happen to us this time. However, at one station I was slow in removing both our tickets from a shirt pocket stuffed with other receipts and notes. So, with my wife entering the turnstile ahead, the cotton-picking horn went off before I could feed the ticket machine! That blast alerted a station employee, who fortunately took but a few steps in our direction before I found and deposited the correct tickets. This done, Carolyn's blocked passage was opened, and her bewilderment turned to relief as we journeyed onward. And I know darn well it was a great relief for the station employee, who didn't have to struggle with a couple of bumbling *gaijin* (foreigners), or their language!

Anyway, Suzuka Station sports a real-live ticket taker — not some high-tech machinery to confuse these *low*-tech American travelers — and he thanks us politely when we hand over our tickets. Our next objective: To find a hotel or inn that is not too far removed from where our granddaughter is residing with her mother and other grandparents.

Just outside the station, we deposit our bags by a bench indicating this is a *Basu Noriba* (Bus Stop). "Please sit and wait here a moment, hon." I ask Carolyn, "and I'll drag this bedraggled body in search of someone who can tell us the actual location of Monica's address."

Nearby, I spot a stairwell leading up three stories with a sign designating that the YMCA is located on the second level. I clamber up the steps thinking, *Aha — this may be the way to some preciously desired information.* The glass door was open to the 'Y' office, but upon entering I see no one at the desk. Spying an open door off a hallway, I call loud enough for anyone near to hear, "Excuse me, please. Is anyone here?"

I look around what appears to be a classroom, and a smiling man approaches. We exchange greetings, then I produce an address book to show this friendly young chap Monica's address. "My wife and I wish to find this location where our granddaughter lives. Can you help us find it?"

He peruses the address written in English, and this supplicant is grateful the fellow seems to understand. But he shakes his head and replies, "Although I know Suzuka well, I have no knowledge of this apartment and street address, it is strange to say."

My face fell significantly lower than the bottom of the stairwell I just climbed. "I'll return soon. I must check with my wife. Perhaps I've copied the address wrong."

Sure enough, there were two small words in Carolyn's address book I'd neglected to copy. Racing back up the stairs, I presented the complete address to the gentleman. He grins, happy that I am now able to enlighten him with two important words: *Hirata Cho.*

I am referred to a map posted on a cork bulletin board.

"You must reboard the train to take you to the next station. Hirata-Cho is a small place at the end of the line. Your granddaughter's apartment will be a brisk ten-minute walk from there, but bus and taxi service is available if desired."

"Thank you very much. My wife and I are indebted to you for your help. Best wishes with your YMCA responsibilities." Whoo — what a relief it is to learn that, even though it means continuing on, we aren't far from our heart's desire on this birthday of a hopeful and eager grandmother.

With renewed vigor, Carolyn and I return to the stationmaster's window to explain the dilemma of having mistakenly exited here. He fished around in a cardboard box of tickets to find and return ours. "You must each pay fifty yen more with these tickets at next stop, end of the line," he explains.

As there was no train in sight, I pause to tell this relaxed attendant where and how we have traveled this day. He is astonished when I show him the complex directions written in Japanese, thanks to the gentlemen at the Kobe Hotel, and draws in his breath in surprise at these two American's arduous travels this day. This fare we are to pay to take us one short hop to our end destination is insignificant when compared to the previous fares. No sweat.

After a wait of perhaps ten minutes, we board our final train on a quiet platform that must be the envy of the beleaguered train employees who perform their duties under the canopy of such noisy, congested and hectic working conditions. "It seems you've heard this song before, babe. But let's hope this is the final 'encore,' and the next stop will deliver us somewhere in close proximity to our beloved granddaughter.

Reusing our tickets and paying the balance with a hundred-yen coin, Carolyn and I step out to a sky above so dense with cloud cover that it seems it will rain any minute (and it's difficult to carry this blamed luggage with crossed fingers).

"Oh how I hope we've finally made it, honey," my exhausted spouse sighs. We are both exhausted by this day's myriad train transfers; exhausted by the heavy luggage we must transfer at each point along the way; exhausted by the diverse questions pertaining to the correctness of this day's destination — a special birthday destination. And the day is waxing late, so it's crucial that these two sojourners from America dare not goof (yet, dear diary — they did)!!

CHAPTER XXX

Tuesday, May 31, Hirata-Cho (Granddaughter's village):

Just as before at the stop in Suzuka (which we thought for sure was Monica's home town), Carolyn and I plunk down our cumbersome bags alongside a bus stop bench at the front of the station. There is an elderly lady seated here, and I ask her where an inn or hotel can be found nearby.

Before this little lady in a lace bonnet could respond, a sturdy, heavily-muscled young man in a sleeveless T-shirt and jeans intervenes. "I know some English," he says. "I show you hotel Americans like." This fellow's speech is husky and hoarse, and upon closer examination - I see his face around the mouth is pitifully disfigured.

Just then a bus pulls up and our volunteer guide bids us step on board, helping Carolyn with her luggage and waving me inside where he sits next to us as the bus lurches forward, then makes a left turn, steadily leading away from the small station we've just arrived. It doesn't bode well....

I become increasingly alarmed after the bus has traveled some distance, yet there is still no sign of a hotel. Carolyn gives me a look mixed with concern and resignation, and I tell her softly, "Gosh, honey, we're getting more and more distant from Monica's abode. I don't like this."

Our not-so-helpful 'helper' speaks up, and I strain to understand his hoarse words, spoken from lips and mouth contorted by a birth defect or a severe accident of fate: "Do not worry," he counsels, "You like this place. It is at world-famous *Suzuka Circuit Raceway*. We soon see tall building called *Suzuka Circuit Hotel*."

Yikes, I think, *that's all we need is another splendid, cash-hungry hotel!* But worse than any money concern at this moment is the fact that we are traveling so far from where the chap at the YMCA told us our granddaughter resided — a mere ten minute walk from Hirata-Cho Station.

This concern is difficult to explain, so Carolyn and I sit resignedly with precious minutes ticking away, thinking that we will have to ultimately return by bus to where we came from. There is nothing out here but flat, unscenic land. The fellow who has led us on this long bus ride goes on to explain that he'd been a champion race car and motorcycle rider before a tragic accident befell him, requiring extensive hospitalization and facial surgery — hence the nature of a speech handicap.

We finally come to the Suzuka Circuit, pay the fare upon exiting the bus, and look about at a good-sized amusement park with turnstiles and ticket takers. There are the usual rollercoaster and carousel one sees at such places in America. But no way in God's green earth do these two senior citizens from abroad desire to stay here in this Coney-Island atmosphere!

So, we are stranded out in an area which would delight

racetrack aficionados or young folks on a date; being neither, Carolyn and I are crestfallen, and dejectedly consider that we must retrace our path back to town. We wave good-bye to our handicapped guide as he enters a park turnstile. "The fellow meant well," I tell Carolyn, feeling sorry for the extent of his condition. "I hope that future plastic surgery will ameliorate this present state of facial disfigurement, but oh, my heavens — where this fellow's led us now!"

Our present 'disfigurement' — that of being stranded after being misguided thus — is minor in comparison (turning to major, however, when we learn that the space of another hour will elapse before another bus arrives to return us whence we came).

Our time is too precious to wait! "Come on birthday gal. Let's grab that taxi and get going." The cab driver pushes his automatic opener and the rear doors swing open — an odd characteristic of all Japanese taxis. Seeing our bags are too large to share the rear seat with his passengers, the driver hits the trunk release for me to shovel the bags therein.

Once seated, I tell him we had come here in error, and desire to return to the train station. He dips his head in acknowledgement, then heads out with the meter reading 600 yen (about $6). Carolyn and I are too fatigued to make conversation, but when the meter ticks away to reach 2,000 yen, I interrupt her thoughts by conjecturing, "I wonder where this guy is taking us. None of this route back to the station looks familiar."

"Why not ask him, Tom?"

"Excuse me," I ask our driver in Japanese, "we want to return to the train station. Where are you headed?"

"To the Suzuka Station," this man responds, not realizing we had come from the Hirata-cho Station.

"No, no. This is a mistake. We came to that racetrack by way of bus from *Hirata Station!*"

The cab driver alters his course. I felt as if he should do

something with his meter, since it was his fault for not asking for the specifics of our destination. But the meter ticked away incessantly until it passed the 40,000 yen mark.

"You know, Tom," Carolyn says quietly, "he may have seen the two of us at the bus stop in Suzuka, before we got directions to go on."

"Yeah, you could be right, babe. We stand out like sore thumbs. Yet I still think the driver to be very uncommunicative with us, when he can rattle back and forth on the radio to home base."

When the driver course-corrected he had some lengthy discourse with his base station and, whatever he said, I didn't comprehend, but there was laughter from both parties. Perhaps my ego is overly fragile, but it rankles. "This is another fine mess you've gotten us into, Stanley!" I tell the cabbie for Carolyn's amusement, knowing he wouldn't understand the English impersonation of Oliver Hardy.

Carolyn grins and the driver smiles as we pull up to where we started from an hour ago, having accomplished nothing from this journey, except that my wallet is diminished in size due the fat-as-Ollie-size yen amount of over forty dollars, a nice fare for a driver-san who made quite a circuit of his own from Suzuka Circuit Raceway.

The weather is humid, yet we are fortunate that rainfall hasn't materialized to further dampen our spirits. A time check reveals that it is 5:45 p.m., and I calculate that we have wasted over an hour during this last miscued adventure. This was valuable time, since our mission is to be reunited with our granddaughter before the sun sets on her grandmother's birthday!

Bags in hand, we leave the station area and round a boulevard mainstreet corner. A short walk along a commercial street of various businesses takes us to a hotel with a nice entrance that leads through two automated glass doors to a well-appointed lobby. At a wide desk counter, I greet a young man in his language to inquire if space is available and, if so, what the rate quote is. After the misadventure in Kobe when I bungled the yen amount necessary for two person's (as opposed to one's) rate, I am more forthright and cautious to ask specifics.

"Yes," the youthful clerk responds. "We do have a room with two beds and private bath for 8500 yen, which includes a 248 yen tax."

It is refreshingly 'up-front' at this front desk, to hear a full disclosure — unlike that experienced when asked for an additional sum when checking out from Kobe Hotel this morning. *Was that only this morning? I muse. It seems as though a week's elapsed, so arduous has been this day's travel.* And while this is not the luxuriously-appointed hotel of yesterday, it is nevertheless an upscale hotel. And, moreover, the price is within reason — both judicious reasons to register now.

Carolyn rests on a circular couch while I sign on for a night's stay, hoping against hope that our Monica is not too distant. After our circuitous circuit of the outlying Suzuka Circuit Hotel, we are thankful to have found this one. "Too bad we didn't check in here an hour ago," I tell my wife as a second clerk appears with the room key and leads us to our quarters on the second floor.

"This room looks great, Tom," Carolyn exclaims. And indeed, it is spacious enough, even with twin beds, to accommodate several chairs and a table-desk with a television. The drapes are pulled shut — and for good reason, I discover; the view takes in a windowed hallway of an adjacent building very near ours. "That's all right," Carolyn affirms when this is brought to her attention. "Don't worry about the view. We're here to view a granddaughter, Tom. Have you forgotten?"

What was best about our hotel we were yet to discover (although I choose for now to keep the reader in suspense, except to hint that it happens to have nothing to do with inanimate objects). It's time to freshen up — and quickly. After a sponge bath, I exit the tiny bath to change shirts while Carolyn makes use of it. We are both in a heightened state of awareness that time is of the essence. These grandparents are anxious to see dear Monica before dark, and it's already 6:00 p.m.

Carolyn is touching up her makeup, then washes her contact lenses — the better to present her grandmotherly self this special evening (ironically, the makeup and clean contact lenses will be negated by tears before this evening is over).

"Since I'm ready, dear, I'll scoot down below and meet you in the lobby." Though weary, I'm reinvigorated by the thought of seeing a grandkid soon. With her address in hand, I return to the front desk to ask the young man there if he can direct me there.

He looks it over, but is unable to offer any help. "I have trouble reading English," this fellow tells me. A distinguished-looking lady emerges from an office to my right. She has overheard the conversation from the inner office and presents herself as the manager. "*Chotto matte kuda-sai* (please wait a moment)," this lady says.

A phone call is made, and in no time a young lady descends a flight of stairs leading from the left front of the lobby, just as Carolyn appears. The manager makes introductions and leaves. The two of us are much surprised to see a young lady walking in American fashion (Japanese women take short, precise steps, whereas the stride of an American is more relaxed and imprecise — some long, some short steps). We are even more surprised to see this lady's very un-Japanese outfit — bib overalls and a T-shirt. At least her name (Miss Matsuo) is Japanese.

"I work here," Miss Matsuo grins, "but am off duty at the moment. How can I help you?"

"You can probably tell from our faces that we are surprised to hear you talk in unaccented American English," says Carolyn.

"Yes, are you sure you're not a tourist like us?" I add.

"Nope. As I told you, I work here. I'm from Columbus, Ohio, and attend university at Ohio State. This hotel just hired me to work my summer vacation months here. A fluency in both English and Japanese were tickets to a good summer job that includes room and board. My only concern at the moment is how my roommate is looking after my pet iguana back in Columbus. Would you happen to know how I go about placing a phone call stateside? I need to check on Gertude.

This refreshing young lady seems as eager to speak in English as we, but doesn't yet realize that Carolyn and I are here, not as tourists, but as grandparents. Our mission has significantly more meaning but, before we are able to explain the nature of this mission, Miss Matsuo continues, "I don't think they are accustomed to the way I dress over here. Matter of fact, I'm sure they dislike it," she says, holding out the suspenders of her overalls. "I told them, 'sorry — no room in my luggage to pack the fancy stuff ladies go for here in Japan.' But enough of my concerns. This is the first opportunity to prove my worth! What can I do for you fellow Americans?"

Overalls notwithstanding, Carolyn and I are absolutely delighted to converse with this fun lady who, of all things, keeps some sort of strange reptile for a pet! I, for one, am glad that iguana didn't accompany her here. Carolyn and I have experienced enough troubles without meeting up with a varmint such as that. But how splendid it is to use plain old English to hasten these minutes leading to our grandchild's door. Dear Miss Matsuo becomes a savior without portfolio!

CHAPTER XXXI

Tuesday, May 31, Hirata-Cho, Suzuka, Japan:
Carolyn and I are much relieved to have selected this particular hotel. After what we have just been put through by a volunteer who almost had us checked in at a race track we are truly glad to be in the company of Miss Matsuo, recently arrived from the unlikely place of Columbus, Ohio. This young lady is our savior now, and would serve in that capacity several times over, during what was to become a two-day stay at the Suzuka International Hotel.

Carolyn produces an address book from her purse, and shows this new acquaintance our granddaughter's address, while I dig from my billfold a photograph of Monica taken two years ago in her San Diego kindergarten class.

"What a cute little girl," Miss Matsuo expresses upon viewing the photo, "however, I'm not at all familiar with this area, having just arrived here several days ago. Tell you what — I'll go ask our assistant manager. She's really nice."

After a conversation in rapid-fire, staccato Japanese, the assistant manager (whose name I greatly regret not having copied down - so hospitable and helpful was she), beckons Carolyn and me to the counter. This kindred soul has drawn us a map.

"Hurray, honey," I exclaim. "This is an easy walk from our hotel, I see; just two blocks to the right, then another right and we'll see the six-story apartment complex."

"I was told it is a newer building," Miss Matsuo explains. "But anyway, follow this map and it should lead you right to your granddaughter's door. "Let's see," she adds, while turning the paper around to gain a better view, "it's up on the fourth floor level. Good luck."

"Thank you, young lady," I say. "You're better than a buttered slice of warm toast on a cold morning." Then Carolyn joins me in a bow and sincere expression of thanks to the assistant manager, who assuredly merits the 'assistant' part of her title, having assisted these American visitors with the last leg on a quest to link up with their grandkid.

We waste no time in heading there walking as briskly as our tired legs permit. I'm grateful not to be shouldering a ponderous piece of luggage, and feel free as a bird who's escaped a cage. Grandmother carries her purse (an object most women feel naked without) and a package of gifts for Monica.

The two of us hasten along, and as we pass a pastry shop Carolyn grasps my arm and backs me up. "I think it would be nice, Tom, if we purchase an *omiyage* (a gift) to take Monica's household."

"A splllennnndid, ideehyah, ol' chum," I reply in the fashion Art Carney popularized in so many of the *Honeymooner* episodes, this wife and I have watched together. "Shall we step inside, little lady, and see what's cookin' on the middle burner?"

After a hurried perusal of pastries (Japanese, by the way, are artists at this enterprise), Carolyn points inside a refrigerated glass case, then looks at me for a consensus of opinion. I nod in agreement, that this pastry 'takes the cake. It's a cake (and/or pie — I never learn which), embroidered with thick, whipped cream, garnished with a lush collection of ripe, red strawberries.

A smiling attendant draws it forth. She's all done up in a white outfit like a nurse, and wears a blue apron. After I see the way this lady deftly slides this strawberry delight carefully into a clear plastic box, without smudging the slightest bit of cream, or losing a strawberry; I decide she's a 'surgeon,' instead.

The sum of $15 in yen seals this transaction, and onward these grandparents travel, happy as a pair — no, a whole *covey* — of larks to be only moments away from a momentous birthday reunion, put on hold for two long years! For one to look upon my wife now, he or she would little suspect the 'wringer' of a test she's been put through in order to reach this destination.

We approach the apartment building that has been circled on our map, and my smiling and excited wife says, "I'll wait downstairs, honey, while you go up to see if they're home."

So, while Carolyn remains at ground level and watches several children Monica's age at play there, I punch the elevator button to whisk me to the 4th floor. Upon exiting, I see three doors to the right, and two on the left.

Monica's door (number 404) is on the right and, with the strawberry cake in one hand, I press the buzzer with the other. The door opens momentarily and my eyes meet an elderly lady whose face bears an unmistakable likeness to that of Monica's mother, Miyoko.

"Good evening," I announce in polite Japanese. "My wife and I are here to see our granddaughter."

With that, the door was promptly shut in my face, then opened a crack with an inside chain securing it, withholding any possible view of others present within. All I could see was the scowling countenance of a short, elderly lady, who hand signals in the manner of Japanese disapproval (a wave of the hand with palm facing the viewer). "Monica isn't here. She's gone to Kyushu to vacation with her mother." Then, for good measure, she gives me a few additional hand waves while shutting the door for good, indicating, in no uncertain terms, that this is the final word in this conversation.

Not even given the chance to present a strawberry pie to sweeten matters, I am in a state of acute dismay, and continue to ring the bell, hoping for some additional consideration. I shudder to consider that *THIS IS IT!* I shudder to think what to tell my wife who waits below, expecting word of her granddaughter! What on *earth* will I tell Carolyn to assuage the grief this situation imports? She'll be absolutely devastated!

A small window to the left of the door is half open, and I can detect muffled conversation inside, some of which sounds like two children's voices.

It's difficult to squelch the innocent spontaneity of children, I muse, thinking that perhaps Monica has a playmate over for a visit this evening. As I continue to wonder thus, I become more convinced this child is in there, in spite of what's been told me. And, indeed, if she is there, it is heartless to tell a blatant falsehood in front of this granddaughter; such an act will hardly gain respect for this grandmother.

And if that woman has lied to me, as I more than suspect, I'd like to take this strawberry-cream pie, right now, and gently, ever so *gently*, push it into her scowling face, with its clenched teeth. Or so I feel now, a victim of rejection, having the door unceremoniously slammed in my face as if I were a common criminal — when the woman understands full well that I am Monica's *grandfather*.

But, diplomacy being the better part of valor, I manage to suppress that pie-throwing notion fleeting through a brain addled by the extreme difficulty, of finally reaching this goal-line — only to be fouled out. How I wish for a fair-minded 'referee' to overrule this! "Please open the door," I entreat, while alternately ringing the bell and knocking. "I have brought a fresh, strawberry-cream pie, which deserves to be eaten. Today is my wife's sixty-first birthday, and she will be bitterly disappointed to have come so far, only to be denied a chance for a short visit with her granddaughter."

Precious minutes have ticked away at the threshold of this door. I must have spent ten to fifteen minutes entreating the possibility of a change of heart; but all is still within. It has become ghostly quiet. No response. Nothing....

So, I finally break away to return downstairs via the stairwell, too agitated to stand still in the elevator. Any animal in a zoo cage knows that pacing is a remedy for frustration, — and that's precisely what I feel like doing. But I am reluctant to pace too far afield, apprehensive that once I'm out of sight, Monica will be led away to some other location to give credence to the lie that she isn't home at present.

Seeing no sign of Carolyn, I judge she is likely doing some frustrated pacing of her own, undoubtedly sensing, after waiting this long, that something is amiss. Three kids about Monica's age are at play, and I strike up a conversation to say, "Since my wife and I have come from America to see our granddaughter, Monica, perhaps you can tell me if she was at school today."

The larger and perhaps elder of the three acts as spokesperson to forthrightly reply, "*Hai, hai* (Yes, yes), She's in Jiro's class. We saw her. I think she's doing schoolwork now with another girl from her class." This lad is staring curiously at the package I carry, and I feel a genuine desire to reward him with a piece of strawberry pie, as compensation for the prompt answer that confirmed my suspicions.

Still seeing no sign of my wife, I hastily scale the stairs and return to the 4th floor, anxious that these meanspirited people might spirit our grandkid away. The remembrance of how that grandmother conspired with her daughter in an act of subterfuge in San Diego, leading to Monica's removal to this distant location, further legitimizes my concern. And, at this point, after being lied to, I don't discount *anything* this woman might do. ("After the event, even a fool is wise," some sage put it best.)

And hang it all, these people need not fear our seeking to get Monica back; only their personal guilt reinforces that nonsense. It's mind-boggling to reflect upon how our astute friend and confidante, Mr. Seyama, did everything within reason to allay such fears, and reassure Monica's Japanese family that Carolyn and I want nothing more than to visit our grandchild for a short while during this trip.

"Indeed, Tom and Carolyn Drake only wish to reassure themselves that Monica is doing well," this thoughtful go-between articulated on the telephone. "As grandparents, they are understandably anxious to know first-hand of Monica's health and happiness and, as retired educators, how the child is doing in school."

These thoughts race through my mind while ringing the door buzzer again, and I think it scurrilous of the inhabitants behind this locked door to be so inhumanely inconsiderate, to have prohibited Monica from answering our correspondence from the U.S., and in the wake of all the effort manifest in locating her, to be so thwarted. I've damned near reached the boiling point, sufficiently outraged to call upon a policeman to intervene here and now. But where to look? How I wish Miss Matsuo were here to enlighten me about what to do.

First, however, I must look for Carolyn, and explain the awfulness of the dilemma confronting us. I observe this dear standing forlornly below, and call to her. It's tough to find words to impart such miserable news to one deserving better, on what should be a joyous birthday occasion. "Monica does live here, dear. I talked briefly to her grandmother, who told me she's not here today, but I know she's lying. While you took a walk about the neighborhood, I went below and talked with a child from her school to ascertain the truth. She's here, all right."

"I just knew this would happen," Carolyn sobs with pent-up emotion. "Let's go on, honey. Take me back to our hotel. They took Monica unjustly, and naturally feel we're out to do the same thing. People lack trust — when they can't trust themselves."

CHAPTER XXXII

Tuesday, May 31, Hirata-cho:

"It's probably useless to try and persuade you to give me one more chance up here, dear," I lament to my wife from a fourth-floor landing, as she looks up with tear-filled eyes —tears of dismay and anger. She is reconciled that we are not to see our granddaughter this evening. There comes a time to give up, and Carolyn has reached the point when one feels it is futile to continue on, and powerless to effect any change. Still, this hound-dog granddad wants to persist. A hound disdains to desert its quarry after an arduous and vigilant chase, and this 'hound' dares not desert such a precious 'quarry' as this grand-child we know and love! "Please take another walk while you're drying those tears, dear. I can't give up just yet. Let me have just one more try at the door, please."

After another ring of the buzzer — and a knock on the door to boot — I hear Monica's voice! She says something in

Japanese I fail to comprehend; then in English I hear, "Grandpa, you can't come in."

"Monica, my little flibberjibbet, it's you! We must see you, dear. We have come so far this day. It's grandmother's sixty-first birthday, and she wants no better present than to see you!" Then, I am quick to repeat this in Japanese, with the hope that Monica's grandparents will be receptive to this visit.

There is no more response from within, however. It becomes silent — so much so that I can hear my heart pounding. How tickled I was to hear Monica's voice, though her message wasn't the least bit encouraging at this point. The elevator door slides open, and a lady of perhaps thirty leads a little tot by the hand, holding a package in the other. She views my foreign face uncritically, so I introduce myself in Japanese, describing my wife's and my odyssey to visit our granddaughter at this door.

"Monica's grandparents think we want to take her back to America," I tell this lady. "That's not so (*machigaimasu*)," I explain. "Yet these strange people refuse to open their door to us now." For good measure, I show this lady Carolyn's passport photo delineating her date of birth (5/31/33), and produce Monica's school photo for additional verification.

"My name is Suzuki, and I live on this floor," my new acquaintance says, then sets her package on the floor and rings the bell while exclaiming, "This is your neighbor, Suzuki. Please open the door." Mrs. Suzuki persists at this for several minutes that seem like hours, while I hold my breath in the hope there will be a response. There is nothing but silence; this kind lady's entreaties, like mine, go unanswered.

Finally, Mrs. Suzuki asks that I follow her, and she will try telephoning from her apartment. As we walk along the railing, I see Carolyn standing on the pavement below. I point her out by way of introduction, "That is my Japanese-American wife, Carolyn, Mrs. Suzuki. And listen, honey," I call to my wife, "this is Mrs. Suzuki, a neighbor who offers to help us by telephoning Monica's home."

Carolyn is too tearful to reply. Speaking in Japanese is difficult under any circumstances, much less these. "I will wait outside your door, Suzuki-san," I tell this pleasant lady as she opens the door and leads her toddler inside. Mrs. Suzuki won't hear of this. She asks me to step in while she phones, so I slip out of my shoes and enter.

After depositing her package on a kitchen counter on our left, Mrs. Suzuki enters the living room, where a play pen takes up a good deal of space. She kneels on a tatami-matted floor and picks up the telephone in hand, then searches in the phonebook for Monica's number.

How kind, I think, *for this busy mother to be taking time to help this stranger. There is much right with this old world, after all.* This person now dialing is like a ray of sunshine wafting through a dark and stormy sky. Her toddler, a little boy of perhaps two, peeks out shyly from his play-pen, and I try to amuse him with a toy truck, while his mother patiently lets the phone ring and ring. No response....

Undaunted, Mrs. Suzuki hangs up and redials, but there is still no answer, and I wonder what on earth's the matter. Finally, she cradles the phone, and stands up to say, "*Shikata ga nai. Mezurashii, ne* (It's no use. How strange, isn't it)?"

"More than strange," I agree. "My wife and I started out from Kobe early this morning, and it has taken four train transfers to reach our granddaughter's home. You were *taihen shinsetsuna* (very kind) to offer us help, Suzuki-san. Please take this strawberry-cream pie for your family as a token of our thanks. We bought it to bring to Monica's family, but I am glad now to offer it to you."

I back to the door and bow, handing her the pie. Mrs. Suzuki, however, staunchly refuses this gift. She tells me it was no bother to have tried to help, and that she is as astonished and perplexed as I by this state of affairs.

Carolyn appears morose but calm, as I return to her via the stairwell. We walk disconsolately back to our hotel without speaking, heads hanging dejectedly low. Strangers approaching must think this couple have been engaged in a spat — such is our demeanor. Perhaps someday they'll read this narrative in translated form and will be enlightened as to the true cause of these woebegone, foreign faces (one obviously tear-stained; the other barely containing his grief).

When we return to the hotel lobby, Carolyn and I are cheered to find Miss Matsuo on duty this evening. It's convenient now to speak English to recapitulate what has just transpired at our granddaughter's dwelling. "I could tell by your faces that something was wrong," says this lady, shaking her head in disbelief. "How shocking! Didn't you tell me that your son was paying $1000 monthly to that household?"

"Which he does," I reply. "But, please tell me, do you think it advisable to call in the police at this juncture?"

"Just a minute," Miss Matsuo frowns, "I'll call in my boss-lady, and consult with her as to what measures you can take. That lady is wise in the ways here, where I am not."

The assistant manager breaks away from what she is doing in her office behind the main desk, and joins Miss Matsuo. The Japanese language becomes the vehicle for such a rapid exchange of conversation that Carolyn and I understand only bits and pieces.

Our American friend turns to us and explains, "To call in the police at this time, is not the thing to do yet, I'm told. The manager wants to notify the child-welfare office first thing tomorrow morning. She would phone right now, but that office is closed for the day."

"What about Japanese law in a matter like this?" Carolyn interjects. "It's a question of justice. Have Americans no rights under Japanese law where seeing one's grandchild is con-cerned?" This is quickly translated for the manager's under-standing.

"There is no question that you have been wronged," Miss Matsuo replies to Carolyn's query. " The manager lady is very concerned to have learned of your mistreatment at the hand's of Monica's grandmother, but I think things will turn for the bet-ter tomorrow. She's got some clout in this community."

The kind manager excuses herself and returns to the in-ner office. We are left alone with an equally kind and con-cerned, yet very different, employee of this hotel. Miss Matsuo still wears her Farmer John overalls, and looks directly at us in the manner of Americans, exclaiming over and over, "This is not right. This is not right."

Carolyn's eyes begin to brim with more tears, but before I take her arm to lead her to the elevator, I insist that this young lady take the package from me. "Please don't wait too long be-fore eating it, Miss Matsuo. It's a strawberry pie covered with whipped cream."

This animated lady's eyes light up as she exclaims: "Yummy! Thanks — there goes my diet, but, *oh boy!*"

As I lead a wife half blinded by tears to our room in quest of a crying towel (her handkerchief is saturated by now), I call back to Miss Matsuo, "It would be nice to share that pastry with the manager. She's been great. Carolyn and I really appreciate the two of you!"

CHAPTER XXXIII

Tuesday, May 31, Suzuka International Hotel (near granddaughter's home):

The two of us are near exhaustion as I unlock the door of our room. Carolyn heads directly to the bathroom to bathe her eyes with a moist towel, and I collapse in a chair, lost in a sea of wonderment. *What on earth did Monica's mother, Miyoko, say to her mother to foster such inhospitality? I ponder. Nothing but lies, obviously. After all, we've earned the respect of many during our long careers as educators.* (There are plaques on the wall of a downstairs den bearing mute testimony to this. Out of several hundred teachers in the Paradise Unified School District, Carolyn was singled out to be feted by the Masonic Lodge as Teacher of The Year in 1984. And, as a school principal for sixteen years, the superintendent thought the world and all of my work in that profession. There is ample evidence of that in letters stashed away in a dresser drawer. And a post-retirement career in the real estate business was equally successful and re-warding.)

"What to make of this, honey?" I ask my spouse as she comes into our room and sits on the edge of the other bed. "Surely, Miyoko's mother must be aware of her mental instabil-ity. There's no hiding that. My guess is that she's being treated for this, and neighbors, like dear Mrs. Suzuki, have probably come to the conclusion that *something* is definitely wrong."

"Tom, I don't wish to even think about it now. Except for some snacks, we haven't eaten since breakfast. Will you take me out to dinner, dear? I'm famished."

"So am I babe. I could eat the hind-side of a water buffalo, assuming I could catch one of those varmints out in the nearest rice paddy." It's high time to lighten this somber mood.

"Silly grandpa. This is not China, you know."

"Just kidding, my love. I've seen those *Kubota* tractors sending up flurries of dust clouds outside train windows. Let's go — it's just possible we can flag one down for a ride to the res-taurant; I'm beat. Better yet, we could dine here in the hotel. Shall I take your arm m'lady?"

We're both hungry, having foregone eating since that mar-velous Kobe Hotel breakfast, such was our earnestness to dis-cover the whereabouts of Monica.

Sprightly Miss Matsuo is still on duty below. "Tom and I are looking for a nice, quiet restaurant," Carolyn tells our friend and benefactor. "Any good ideas?"

"The hotel restaurant isn't that great, and it's pricey," this young lady asserts. "Turn left, and you'll find all kinds; there's even a McDonalds about three blocks down along the main street. By the way, your pie was scrumptious. Thanks!"

"Thanks to you," I correct. "That dessert was originally in-tended for Monica's grandparents. But it's in better hands with Allstate... I mean, *Ohio* State.

She grins us out the door, then my rejuvenated wife and I

strike a left on a warm and humid evening, this last day of May. Within a short distance, the unmistakable aroma of *soba* and *udon*-noodle dishes springs the olfactory senses to attention.

We pause at the door of a typical Japanese noodle restaurant. These all seem to have been built on the same scale — small. No more than thirty or forty feet wide, the entrance in the middle is invariably curtained in royal blue material with deep red accents, and large, bold *hirigana* script, spelling out *UDON* and *SOBA*.

Some big-city noodle restaurants sport a window display to the left or right of the entry, with plastic models of the many ways *soba* and *udon* dishes can be embellished. But there is no plastic here; and none is needed. The door is open, and the entry curtains flutter a tempting aroma on the wings of a light breeze. Such a fan of this type dish am I, this place is worthy of attention. I'm hungry enough now to order the works: shrimp octopus, fish-catch of the day — in truth, every seafood item catchable in these parts, including lobster. I believe our American pizza parlors were modeled along these same lines; in a favorite, called *Mountain Mike's*, back home in Paradise, one can even have his pizza garnished with anchovies.

But we don't linger long. This is to be a birthday dinner and, no matter what the menu specialities are here, it won't answer this evening. I take my wife's hand, and we round the corner to view the small train station of *Hirata-cho* once more. A side street to the left angles right, where we see twinkling lights of business enterprises, revealing a picture of commerce down a lane uniquely Japanese. You see, there is no in-between-size here; it's either large in the extreme — as in the urbanized centers of commerce, with acres of shops under one roof — or, as the case now in this rural village — postage stamp-size shops, with a side-walk-size gap of a lane in between.

Following our noses, we stumble upon a *sushi* restaurant and go no further. Carolyn hasn't dined on this vinegared-rice and seafood since her second cousin treated us to *Mastah's Place*, near Hiroshima. We're both well trained in the proper exercise of eating *sushi* with various salads and thinly sliced *shooga* (ginger root) on the side. A *sushi* meal is not complete, either, without an accompanying dip of soy sauce and *wasabi* (horseradish) to bring out its flavor.

I escort my hungry wife inside, ready to receive the blessing of *O-sushi*, to celebrate a birthday that has been more hellish than heavenly to this point (and certainly one the two of us aren't apt to ever forget until the day we are transported either *up*, to receive wings — or *down below*, to be pitchforked into service in an over-heated workplace).

I decline a table, one of only a few here, so tiny is the restaurant. Part of the ambience of a *sushi* place is sitting at the counter, where one can view the chef at the craft of blending fresh (one would hope) seafood ingredients into *nigiri* (rice-topped seafood), or *maki* (sushi wrapped with *nori* — wafer-thin seaweed). This is an age-old art, and a magical act to observe for one like me, whose culinary claim to fame, is dependent upon a microwave oven back in America.

The chef salutes us with a welcoming smile, while he slides small dishes of the aforementioned ginger toward us. A waitress pops out of a side room with her order pad, and removes a pencil, doing double duty as a hair barrette, and takes our order. "Let's start with some *maguro* (tuna) *sushi*, which we both like. My wife enjoys the *sushi* with vegetables, called California Roll back home. There isn't anything *I* won't try. Our son works near Tokyo, and we dined several times at a large *sushi* place that employs a mechanized carousel for one to take whatever dish looks good. So we've tried almost everything. I think I'll try the sushi dish with fish eggs, as well."

Our polite little waitress brings a pot of steaming green tea, and I order a glass of cold white wine for Carolyn, and a bottle of *Kiirin* beer with which to toast her birthday. "*Saa*, she can't be sixty-one today," exclaims the waitress while giving Carolyn a closer look. "She looks *wakai* (young), *neh?*" (And it's good to see my wife turn loose her broadest smile of this entire day.)

Carolyn and I chat in English. We surmise that our waitress is the owner's wife; she is not young, and has more of a casual air about her than an employee. In these small, family-run enterprises — particularly where restaurants are concerned — family members play prominent roles. "It's sort of nice to be far afield from a typical American restaurant-business center, honey, isn't it?"

"Yes, I know what you mean," my wife answers. "When driving that long freeway from our house to my mom's in Los Angeles, all one sees are chain after chain of fast-food restaurants with young kids working for minimum wages. This *is* nice. Order me a cucumber salad, would you, Tom? I've had about all the *sushi* I can handle at one sitting."

The waitress has kept a running tab of our orders, so it comes as no surprise, when finished, to find our bill in excess of $40 yen money. "This is the wrong place to come when diners are as famished as we were, honey," observes Carolyn.

"You're just not an urban gal, honey. We're spoiled by the modest prices our small, hometown places charge to eat out. But it's nothing to spend this sum for first-rate fare here, or at your average, big-city restaurant in America."

While paying the bill, I chat with the owner in Japanese. "I have some very old Japanese paper money collected over many years," I tell him.

Upon hearing this, he asks us to wait a moment, then exits to a side room where the waitress stays when she's not busy — like now. There are only a few patrons here, and most of them are drinking *sake* or beer as nightcaps to rinse the delicious *sushi* down. "If those seafood critters were still alive, they'd be swimming about half-zonked," I joke with Carolyn as we watch and wait.

The owner jogs to an empty table and spreads out a number of old Japanese and foreign currency like so many playing cards. What really arrests Carolyn's and my attention, however, is an entire page of American one-dollar bills displayed behind a clear plastic film. "Wow, would you look at this, babe? I've never seen currency affixed together like this. These American 'greenbacks' are all in mint condition, yet spliced into single-dollar denominations. There must be at least twenty on this page. Count 'em." But, not being an authority in this field (money has always passed too quickly through these hands to have gained any expertise), I can't now decide if this stuff is genuine, or the artistry of some ingenious counterfeiter.

It must have been the real McCoy; this genial proprietor looks too honest to have come by this under false pretenses (even wrapping up a box of ginger for us to take along, having noticed how much Carolyn relishes that item).

We make good-byes at the door by an exchange of bows with the owner, the chef, and the waitress, and step outside on a narrow street, where pedestrians compete for space with bicyclists. "Walk carefully, honey. I want you to live to see birthdays grander than this."

The evening air is cooler and refreshing now. For the space of an hour we had put the sorrow of not seeing our granddaughter this day almost, but not quite, out of our minds. We elect to take a different route back to our hotel, a benumbed silence settling in upon two individuals whose quest went unanswered, and whose emotions during this quest rose and fell like the tides earlier this day, only to reach rock bottom little more than an hour ago.

We stroll this back street until we come to a concrete walk-way leading toward the main boulevard. "Let's try this, babe. I think it leads to the right of our hotel." And it did. Carolyn was just entering the first of two glass entry doors when I glance to the right and — lo and behold — who is this I see strolling down the sidewalk towards our hotel, but our grandchild?!

Monica grins like a possum, her hands firmly in the grasp of an elderly grandfather on her right, and grandmother on her left. I practically shout to Carolyn, "HONEY, I DO BELIEVE I SEE A MOST WONDERFUL APPARITION IN THE FORM OF MONICA! HOLD UP — SHE'S HEADED THIS WAY!"

CHAPTER XXXIV

Tuesday, May 31, Suzuka International Hotel:

For a grandmother, Carolyn can sure move fast when motivated. She sails right past me like a shot, stopping Monica and her escorts in their tracks, then kneels at Monica's feet and warmly embraces this child of eight, who smiles angelically. My wife and I only have eyes for Monica - Not a 'hello', 'how do you do,' 'nice to meet you' — not a word is extended by way of greeting to the two who still hold tightly to Monica's hands, making it impossible for the child to return her American grandparent's hugs. At this stage, I actually believe Monica's escorts fear we will abscond with this grandchild; there's no other explanation for such behavior!

Nevertheless, I see the situation calling for tact. While still harboring enmity for a lady who lied and shut the door in my face, and whose facial expression still doesn't evidence the slightest hint of a smile, I do see the need for some cross-cultural diplomacy. The granddad, at least, has a twinkle in one eye (I learned later that he lost the sight of the other, due a stroke last year). With Carolyn still embracing Monica, I bow to the granddad, introduce Carolyn and me, and invite them into our hotel. "This hotel has a nice, comfortable reception room where we can sit and visit," I add, as they steer this welcome sight of a grandkid forward.

Carolyn's and my timing in meeting these three was something of a miracle; had we tarried longer at the *sushi* restaurant just now, we would have surely missed them! Two, young, male employees behind the main desk are now joined by Miss Matsuo and the manager lady, all beaming smiles of satisfaction at this scene — smiles that mirrored our own and, I think, smiles of happiness that their hotel is the site of such a touching reunion.

I later learned that the manager lady had taken it upon herself to drive to Monica's apartment. Unable to get anyone to answer the door, she spoke with one of the tenants, explaining how painful an experience it has been for two worthy guests of her hotel to be denied the privilege of visiting their granddaughter. She then returned to the hotel and began phoning Monica's number, finally getting through to inform the grandmother, "This is serious business. As the manager of this hotel I will seek on the morrow to inform the Child Welfare Office in this precinct-ward. I will disclose the facts concerning your concealment of this child from her close relatives, who want nothing more than to see her."

"In the absence of a restraining order," she forthrightly explained, "you are being inhumane! It is a terrible wrong you do these American grandparents. Theirs is a valid request."

"Theirs is a righteous cause," continued this resolute woman, "and your fear of these two Americans is unwise and unbased! And finally, there will be recriminations if you continue at this. You must, by all means, meet Mr. and Mrs. Drake and permit a visit with a blood-relative grandchild, who has not even been permitted to answer correspondence sent her from America during a two-year stay in your domicile!"

What a lady, this!! And what a godsend she has been to intercede so determinedly on our behalf. We will never forget this gracious and intelligent person!

Of course, without the aid of a certain young lady (who continues to beam at an equally radiant American grandmother and her granddaughter), it might have been impossible to relate the nature of our earnest quest to the manager. Truly, Miss Matsuo has done so eloquently in that lady's language, and Carolyn and I owe both these ladies an enormous debt of gratitude for this evening's tryst with our grandchild.

Monica is unbridled in the joyousness of this occasion (and noticeably taller than when we last saw her). She hops and skips about, pausing to show off some school papers she's brought, displaying a mark of '100' at the top, indicating a perfect paper. "I'd like to run up to the room and fetch my camera, Miss Matsuo," I say at this point. "Would you mind snapping a few photos of these two overjoyed Americans in the company of their grandkid?"

"It would be an honor, sir," she answers from behind the counter, peering over the top of her glasses to focus on how things are going with this reunion. "And Monica looks just as delighted as you two. I hope her Japanese grandparents are taking notice."

After a brief photo session, I think it prudent to join those two. They are seated off to the side on an L-shaped couch, a kidney-shaped table in front of them. "*Tanoshii honto ni* (truly merry and delightful)," I remark, wishing that I knew other words to express the total glee exhibited by the actions of the granddaughter we share in common. I am not ashamed to admit that I direct all conversation to the grandpa, who smiles and nods, and ignore the sourpuss demeanor of the grandmother.

"We will also spend tomorrow night at this fine hotel," I apprise this pleasant-seeming man, "and it's our wish to spend some time with Monica tomorrow after school. My wife and I want to take her shopping, then treat her somewhere special for dinner. How about a three-hour visit?"

This elderly (senior in years to Carolyn and me) gentleman nods, after first looking (henpeckedly) in his wife's direction for approval. Then that stern lady stands erect, her face unsmiling, and announces, "We will bring Monica here at 4:30 tomorrow afternoon. It's time we go now."

It was an hour-long, joyous and surprising reunion that Carolyn and I have just savored with a grandkid we know so well! With the exception of having become fluent in the Japanese language, she hasn't changed that much. "Oh, Tom, I'm so delighted to see Monica looking well! I think she's happy here, in spite of our misgivings based on her mother's mental state."

"Yes, honey, she's obviously being given care and concern by the grandparents. She seems the same happy and animated kid we knew in California, and is apparently doing well in school. The little flibberjibbet was so proud of her schoolwork she even held those papers up to the camera. Did you notice?"

"I can't wait to write our friends and relatives back home! Shall we go upstairs now, Tom? My, what a day this has been!"

"Let's take just a moment to thank Miss Matsuo for being such a dear. And we'll certainly ask that she share those same sentiments with the manager! My, what a super twosome they've been — even better than Batman and Robin!"

Inside our room, Carolyn embraces me and sobs with joy. "This turned out to be the happiest of birthdays!" Then her words fall off unintelligibly, so tearful has she become to have consummated our glorious quest, described in this journal I sit writing now -- glad that any readers out there can't see how funny-looking this kimono makes me feel. Glad, also, that no one heard Grandpa singing at the top of his lungs in the shower a few minutes ago: "NO MATTER HOW HOPELESS — NO MATTER HOW *FARRRRR* . . . TO FIGHT FOR THE RIGHHHT, WITHOUT QUESTION OR PAUSE — TO BE WILLING TO MARCH INTO HELL FOR A HEAVENLY *CAUUUUSE.* . . ."

...Rap, rap, rap comes a knock on the bathroom door, and I slide the shower curtain aside and peer through the steam to view a scolding frau. "Tom, will you *hush!* People may be sleeping, you silly grandpa. *Enough* of that. Besides, I can't concentrate on these postcards I'm writing in the next room."

"Sure, babe, I'll tone it down." Then, in a more subdued and muffled pronouncement, this singer of little renown adds what he thinks a finishing touch while toweling off. "*To Dreammm, the Imposssible Dreammm!*"

CHAPTER XXXV

Tuesday, May 31, Suzuka International Hotel:

My wife completes five postcards ready to mail home tomorrow, and I finish a half-dozen pages in a compact notebook doing service as a diary. Both of us have highlighted the remarkable conclusion to this unforgettable day. "God, I'm glad that grandmother of Monica's came to her senses and brought her here to see us, Carolyn."

"You must write thank-you letters to Miss Matsuo and the manager, Tom. Particularly, that dear manager lady. It took her to break down the obstinacy of that little woman who slammed the door in your puss."

"And just in time, too — for I was ready to let go with a strawberry-cream pie in hers, Toots. And you needn't giggle — I mean it! I don't think...who was it — Commodore *Somebody* — had any more trouble opening his history-making door to Japan, more than a hundred years ago, than we did in opening Monica's door today."

"Commodore Perry, honey."

"Oh, yes, Perry — and that dude had a squadron of Black Ships with mucho cannons to pry open *his* door. All *this* poor grandpap had was a cream pie! So we did pretty well, considering, don't you think?"

"You mean the hotel manager did well, *considering*. Why are you getting dressed, honey?"

"Because they'd arrest me for parading outdoors in a kimono that doesn't manage to cover all of me all too well, sweetie. As fatigued as I feel, I'm still too keyed up to sleep. Wanna join me? I plan to trot back to that *sushi* place and show the owner this collection of old Japanese money and have a beer to, hopefully, put me into the mood for a good snooze."

"Nope; I'm in bed to stay. Don't stay out too late, dear. And how 'bout a goodnight, birthday-kiss first?"

The sushi place had a late evening crowd, obviously a gathering spot for the citizenry hereabouts after dark — a place to chew the fat while imbibing one's favorite beverage. A man and a lady are seated at the counter, enjoying a *sushi* repast. Two men occupy stools next to them, and three other guys are on the right. This leaves only one stool in the center for me to squeeze in, and I receive a grin from the chef who so ably satiated our appetite two hours earlier. "Where's your wife?" he asks in Japanese.

"Sleeping. She's had an unbelievably busy day. I'd like a bottle of Kiirin, please." The middle-aged waitress is apprised of my order and brings it round the front of the counter, pouring me a glass of that amber liquid.

After a few refreshing swallows, the owner comes out to greet me, happy that I've returned with an envelope of the old Japanese currency we had discussed earlier. One table is vacant behind me on which to spread the bills out side by side. The proprietor draws in his breath in the manner Japanese do as an expression of surprise....

The other patrons vacate their stools temporarily to take a look. "My," one man remarks. "It's strange to see 1, 5, 50, 100 and 500 yen currency, which for many years have been replaced by coins."

Another onlooker says, "Yes. Some of this money is fifty years old."

"More," suggests another. "None of it is in circulation, that's a certainty."

While these folks take a gander at this collection, I enjoy the uncrowded counter and sip my brew in peace — but not for long. All re-congregate there, and the owner returns my envelope with thanks. "Here," he says while handing me an old 500-yen bill from his collection. "Keep this for *presento* (using the Amercanized word for 'gift')." I, in turn, extract a bill from my envelope before inserting it in an inside jacket pocket, and make this man a gift of currency, of which I had two of the same: A five-peso note used during the Japanese military occupation in the Philippines.

Halfway through my tall bottle of beer (which always seems to last longer when quaffed from tiny glasses), I hear the voice of a man occupying the second stool on the right, while pointing this direction. "You from Kentucky."

Three words in English, and that was it. "No, not from Kentucky," says I in Japanese. "I was born near Kentucky, in the state of Missouri, but now I live in California."

"No — you Kentucky," counters this fellow of rosy-colored complexion, whom I judge to be slightly inebriated.

"Well," says I, "what makes you think I'm from Kentucky?"

With that, he slips off his stool and approaches me, *sake* bottle in hand. "You Kentucky," he tells me in English; then, in Japanese, "because of your white hair, white moustache and eyeglasses." He points to each in turn, in the event this foreigner doesn't savvy those Japanese words.

"You Colonel Sanders (which comes across *Ko-ru-nu San-*

doru)," this fellow insists with a grin. And other patrons, over-hearing this, erupt into laughter.

"*Ah — ima yoku wakarimasu* (now, I understand well what you mean)," I respond, returning this man's broad smile.

Although rather unsteady of movement, he nevertheless manages to place a shot-sized *sake* glass at my right, and wants me to join in a *kanpai* (toast) with him. There is much laughter in the house already, and it increases in tempo when I refuse this new acquaintance. "I don't like *sake*; only Japanese *beer* tastes good."

Looking amused, he grips the right hand of this pseudo-Colonel Sanders in a handshake that tells me this dude must be in the employ of a bricklaying firm! He proceeds to fill a sake glass, adamant that I join in a neighborly drink. *Well, one won't kill me.* I shrug and clink glasses with this fellow to ward off the possibility of another 'persuasive' handshake. I swallow that clear but potent liquid in one gulp, then quickly follow up with a few slugs of cold beer to extinguish the fire in these innards.

My questionable benefactor retires to his stool, and others take up the gavel, asking various questions about life in the U.S. Having seen news clips on television, documenting how certain of their countrymen were gunned down recently in America, they want to know why there is such laxness in gun control there. (I can appreciate the nature of this concern, having seen reenactments of the horrendous crime when a young Japanese student was gunned down by some jerk in Louisiana who was excused from judgement there on the pretext it was accidental. And another, more recently, whereby two young Japanese were shot and killed by a thief in the act of car-jacking their vehicle.)

So the conversation invariably turns, in the company of Americans, as to why these things happen. "Why is living in the U.S. so fraught with danger?" "Do you have a gun?" etc. My feelings on this subject are as lacking in understanding as theirs, and my concern equally compelling. I can only tell them, "Yes.

Living in *tokai* (big city) areas is dangerous in America due to the proliferation of guns, drugs and gangs. But the rural *inaka* areas are mostly law-abiding and peaceful."

Anyway, these folks here this evening seem visibly pleased at the opportunity to converse with a foreigner in their midst, who has some knowledge of their language, so they may better understand the topics under discussion.

But it is time to staunchly refuse any additional refills of beer these residents of a granddaughter's village seek to bestow in exchange for conversation. It's been an exceedingly long day, and I'm dog-tired. Time to say *sayonara* and beat a path to the finest hotel this side of Kentucky...

CHAPTER XXXVI

Wednesday, June 1, Suzuka International Hotel: All is deathly still and silent as I awaken to greet a new month...but what's this munching sound I hear? I lean over the edge of the bed, open one eye and peek under to see if a mouse is the cause of this munch-crunch business. Nothing there. Still the sound persists, so I sit up to reconnoiter the room for signs of a rodent.

Well, it's neither Mickey, nor any of his kinfolk, I discover — merely a wife, dressed to the nines, and perched on the end of my bed; her bed is already made up, I see. The munching sound is being emitted due to Carolyn's sampling of a bag of *senbei* (rice crackers). "Holey-Kimoley, babe — it's you! I thought for a minute a mouse was under my bed — which wouldn't surprise me; last night, upon retiring, pink elephants were rehearsing for the next Disney film. Funny, what *sake* wine will do to one's perception."

"You silly goose — I thought you couldn't stand *sake!*" this foot-of-the-bed wife remarks in astonishment.

"Nothing has changed, dear; what you say is true and factual. Oh, my gosh," I yawn, "what day is this? What *town* is this? I hope it isn't raining."

"Nope. I've already taken a long walk outdoors this morning, and June the first has come in like a lamb " My dear wife frequently uses expressions to designate dates, places, or happenings that confound a listener's comprehension. So I let this pass, grateful she's let me sleep in while gallivanting on her own.

"Well, I'm glad to hear it's not raining, honey, because I have plans for this second day in our granddaughter's home town."

Before I'm given a chance to delineate those plans, Carolyn stands, seals the top of her *senbei* bag and goes off on a tangent. "Oh, Tom! she exclaims, "While you slept, I walked to the corner, crossed over a bridge that spans the street, and spotted a toy store. It wasn't open yet, but I could see some interesting displays in the window. They have children's clothing as well as toys there. We must return and look for bargains for Monica and Kirby."

"Sounds okay to me, babe. We have a half-dozen hours to kill before our 'visitation rights' begin. But first, I propose that we make a visit to her school. I didn't disclose that to Monica last evening, wanting it to come as a surprise. And, needless to say, I held off apprising her Japanese grandmother, fearing she'd cook up some reason for Monica to stay home from school if she knew."

"Super idea, Tom; the wine must be wearing off. C'mon, get dressed and ready quick. I can't wait!"

"Silly grandma, don't be impatient! And moreover, I had but one small dose of that clear liquid before gagging. Honey, I swear that stuff is identical to the fuel used in cigarette lighters."

"It's not nice to demean the Japanese National Pastime, honey. What's sauce for the gander, isn't always sauce for the goose."

"In a way, you're right on target, babe. That 'sauce' *is* for the birds. But *pastime*? You've gotta be thinking of baseball or *sumo* wrestling. Matter of fact, I read where most Japanese today prefer other drinks to *sake*. But, be that as it may, how would you like your chicken? Regular or Extra Crispy?"

"Tom, your idea of visiting Monica's school is great, but what's gotten into you with the *chicken*? You know it's too early to eat chicken — but, if that's what you want, as soon as you're ready, we'll go out and look for a Kentucky-Fried place. You know good and well that there's one to be found within a short radius of anywhere in Japan, just as in America."

So that my wife doesn't continue in this vein, I bring her up to date on what transpired at a certain *sushi* restaurant while she dozed tranquilly in this room. "You misunderstand, Carolyn. I mentioned chicken merely as a lead-in to telling you about my late-evening encounter with a brick-laying fan of Colonel Sanders." Before she became totally confused, I recapped that event, and her puzzlement turned to amusement.

The hotel manager was downstairs, and cordially provided us with a map of the area, penciling in the route to a street some eight or nine blocks away, leading to the public school building serving this neighborhood.

Before heading in that direction Carolyn and I jump-start our batteries at a *kisaten* (coffee shop) near the train depot.

"Wow — that's strong stuff!" my wife gasps after a first sip. Here, let me pour some of my coffee in your cup, Tom. Then I can add more cream to mine."

"This is a *deja-vu* of last night's drama, hon. Why are folks plying me with strong drink? Is it because this foreign face looks that gullible to the almond eyes of Orientals like yourself and a certain bricklayer? Given a choice, I'd rather have half your doughnut and, definitely, the other guy's *sushi*!"

Dressed in our Sunday best, Carolyn and I now journey

out on a day turning warm and sultry. She sets a brisk pace and I scurry to stay abreast. In fifteen minutes, we see two large and imposing school buildings, reachable by crossing over a pedestrian bridge spanning a wide street. "Little Monica must have climbed this stairway dozens of times to cross the bridge to her school. It seems to be a safe route," this grandmother sighs.

Finding the doors of both buildings locked, and seeing no sign of children, our smiles vanish. "Do you suppose the kids have been bused somewhere today to celebrate a festival?" a disappointed granddad frowns.

"If so, it's strange that Monica didn't make mention of it last evening, Tom. Oh, there's a maintenance man walking between buildings. Hurry and ask while I rest here."

"*Kyoo was gakko no yasumi* (today is a school holiday)," this man explains after I tell him of our mission to visit our granddaughter's school.

Returning to Carolyn, I shake my head in dismay. "Well, babe, it's been a wild goose chase, darn the luck. But what say we come here tomorrow before departing on the train? And cheer up — Monica will pay us a visit later this afternoon, remember?"

"Phooey!" exclaims my dejected spouse. "That won't be until 4:30." Then we retrace our steps with the same apathetic air of disillusionment we affected when we finally threw in the towel and left our grandkid's unyielding door late yesterday afternoon.

Up a stairwell and across a bridge we trudge in funereal mood, in opposition to the eager and sprightly steps taken while advancing from the reverse direction only minutes ago. Along the way I pause to show Monica's photo to a shopkeeper. "*Saa*, I've seen that child before," she tells her husband when he comes to look.

"Well, it's my grandchild. My wife and I had a short visit with her yesterday, and hoped to visit her school now, but discovered the students have a holiday. It's strange she didn't tell us of this." But then, I didn't ask Monica either, primarily because this was to be a surprise visit and, secondly, it was not my intent to apprise her Japanese grandma of our school visit; she might have devised some stratagem to keep the child from attending school today.

Oh, well, it's worked out the same in either case, I muse disconsolately. Yet I'm fortified to reflect there's always tomorrow. Unfortunately, Carolyn and I can't tarry beyond then. Mr. Seyama has invited us to the resort city of Hakone this coming weekend to play tennis with him and son, Takanori.

CHAPTER XXXVII

ednesday, June 1:

"Wait up, babe," I yell to my wife who continues slowly on to reach the next corner while I pause to ask why this is a school holiday. Jogging to catch up, I grasp Carolyn's arm, breathing in deeply to get some encouraging words out. "Guess what? The shopkeeper back there informed me we'd been at the wrong schools. Those buildings are for intermediate and high school kids, and (puff, puff), they, indeed (puff), have a holiday. But the primary school is in session, honey. It's located at the end of a narrow street on the right, not very far from where we stand (*whew*)!"

I managed to get this out by waving my arms effusively in the direction of Monica's school, and we are both all smiles now. Traversing an alley-like lane, with small cottages lining both sides, and without breaking a step, we grin at each other as we observe a mother cat licking her two kittens.

"I bet Monica stops to pet those cute kitties along this path to her school," Carolyn beams.

"Silly grandma. Remember what you said earlier when you thought that stairwell and bridge leading to the other school bore significance to our grandkid's route? Who knows? This route we travel now may lead us to a Toyota Factory, or worse — a brick manufacturer!"

But no such ill luck throws us off this time. Even before reaching the building, the shouts of young children on a playground can be heard mingling with the sweet voices of others singing a song to the accompaniment of a xylophone and some sort of song flute. Then a two-story school building comes into view. Dame Fortune has finally smiled.

Carolyn and I search out the front entrance, and it's open, so we enter into a vestibule lined on both sides with a latticework of storage boxes. Myriad pairs of tennis shoes and sandals of every description are tucked inside these compartments. "These lucky kids get to go barefoot in school, hon." I grin at a wife who knows better. And to further confirm her doubts, we see several slipper-clad students come into view in a hallway one landing up. "Well, not altogether barefoot," I add. "And this building has got to be a school custodian's delight! You saw that spacious but dusty playground with a soccer game in progress just now, didn't you? Thanks to this 'shoes off and slippers on' arrangement, that dust and dirt is restricted from showing up on classroom floors, or in the Principal's Office." And since it's the latter we now seek -these schoolchildren gleefully point that door out on our immediate right. A secretary is there to run interference for whoever bears the title of Principal. "My wife and I would like to visit our granddaughter's class," I explain to this young lady, whose brow is furrowed and expression quizzical as she returns an envelope to a filing cabinet.

Without responding, the secretary summons a slender man in his thirties, who greets us as Mr. Koichi, the vice-principal. "I am sorry not to understand English very well," he explains, after I tell him we're here on a visit from America to see our third-grade granddaughter's school.

Mr. Koichi bids us sit down on a reception area couch, and another secretary smiles and pours us hot tea. "My wife retired from teaching children this age in California," I apprise this gentleman, to break the ice while my tea cools. He hands me a business card printed only in Japanese but, short of a Social Security card, I have none to exchange with this gentleman. However, I think to show Monica's photo in my wallet, and a family photo with her dad, our son David. This gentleman looks at these without commenting, so I continue, "Ours is a family of teachers, you see. The young lady in this photo is our daughter, Andrea, also a teacher. And Monica's dad is a teacher in a way; he's often called on to explain computer operations. And Grandpa, here, served as a principal for sixteen years before retiring. Carolyn and I have been married almost forty years, and Monica is one of five grandchildren. Can you tell us how she's doing in school?"

"Just one moment," Mr. Koichi remarks at this point. "I will bring Monica here for her to visit you."

Carolyn understands this spoken Japanese and is much chagrined. "Tom, please ask if it's okay to visit her classroom. I want to see her in a schoolroom setting if possible."

That request is cheerfully granted, and our host takes on an amiable quality while he leads us to the second floor. "Monica does well in school. She has a good teacher," he says quietly outside a windowed classroom door.

The three of us silently steal inside. Carolyn and I stand at the rear until provided with two chairs. Then we sit and observe a lesson in progress. The desks of this third grade class are arranged in typical American-school fashion: Three rows of paired desks face a front wall of chalkboard where the teacher presides with a stick of chalk in hand. A male, whom I judge to

be younger than our son, is apparently teaching a Japanese language lesson. Our granddaughter sits at a middle-row, rear desk.
She gives her grandparents a fleeting side glance of recognition
before obediently facing in the direction of her teacher, who is
being apprised by the vice-principal of the reason two visitors
are seated at the rear of his classroom.

I am truly astonished at the self-discipline of these young
students; not one head turns around to stare at these visitors.
They give undivided and rapt attention to their teacher as the
lesson continues.

There is a list of Japanese *kanji* words written vertically on
the chalkboard, and the students are asked to recognize these.
Instead of progressing in orderly sequence from top to bottom,
the teacher skips around, and the children animatedly seek to
identify a word as quickly as it is pointed out. There is no need
to wait for a show of hands; these pupils are swept up in a gleeful
and spontaneous whirl of enthusiasm, anxious to be the first to
call out the word before a chorus of other voices follows suit.
And if an 'eager beaver' cries out a wrong definition, mirthful
giggling erupts while the teacher waits patiently for that to subside, and a correct response to follow. Yet, I see no 'put-down' or
embarrassment intended; it's obviously quite all right for one to
err now and then, and it's this ex-educator's hunch that this
teacher is much admired by these children. I doubt that he seldom, if ever, needs to dispatch a student to the principal's office,
thinking it likely that a stern look by this teacher in the direction of a pupil who is wont to step over the bounds of decorum
will suffice to rectify matters. As one who has observed many a
classroom lesson, I like this man's style! And Carolyn, also with
many years experience in the classroom, concurred in this assessment later on while discussing our visit to Monica's classroom. It's almost noontime when the vice-principal, Mr. Koichi,
returns. "*Ima, kodomo no usa wa oshieru koto ga dekimasuka?*
(Is it possible to teach a children's song now)?" I whisper to him.

The next thing you know, Monica's grandpap is at the chalk board as in days long since past — and his fervor is still there. I write such explanatory things as our names, where we come from, etc., all in Japanese syllabary. Except for some squeaky seats, the room becomes strangely quiet, and when finished at the chalkboard, I turn to view a sea of smiling faces on the horizon. "I will write the words of a short American song in English now. When, after a practice reading by you students, I will ask my wife, Monica's grandmother, to join me." I bow with a flourish to this attentive bunch of kids. "Then, if your teacher will lead the middle row, my wife and I will take the left and right rows to lead you in song. It's one you probably already know in Japanese words."

All is silent as the English words to *Row, Row, Row Your Boat* are written on the chalkboard. For certain words such as Boat, Stream and Merrily, I write in the corresponding Japanese names: *Fune, Kawa,* and *Tanoshii.*

After steering these third-graders through a recitation of these words for a few minutes, it's time to strike up a three-part round! Carolyn comes forth with the teacher, and the three of us guide our respective bands of 'canoeists' down a fanciful, but assuredly merry stream.

These kids have obviously sung in rounds before. And at this point in time, life *is* but a dream to hear a suffusion of children's voices filling the air. After several encores of energetic rowing, we're done. Grandpa bows to the teacher, then the class, and thanks all for a *subarashii* (wonderful) visit this day.

After exchanging an American-style handshake with an exuberant child up front, his neighbors stretch out their little hands in an effort to participate in this ritual. So I 'row' up one aisle and down the next, missing nary a one along the route except Monica. These are gleeful handclasps from ecstatic youngsters, whose day was made slightly more unusual by the presence of a foreigner from abroad (and fortunately for him, there wasn't a bricklayer in the crowd!).

But what of Monica, you ask? That kid got a *hug* from her gramps. A mere handshake wouldn't carry the day for a child who looks so radiant while basking in the shared limelight of her grandparents. "We'll see you later this afternoon, little pumpkin," I tell her with a squeeze. "It's time for Grandma and me to be on our way now." We exit to a chorus of good-byes, and wave back to these delightful youngsters.

After this exhilarating experience, Carolyn and I repair to our hotel. The cockles of our hearts are as warm as this day, and Grandpa's spine tingles anew as he relates the nifty back-to-school experience to Miss Matsuo. She immediately translates this to her cordial employer, who seemed intent upon learning the reason for two American guests of her hotel to be so effusive while conversing with Miss Matsuo just now.

"Whew, honey," Carolyn says, now that we're resting in our room on the second floor, "that was quite an experience."

"An enjoyable one, for sure, babe. But what's stirring in that active mind of yours now that it's a *fait accompli*?

"You look tired, Tom. I won't mind if you don't go shopping with me. Why don't you rest up until Monica comes for a visit? I'll bring you a sandwich or something in the meantime."

That statement was music to my ears, and I collapse on the bed, adrift with reflections of other music pouring from the windows of a certain school nearby, and the little round of music we participated in with a grand-kid and her classmates. Row, row, row your boat....

CHAPTER XXXVIII

ednesday, June 1 (Suzuka International Hotel):

The phone on the nightstand jangles to arouse one who sought a midday siesta. It is a downstairs clerk announcing that our granddaughter is here with her Japanese grandparents.

Whew, I reflect with a quick check of the watch, *they've brought Monica an hour earlier than we were told, and Carolyn must still be out looking around town.*

So be it. After jumping into a change of clothes and administering a quick brush of the hair and a swipe across the puss with a moist washcloth, in no time at all I'm down in the lobby to greet a giggly grandkid.

I return the greeting bow of both grandparents and remark, "You're here earlier than expected. Thanks, that's fine, but Carolyn, thinking you were to come at 4:30, went out this afternoon to look about the shops."

"*Ima Monica daijobu* (is it okay for Monica now)?" asks the grandmother.

"Yes, yes," I answer in Japanese. "She can sit here in the lobby until Carolyn returns. It will be interesting to hear what she did in school today, after paddling about in a stream, that is." That last aside remark, I think will appear nonsensical to these two elders unless, of course, Monica related a certain school visit to them.

With that, these two exit, after reminding Monica to be ready when they return at eight to take her home. "Grandpa, you were funny at school today. Kids ask me if you coming back."

"I'm afraid not, dear. Remember the exchange student from Japan who stayed with Grandma and Grandpa in Paradise? We took him to your condo in San Diego to celebrate your mutual birthdays."

"Takanori?"

"Yes, Takanori. Day after tomorrow, your grandma and I are being treated to a trip by Takanori and his father. We're going to Hakone, a hot springs resort."

"Hot springs?"

"Yes, hot springs — *onsen* — and we're told there are tennis courts for us to play on with these dear friends."

"I remember tennis court in Paradise, Grandpa."

"You should, dear, the newspaper man took your picture there."

"Bouncing big rubber ball," Monica interjects with a giggle.

"Bouncing, my foot! You were smacking the daylights out of that beach ball with your little tennis racket, Monica."

"I no understand everything, Grandpa. Tell me again Japanese, please."

"You tell grandpa that *he's* funny, " I continue in English, avoiding her entreaty to switch language gears, "*You* are the one who's *funny*, little flibberjibbet. In America, Grandpa tried his best to get you to use Japanese words — and guess what? 'Speak American, Grandpa,' you scolded me every time."

Facing the door from this lobby, Monica spots a familiar figure and jumps up to dance around. "Whee - Here comes grandma. *Kaimono e ikimasu* (we go shopping)."

Both embrace in an old-fashioned bear hug. "Gosh, Tom, when did she arrive? I thought we were told four-thirty."

"Fifteen minutes or so ago, babe. With Monica coming here earlier than expected, I'm glad to see you now. It's boring to have to baby-sit this grandkid all by myself."

Monica recognizes an oft-used word of hers — *boring* (as in, "This TV show is *boring*, Grandpa. Can I change stations. Grandma, do I have to eat these beans? They're *boring*"). So, hearing this, she gives Gramps a glare of a stare, hands on hips, and raises her right hand as if to swat him one, but stops short when he grins and apologizes, "Just teasing, dear."

"Come see Grandma's room now, Monica. I need to freshen up before taking you out to the store and dinner."

"And bring the camera down with you, honey. I'll rest here in the lobby, and maybe ask some questions of the clerk."

But I do neither. Instead, taking out the notebook serving as diary, I record some still-fresh memories of the fulfillment of these grandparent's quest, and my spine tingles in the manner it does when exiting a movie theatre after viewing a particularly moving scenario.

"How I wish David were here to see this effervescent little daughter of his," I write. "She would dearly love to see her dad. The rascal didn't give his mom and dad but the slimmest of chance for them to be visiting her like this. And you know, dear diary, he was damn near right! Were it not for a supporting cast that included Mr. Seyama and two ladies at this swell hotel, Carolyn and I would likely have run out of time, and left this place with nothing but bitter memories."

"Okay, Grandpa," exclaims Monica as she prances from elevator to lobby, "I show you *Hunter Store*."

"Hunter Store?" I look questioningly in Carolyn's direction for clarification. No weapons like guns are sold in this safe country; does she mean some place where bows and arrows or fishing gear are sold?

"Hunter Store, Tom. I spent a lot of time there today. It's a good-sized department store. You and Monica can go to the book department and find something she likes." Turning to her grandchild, she says, "I bet you know just where the toy section is on the second floor."

We captured Monica on film this afternoon. She's a little ham — not shy at all about posing for snapshots, gleefully grinning like a possum at every turn of the corner and every click of the camera.

For a too brief interlude on this first day of June, two Americans who have journeyed to this unlikely place are in Seventh heaven. Not because this area is a fabulous vacation resort, like Kyoto, Nara, Nikko, Hakone, or all those other cities and villas singled out in travelogues, where the subject of 'what to see and do in Japan,' is of uppermost and consummate interest to the traveler. On the contrary, this particular area is an anonymous, working-class neighborhood — a highly unlikely place to be accorded any recognition in travelogue testimonials.

Yet, the reality, here and now, is that this *is* Seventh Heaven for these travelers. And if it is hinted that to remain longer is acceptable, we will assuredly postpone what is projected on our calendar of events for the almost two-week stay remaining — and pause to stay longer in a village situated in the flat lands, at the tail end of a wee rail line.

CHAPTER XXXIX

Thursday, June 2 (Suzuka International Hotel):

"The proprietor of this hotel is a swell lady, honey, but she neglected to provide us with a mop in this room," I kid my wife upon arising late on this last morning in a rather ordinary hotel (as hotels go), but an *extra*ordinary one for these grandparents.

Carolyn sits up in bed, rubbing her almond eyes awake and asks, "Why, Tom? Is water leaking on the floor somewhere?"

"Oh, not that, Carolyn. I was making reference to the bucket of tears you've shed in this very room over the course of two days."

"Silly grandpa, come over here and rub this sore neck and back of mine. And, oh, what time are we leaving?"

"No hurry. Check-out time is at eleven," I reply, while administering a kneading massage, learned years ago from this patient's father, Pop Matsuda.

Monica's grandparents came to pick her up promptly at eight last night. I wondered why Carolyn was giving Monica a last good-bye hug in this room, instead of downstairs, but it readily became apparent: That last hug tripped a switch, setting off such a flood of tears that Carolyn was unable to see Monica off down in the lobby.

Anyway, dear diary, during the course of that final parting, Carolyn's tearfulness almost got mine going. Not wanting to ask Monica to go alone, I pulled myself together with Carolyn sniffling, "Go on please. I'm sorry, Tom...I can't bear...."

So, with moist eyes, but managing some semblance of composure, I squired Monica to the lobby, where she was led away by two elderly grandparents, entrusted by some quirk of fate, to that child's guardianship. I walked as far as the sidewalk and stood there waving to a grandkid who looked back to wave in return. I kept at this until the three figures receded in the distance down the street.

Carolyn was still sniffling when she responded to my knock at the door. I held her close for a long while, neither of us able to manage any conversation. We've had a rollercoaster of emotional ups and downs these past two days. That parting was a combination of both, for you see, although that moment in time signaled a good-bye to an eight-year-old grandkid, before this day is over Carolyn and I will be greeting a one-year-old, who is also our grandchild.

But, returning to last evening — Carolyn sniffled, "Tom, read the letter Monica wrote to her dad and Isabel. It's on the desk there."

"I can't bear to yet, honey. It's too poignant right now. I looked over her shoulders while she was writing it, and the little dickens covered that sheet of stationery with both hands, scolding, 'Grandpa, don't peek. This is for my dad!'"

"That was a cute box of stationery you picked out for her, Thomas. I hope we will hear from that dear in the future."

The stationery was one of several items shopped for last evening at Hunters Department Store down the street. Almost three hours were consumed there. Monica, being familiar with this major home-town attraction, proudly guided her grandparents about, showing them this or that area, and bowing a greeting to a salesclerk known to her. That sprite was also elected to select one of the several restaurants sharing space under the canopy of the Hunter Store's abundant roof, before going to the hotel to spend the final moments of a treasured visit. A visit, however short, that had almost passed short of realization.

"I think I'll wear sunglasses this morning, honey. Can we leave right away on the train and eat breakfast when we transfer somewhere along the line.?"

"Thy question is betoken m'lady. Methinks a chariot ride shouldst serve to summon an appetite for thee, lass. But why, pray, dost thee propose to shade thine pert eyes on this cloud-shrouded day? And, forsooth — yon Hollywood is far too distant for thee to be fain looking 'Hollywoodish' here in Sherwood Forest ... Nay, *Suzuka* Forest tis what I mean."

"My eyes look red this morning, Tom. People will just know I've been crying."

"Yes, and think me the heartless knave responsible for thy tears. True enough: methought to conquer a dragon just yesterday ... But thou knowest, m'lady — *it*, not *I* — was the cause of thine abundant tears shed in this castle."

Departing our hotel this morning, Carolyn and I seek to find two grand and special ladies, but they're off duty. Without The help of Miss Matsuo and that wonderful hotel manager, our mission would likely have been incomplete, and this narrative never written.

"Wait just a minute, Carolyn, and I'll leave the manager a note in Japanese to say good-bye. Since we have Miss Matsuo's phone number in Ohio, we can give her a ring there after she returns to the U.S." I start out: *Moshi hitobito ga* (If people were) *motto kandai de* (more tolerant, and) *seijitsu ni tasuke au naraba* (sincerely helped one another,) *kono yoo wa motto sumi yoi tokoro to naru deshoo ni* (the world would be a much better place in which to live). Then, with payment made to the young chap at the front desk, I tell him my wife and I will never forget this place. We exchange bows and venture forth to the tiny station of Hirata Cho, from where we will return to our son's house, near Atsugi Naval Air Base.

Among the varied contents of Carolyn's purse is the letter of greeting to this family at Atsugi. "I was tickled to see you encourage Monica to sit and write a letter to her dad, honey. I noted that she told Isabel hello, and wished she could see her baby sis, Kirby."

"How incredible it was when Monica told us that she was unaware he had been working in Japan for over a year, Tom."

"That stunned us both, babe. She knew her dad had remarried, of course, but thought all along he was living in San Diego. Boy, does that family of hers keep a tight lid on communication."

"All the more to estrange her from all of us, I guess. But let's not talk of that heartlessness on this train. I don't dare break out into another tearful session here."

"Bet you can't if you tried, dear. The reservoir's got to have run dry by now. Gee, you look chic in those sunglasses; these folks on the train probably think you so important and famous a personage, that you wear those shades for reasons of privacy."

"You silly dreamer. This plain luggage and rumpled clothing give us away immediately for what we are — plain old, everyday-ordinary, middle-class travelers."

"Shucks, babe, I merely thought to entertain you with that notion. You're right, though. If anyone peeked inside your yen-depleted purse or my billfold, they'd be quick to conjecture that the both of us have ceased to even fit the middle-class description, you accorded us just now. We're paupers, baby."

"You needn't fret, honey. Tomorrow we can go to Isabel's bank and exchange some more traveler's checks for yen."

"Too bad you didn't borrow the *Do Not Disturb* sign from the doorknob at our hotel, babe. You look as though you could do with a bit of rest now."

And, sure enough, this lady begins to slumber — a convenient time to take friend diary in hand....

Touring about Hunter Store yesterday afternoon and evening was an exhilaratingly time for this old fogey, who couldn't care less about shopping. Monica spelled the difference. One of the books she wanted Gramps to buy her was a thick paperback, featuring a blonde-haired Wonderwoman of a cartoon heroine, popular these days with children in Japan.

"Monica, you see enough of that on TV, I bet. Let's find some books with more *meat* to them."

"Meat? You silly, grandpa. Hamburger meat in restaurant down first-floor — not here, bookstore."

"By meat, I mean something of substance — nature books like these on this shelf," I point out, "or old Japanese fairy tales here, with these wonderful illustrations. Find some books that your Japanese grandpa will be proud to see when you return home this evening."

Dissuaded thus, the little dear went along with that idea, and found several books before venturing on to the toy section, where we are joined by the real-live Wonderwoman Monica refers to as Grandma. This time yesterday, that lady wore such a doleful expression one might suppose she'd eaten a blowfish the Japanese call *fugu*, and was ready to make out a last will and testament. *Fugu*, although a delicacy must first have its deadly poison removed by the dexterous hands of a skilled chef before one partakes of that Russian-roulette of a dish favored by the local gentry here.

Today is a horse of a different color. This grandmother is

all smiles, and tells Monica: "Since we can't be here for your birthday and Christmas, let's look around among these toys and find some goodies for you to take home."

Monica is on Cloud Nine. Grandpa thinks to leave it up to the womenfolk to find suitable gifts to please a little girl. A shelf of model cars and airplanes pique his interest, and upon returning to the ladies with a beauty of a hook and ladder firetruck, Monica's grandma waves me off, not unlike her other grandma did yesterday. "Gosh, Carolyn, what do grandma's have against such innocuous objects as a toy truck and a strawberry cream pie, anyway?"

Our little pumpkin, Monica, had paused at a doll display, looking adoringly at a plastic doll I recognized as the same blonde Wonderwoman she coveted in book form awhile ago. I held it up for Carolyn to inspect. "This is the Japanese answer to the Barbie Doll, honey. Monica wanted me to buy her a huge paperback book that depicted this lady engaged in heroic feats of strength and ingenuity, going head to head against various and sundry villains."

One of the toys Monica selected was a cute, plastic fruit and vegetable cart filled with miniature wax produce. "Look, Grandma — it says *Paradise Market* on the sides. I like it to park next my doll house."

"Of course, Monica. How darling. Tom, put this on the counter. Wasn't it cute of her to find a toy with our home town written on it?"

Monica heard this and basks in the compliment, then added a touch of pathos that gripped her grandparent's heartstrings. "Someday, Grandma, I like go your house in Paradise again."

Carolyn took out a hanky and dried her eyes, but finally responded, "It's so very far away, Monica. But yes, you know you are welcome anytime, dear." Turning to me, Carolyn continued, "You know, Tom, let's talk with Takanori's dad about the possibility of the Seyama's bringing Monica with them when they come for a visit."

While Monica continued to browse, Carolyn and I mulled that very idea over together. "We're stashing away a U.S. Savings Bond each month in Monica's name. But that's to help with college, Carolyn. If the Seyamas bring Monica for a visit, we need to set aside a separate savings account to defray the cost of that proposed trip. But your idea is super, babe."

"And your idea of a travel savings account is super as well, Tom. I'm sure the Seyamas will be agreeable to bringing her. Monica is a mannerly child."

"That's the easy part of that scenario, honey. But do you think these relatives of hers will permit a visit, even though we fund it? Not a chance, I'm afraid."

"Don't be a pessimist, Tom. Remember — that's what David told us at the outset of this trip to see his daughter — *not a chance* — yet, here we are, dear."

CHAPTER XL

Thursday, June 2, (Enroute Atsugi):

There is a wait of fifteen minutes at the minuscule Hirata-Cho Station before a two-engined train arrives. As this is the end of the line and there is no turn-around, the train simply pulls in with an engine in tow, then the tow-engine becomes the main engine. "...a see-saw arrangement if I ever saw one," I remark to Carolyn when we step on board.

"Some years ago we took a train like this in the U.S. Where was that, Tom?"

"In New Orleans, I think...yes, that was it . The thing shuttled back and forth along the Mississippi Delta, from the downtown area to the old French Quarter."

With no luggage rack to stow our bags, mine sits between my legs, and Carolyn's is placed on the floor, as the train creeps out and slowly gathers speed as it heads in a northeasterly direction. "*Whew*, Carolyn, I'll be glad to reach Nagoya, where we can link up with the Tokaido Bullet Train. Then we'll be able to use our JNR Pass." Examining that pass now, I note it will expire in the space of four more days. These passes cost the dear sum of $850 — almost as much as the expenditure for the roundtrip air fare....

...funny, where thoughts take one when reminiscing. Thinking on our air fare/train fare business just now brought to mind our trip from Los Angeles to Tokyo in 1983. Carolyn and I secured tickets via *Varig* Airways, a Brazilian-owned airline. That flight had originated in Rio de Janeiro, Brazil, making one stop at Mexico City, then Los Angeles. The most memorable thing about that trip across the Pacific was the passengers. Though wearing Japanese faces, these were *Latino*-Japanese, born and raised in Brazil, and now seeking to tour the land of their ancestors. I distinctly remember shutting my eyes to listen to the cacophony of excitable Latin voices permeating the air of the seat space occupied then, and conjecturing that we must be bound for Holy Toledo (Spain, not Ohio) instead of Honorable Tokyo. Carolyn and I were nonplussed to observe these passenger's very *un*-Japanese behavior. In stockinged feet, the young folks would stand on their plane seats, and jabber constantly back and forth with *amigos*, front, back and sideways. The Portugese language flowing back and forth was incomprehensible to my wife and me; like most foreign tongues, it seemed to clip along so fast apace that the words ran together like one vast sentence.

Conditioned to a Japanese-American cultural background, Carolyn was in a state of shock to observe this, I recall. I would have dearly loved to see those passengers interact with the quiet and stoic demeanors I see all around me on this Nagoya bound train. I bet that Japanese-Brazilian tourist group posed quite a revelation for the locals — a real wake-up call!

Heredity plays a small role, I think, where behavioral mannerisms are concerned. It was proof in a nutshell, to anyone viewing that scene, that one's environmental conditioning will win out every time. And if the interloper who reads this last excerpt doubts this, fly *Varig* from L.A. to Tokyo.

We reach the city of Nagoya to change trains, and I think what a contrast this is to the five days just spent in the countryside of Kyushu and granddaughter's village of Suzuka. And what a contrast this bullet train is to the Toonerville Trolleys serving those areas. After braving the swarms of people thronging Nagoya Station, Carolyn and I are so comfortably laid-back that, in no time, she is out like a light and sleeps soundly until the ol' Bullet shoots into Shizuoka for a brief stop.

Shizuoka is the home of our dear Mori friends. "I wonder what Mr. and Mrs. Mori elected to do with that collection of maps you brought them, Tom?"

"It's strictly up to them, babe. Those old but well preserved books need to be stored in a glass case for viewing. I'd like to think they were called to the attention of the Mayor for that purpose." We gaze dreamily out of the window, hoping to catch a glimpse of majestic Mt. Fuji to the west but, as usual, its peak is elusively shrouded in cloud cover. Carolyn injects an interesting thought to ponder. "You mentioned not seeing farm animals throughout the course of our travels Tom, but there's something else one doesn't see here that is so prominent in every city, town and village in America."

"What's that, dear —'fat Americans?"

"No, silly — graveyards...cemeteries."

"Graveyards? Honey, I know people are dying to get in them, but if this nation parceled out burial plots in the manner we do back home, it would have run out of living space long ago (which is true)." Being laid to rest embalmed, coffined and six-feet under is not the *modus operandi* here, where cremation urns take up far less space than the cemetery grounds encumbering an incredible vastness of acreage across the U.S.

Carolyn and I have willed that, like her father, an undertaker is to scatter our ashes over the Pacific Ocean, rather than inter these bones in burial plots. Now that that lady has intruded into my thoughts with burial practices here and at home, she catnaps again. And here in solitude, other thoughts give sway to pass the time...

My adopted state of California is populated by numerous 'red-neck' types, who emigrated there in the dust-bowl era of the 30's. And although I didn't arrive in California until 1948, I can imagine how the hard-working, law-abiding Japanese-Americans were treated by these red-necks before they were sent away from their homes and farms in California to relocation camps early in 1942. Perhaps even their burial practice was an excuse to vilify a people I have grown to admire so much. Sud and Irene Itamura in Yuba City, Bob and Joyce Honda in Sacramento, Sei and Ellie Inamine in Visalia and, of course, the family of a wife reposing in comfort on this fast moving train.

Yes, the ignominy of man's inhumanity to man was never more evident than that of the maltreatment visited upon Japanese-Americans during WWII. A Chinese lady once told me that, during those days, a Caucasian woman slapped her across the face while she was taking a seat on a train, a case of mistaken identity. I hope there's no mistaken identity at the Pearly Gates, and that racial bigots of that stripe will be turned away to be directed to a warm spot in Hell.

This day has filled me with a vague sense of melancholy. The sky is overcast and threatens rain; June and July encompass the rainy season in this part of Japan. The Japanese call the onset of the rainy season *tsuyu iri*, and the end of the season, *tsuyu ake*. Where Carolyn and I reside in Northern California it's merely *fall* (if we're lucky) and *spring* (if we're doubly lucky). We're hoping for abundant rain this winter to break the pattern of drought afflicting that area recently.

Rain hasn't fallen, but night has, before we reach the familiar train depot of Sagami-Otsuka. We phone number-one son to come fetch us, but nary a soul is home this evening. "You know, honey," I tell Carolyn, "Dave and Isabel expected us home *tomorrow* evening. Oh, well, let's haul our bags to the bus, and I'll ask the driver if it stops at the Atsugi Main Gate."

"Oh, Tom, even if it does, you don't mean we're to carry this luggage from there to their apartment, do you?"

"No, dear, I assumed you'd walk behind me, carrying yours and mine both, as proper Japanese women are trained to do for the sake of their husband's comfort." Carolyn extends me a 'silly-grandpa' look and doesn't take that last remark seriously; otherwise this husband would be eating beans out of a can for at least a week!

CHAPTER XLI

riday, June 3, Atsugi:

Upon reaching the Main Gate via bus last evening the sentry on duty pointed out a phone for us to ring up Dave and Izzie's number. Isabel caught it on the third ring and I could hear Kirby fussing in the background. "Gee, Dad, we weren't expecting you until tomorrow. David will be there to bring you home in five minutes. We're eager to hear about your trip."

'To bring you *home*' were comforting words for a weary traveler to hear. The four of us stayed up late chatting, and occasionally, I'd go to the voluminous notes of this diary when referring to visits with the Mori's in Shizuoka and the kinfolk of Carolyn near Hiroshima. But the main topic last evening had to do with our visit with Monica. Her father hadn't had a progress report like that one since his daughter had been shanghaied to the remote village of Suzuka-Shi.

"You pulled it off, Dad. I'm impressed. Thanks, Mom, for this letter from Monica. I'm glad she seems to be doing well, the little rug-rat."

"How neat that you got to visit Monica's school," Izzie chimes in while she prepares her little rug-rat for beddie-bye.

"As soon as we can get these photos developed, you'll have pictures of Monica," Carolyn affirms. "I wouldn't mind a cold drink, David. Do you have a soda pop?"

"That mother of yours will be dehydrated for days, son," I remark. "She cried enough tears over your child to irrigate an acre or two of rutabagas."

"What in the world are rutabagas, Dad?" asks Isabel, with eyes wide in an expression of disbelief that there is such an animal.

"It's a turnip-like plant I grew up with in Missouri, Izzie. You know how popular the *daikon* turnips are with Japanese. Well, rutabagas are the *daikons* of Midwesterners. But you know, I haven't eaten one in years, and don't need to, since there's always plenty of *daikon* available."

The single bed next to Kirby's playpen won't accommodate both Carolyn and me, so I generally sleep on the couch. Not always, though; if some late evening program on TV has captured Carolyn's interest, she'll remain on the couch, often dozing off before the program ends. Whichever of us arises during the night to use the bathroom will peek in to see if the other's eyes are open and, if they aren't, flick the TV off.

Since it was the first time for us to view programs in English in over a week, Carolyn was glued to the box last night. Around midnight I got up to use the bathroom and found her fast asleep. Turning the set off awakened her and we switched bed places, and I was perfectly comfortable on the couch.

Awakening this morning after a good sleep, I bounce off the couch, fold the sheet and blanket and head for the bathroom to take a warm shower, after which the four of us, with baby Kirby in tow, depart to breakfast at the golf course restaurant. Our young waitress there looked (to me) to be of Korean ancestry, and I politely asked if she were (after all — many Koreans live and work in Japan). Yet it was the wrong thing to have asked of this gal, I reckon. She almost poured hot coffee in my lap while agitatedly remonstrating, "I Japanese, not Korean! *Pure* Japanese! Whassa *mattah* you think like that?!"

Isabel suppresses a giggle, but David and his mother look concerned. "Does it surprise you that she's resentful to be thought Korean, Dad? Many Japanese don't take too kindly to the Koreans who live among them."

"Sure, I realize that, Son. But I didn't ask her that question with the intent of a joke or a put-down. Simply put, she had the Korean-looking appearance of some folks of that ethnic background I've known through the years. And if she's prejudiced — as her actions so indicate — then that's *her* problem."

"Did I ever tell you about a visit to a small restaurant in Reno, Izzie?" I ask, purposefully addressing my daughter-in-law's smiling face and ignoring the frowns of wife and son. "Carolyn and I were paying one of our three or four times a year visits to nearby Reno (*paying* is an apt verb here), and while she was working the levers on a machine at Harrah's, I strolled a half block to come upon a small storefront, with a sign stating: Grand Opening — *Sushi* Restaurant. Anyway, it was a bit too early for lunch, so I asked the proprietor if I could look over a menu while having a bottle of Japanese beer. I told the man my wife and I both like *sushi*, so we'd likely return. Though this restaurant featured Japanese food, the young man and lady here looked Korean, rather than Japanese, so I inquired with one of the few phrases I know in Korean, *Chee goom messeem nee gah* (what time is it)? And you know, Izzie, I was right that time; hearing that, the man immediately checked his wristwatch to apprise me of the time."

"Notice our waitress isn't *checking* our empty coffee cups, Mom?" was son David's response to that anecdote.

The time has come, dear reader, to skip over these anecdotal asides Carolyn and I experienced here in the company of our dear son and his family. I slipped that last one by you merely to point out that the problem of ethnic prejudice is not peculiar only to Americans. It occurs the world over when ethnocentric attitudes prevail over common sense — pitting race against race and nation against nation — to feed the military-industrial complex and its preoccupation with making bigger and better bombs.

As an American, I was taught to despise the Japanese race after Pearl Harbor. It took many years to discover that the 'Pacific War,' (as Japanese refer to W W II) had more to do with *economics* than race, and more to do with patriotism than common sense. And it's the most abysmal legacy of that war to consider that so many young participants, on both sides, were consigned to early graves, unable to share in the many conveniences that make modern living easier than what those men knew prior to serving their countries. What a *damnable* pity!

I don't propose to know the answer of how to squelch the ethnocentric fire that fuels wars, except to suggest that traveling abroad from one's native shore can be an enlightening eye-opener. I'm deeply grateful for the opportunity to be doing that now.

For several months prior to making this trip to Japan, Carolyn and I brushed up on Japanese by viewing a program called *Nihon Go* (Japanese Language). It came to us via a PBS station in Redding, California, taught by a young chap named Tim Cook, through the auspices of the University of Nebraska. Having taped most of these, I mailed some to son, David · and brought the up-to-the-minute ones here in a suitcase.

Upon returning from breakfast I asked Dave if he had

been watching these while we were away. "No, Dad," says this son, (who seems in a bit of a sour mood since awakening — his work stressful this week, perhaps), "that teacher turns me off with the way he raises his eyebrows. That boy has an enormous ego, and that haughty attitude coming across on your tapes was too much for me. I enjoy the night school courses available here at Atsugi, however." The reader must not construe David's caustic remark as having anything to do with prejudice or ethnocentrism. Television teacher, Tim Cook, and son David share an ethnic identity in common — that of having a Caucasian father and Japanese mother. "I think you're jealous, Son. If you'll practice raising your eyebrows in the bathroom mirror every morning, maybe you'll get the hang of it," I grin at a dear boy who makes his parents feel eminently proud. Thirty-eight years ago last March the eighth, this dad and mom were the only ones present at his birth. Carolyn's obstetrician, the good Doctor Leland Fillerup, was in surgery that morning, and this rascal son saw fit to debut too early for the doc to deliver him. Fortunately it was an easy birth for his physically-fit mother, but a harrowing experience, dear diary, for his dad. I was rubber-legged with worry that morning. Yet, believe you me, there's no better music on earth than when a parent hears his child letting go with a healthy cry while drawing its first breath. Carolyn and I have much to be thankful for.

CHAPTER XLII

Saturday & Sunday, June 4th & 5th, Hakone:
This was a weekend Carolyn and I had looked forward to — a journey to Hakone. Hakone is to the Japanese what Yosemite is to Californians; both are scenic mountainous National Parks; both are favored vacation get-aways, taking one away from the urban pall of smog to commune with nature.

Even better than communing with nature was the chance to commune with the dear friends who so generously made this weekend possible — the personable and affable friend from Yokohama, Mr. T. Seyama, and his sincere and unaffected son, Takanori. Father and son arrived here at the main gate this balmy Saturday morning, to notify by phone that they await there.

David would have dearly loved to accompany us, but there is just so much room in a BMW sedan. He delivered us to that vehicle with our overnight bags, and I thanked number-one, "When we return, count on your mom and me to do some baby-sitting while you and Izzie go out, Son. See you tomorrow night."

As before, when the Seyama menfolk returned us to Atsugi late one evening two weeks earlier, Takanori assumed the role of navigator for his dad. Map in hand, he dutifully scanned these narrow and sometimes winding streets, looking for an entrance to the Tomei Highway. Driving through this complicated maze is serious business for anyone, and particularly so for this driver, as it is not Mr. Seyama's regular route to Hakone. Carolyn and I, therefore, keep the conversation to a minimum, while listening to the 'navigator' signal instructions to the 'pilot:' "*Migi, migi* (right- right) *ima hidari*, (now left), *massugu* (straight ahead)."

Their BMW must be as thankful as we to reach the Tomei Superhighway, where it proves its worth as a 'muscle' car, designed for speeding along the similar *autobahns* of its ancestral beginnings in Germany. Two expensive toll gates are the only deterrents to slow this vehicle on the Tomei Highway.

In no time, we branch off and head south to ascend a series of curving hairpin turns up Mt. Hakone, then pull off into the parking area of an American-looking condominium complex perched on a hillside. It's eerily, ghostly quiet here. "Since the economy's turned sour, many of these condos have fallen into disuse," our host explains as the reason behind this dearth of activity. "The market for middle-class second homes like these bottomed out in the last two years." Indeed, the swimming pool is surprisingly unready for use on a summer weekend, its water green with algae and leaf material.

But swimming is not the goal of this foursome; *tennis* is. We remain here in a cozy one-bedroom, kitchen/dining area, living room and bath just long enough to deposit our bags and change into tennis togs. Then we're set to keep a date with the tennis courts located a short distance away at the lodge of a friend of Mr. Seyama. The friend descends from a ladder propped against the sloping roof of a carport-like attachment to the main building, serving as a vehicle exit and entry for guests in inclement weather. This gentleman has been doing some touch-up paint work to the eaves. It is evident by their smiles that he and Mr. Seyama are friends of long standing.

We could not have picked a better day or, for that matter, a better place to play tennis. The court fence is entwined with green ivy, making the ball so much easier to see than the high school courts Carolyn and I play on back home.

Mr. Seyama, a man in his late fifties, is a skillful player, and Takanori, though lacking his dad's tennis experience, has youth going for him at age twenty-two. He's quick as a cat, and has to be; on the other side of the net are two Americans whose lob shots keep this fellow darting in reverse gear to run down the arching rubber missiles which are their fortes. On the courts back home, retired L.A. Police detective, Bill Alexander groans every time he sees one of these patented lobs sail forth over his head to drop near the baseline. Bill has added too many pounds to chase these down, but the man was once as trim and svelte of body to be classified as an "A" tournament non-professional player. "There was a time," Bill remarks now and then, "that I took on Billie Jean King in a mixed-doubles match and won." (When he boasts thus, someone is always quick to take the wind out of his sails by asking, "Oh yeah? Who was your partner, Bill? Chrissie Evert?")

This matchup of the Seyamas and Drakes has been great fun, and our fingers are crossed in the hope that the sky will be as invitingly free of rain on the morrow, when these courts are again reserved for our use at ten a.m.

There are natural hot springs feeding into spas at almost every lodge in the Hakone area, and there's no better spot to soothe away the aches and pains inherent in strenuous activity such as this senior citizen has just undergone. The spa at this lodge sports a jacuzzi that vibrates pulsing warm mineral water over the body to rival the prowess of a top-notch masseuse. "I'm going to give this jacuzzi just twenty-four hours to stop this," I joke to our hosts, who've just instructed me to shower the mineral water off with tap water afterwards.

Rejuvenated, we all set out on a drive through the *Fuji Hakone Izu* National Park, making leisurely stops to tour the grounds and main buildings of two Prince Hotels, where affluent honeymooners can check in for a *paltry* sum — ranging from $420 to $620 per night. The Prince *Hakone* and *Hakone Sengokuhara* are not highrise hotels. Both have no more than two or three stories above the high-canopied ground-level, where one enters to enjoy a walkabout through portaled vistas of gorgeous plants, exquisite furniture, paintings, statuary and porcelains.

A true highrise awaits on the afternoon of our second day, when we depart from Hakone to be taken on a journey to see the Landmark Plaza on the Yokohoma waterfront. Seventy stories high, it dazzles the eyes, so grandiose is its design. Indoor streams course about over immense granite boulders and realistic looking waterfalls.

There is a teeming mass of people sightseeing here on a Sunday. After securing tickets to take an elevator tour to the top, we wait in line for almost a half hour before being dispatched to the sixty-ninth floor. "This is the world's fastest elevator," Mr. Seyama informs us, but what is even more startling than its speed is that *there is no sensation of movement!* It gives us the impression that our ascent in this commodious but packed elevator, has been done with 'smoke and mirrors,' and we've actually advanced upwards only one or two floors before the door opens into a large circular room. A look through the windows here convinces otherwise, however.

A 360 degree walk affords us a view in every direction. We can see Mt. Hakone from whence we've just come. In another direction, the area where our son is likely playing tennis on the court next to his apartment on this Sunday afternoon is visible somewhere out there to the northwest. It was a super undertaking to erect this building, I ponder, here in the rarefied atmosphere of this sixty-ninth story. It must have taken the courage of trapeze artists for the engineers and construction workers to complete this section of the Landmark Tower.

The elevator is situated dead center, like the spindle on a phonograph record changer. What's more, it returns us to the ground floor in less time than it takes a record changer to drop a record in place and commence to play another. "We must hurry on," advises our host as we exit. "We will be meeting my wife and daughter, Satoko, in Chinatown."

We cruise up one street and down another before finding a parking spot for the Seyama's BMW then we set out on a brisk walk along a passage between shops. Carolyn's and my experience at large train stations has been a useful proving ground from which to learn the art of deftly dodging other pedestrians, as we scurry for blocks before reaching the Chinatown gate. On its right side stands an imposing Chinese temple, where the overpowering aroma of smoking incense assails our nostrils.

The smiling countenances of Mrs. Seyama and Satoko greet us here. They have arrived after a weekend of scuba diving, and we have much to share together, both in food and dialogue, at a table in the back of a Chinese restaurant.

Ultimately, the conversation turns to our granddaughter, Monica. Almost every detail the reader of this narrative has gained in earlier chapters is revealed now to these dear friends. Afterwards, Carolyn thinks it a propitious time to pop a question (as equally compelling as when she asked, two weeks ago, if Mr. Seyama would place a phone call to Monica's house in Suzuka). Now this request carries the same breathless urgency, as Carolyn asks, "When you next come to America, do you think it possible to bring Monica with you to visit us? I understood you to say you'd be coming in two years. Monica will be eleven then, and won't be any trouble. She's very well mannered."

Carolyn and I both wear a look of cautious optimism, and Mr. Seyama quickly assents. "Of course, dear friends, we'll plan to do that. I will continue to maintain touch with her mother and grandparents by phone in the meantime."

WHAT'S A WORLD WITHOUT FRIENDS LIKE THIS!?

CHAPTER XLIII

Thursday, June 9 (A Sunrise Tour of Tokyo):

A narrative purporting to enlighten the reader, with what the author thinks (foolishly or otherwise) are interesting sidelights of travel about a foreign land, is somehow incomplete without focusing upon its capital city. As this day dawns I am given the first opportunity to visit one of the world's key centers of commerce — Tokyo.

The reader is already acquainted with the young lady who has planned this day for Carolyn and me. Yet that was so long ago in this narrative, it strikes me as time to re-introduce her: Miss Tomomi Sudo, age twenty, and presently employed by a travel agency in Kawasaki. She resides with her mother and sister in Yokohama.

Having been a visitor on two separate occasions to our home in the U.S., this lass is eager to do something out of the ordinary for her American 'mother' and 'father.' The three of us are scheduled for the *Sunrise Tour of Tokyo,* courtesy of the *Hatto* (Dove) Tour Lines, with advance tickets purchased by dear Tomomi on her (only) day off work.

Thank goodness our son David is an early riser for work. He doesn't object in the least to dropping his mom and dad at a nearby train station at the early hour of six a.m. Carolyn and I have been instructed by Tomomi to meet her at the *SotetsuSen* Line in Yokohama. We arrive there at 6:45 a.m., relieved to have made it in ample time to meet Tomomi at 7:15.

By 7:15, this waiting area of the station becomes unbelievably busy. With the arrival and departure of each train, hundreds of people, hell-bent on making it to work on time, pour past the circular bench where Carolyn and I wait; yet we see no sign of Tomomi in this sea of bodies streaming by. At 7:45, Carolyn suggests I phone her mother to determine if there is some mix-up about where we are to meet. Mrs. Sudo informs us, "Tomomi should be there. She left home over one hour ago."

Before hanging up the phone to rush back to Carolyn, I ask Mrs. Sudo, "If your daughter should phone you, please let her know that my wife and I are downstairs at the *Sotetsu* Line turnstiles. It's too crowded on the train platform."

Luckily, Tomomi did phone her mother and ascertained exactly where we await. She rushes down a stairwell, wiping her brow with a handkerchief. We quickly follow her, weaving our way through an amazing crowd of rush-hour passengers to an indoor, high-ceilinged platform.

"I so afraid we cannot make it on time to catch tour bus at nine o'clock," gasps our dear 'daughter,' above the din of the unbelievable crowd jamming this station platform (yes, jamming beyond belief). Each train is packed to its sardine gills — so much so that we watch in amazement, as in certain of these train cars, trainmen literally push and shove onboarding passengers onto them, to where the last one's behinds are squeezed against the doors! And squeezed some more to permit the doors to close — an awesome sight! Tomomi makes the hair-raising remark, "Some women get hair caught in doors. They can't get hair loose until next stop."

On the surface, this exercise looks like maltreatment, but is obviously very necessary abuse, if one is to reach his or her destination on time. These folks become inured to the logjam of humanity, and come to regard this experience as one of life's necessities.

The particular train for our Sunrise Tour is packed — but fortunately not jam-packed. While there is no place to sit, at least the three of us can hang onto straps and look out the windows. We view a sea of pedestrians scurrying along in lightly falling rain, umbrellas of every color shielding their bodies. Even bicyclists manage umbrellas in one hand while steering with the other — a remarkable feat of dexterity.

At one point, Carolyn apparently doesn't have a secure grip on the hand strap, and when our train lurches forward she is unceremoniously launched onto the lap of some little man with glasses, knocking the book he's reading onto the floor and his eyeglasses askew, and causing a major viewing attraction for many nearby onlookers. I couldn't conceal a bit of laughter, nor could Carolyn, yet, strangely enough, the *other* passengers didn't change their facial expressions one whit! I expected, surely, that there would be some bemused looks or even quizzical stares. Not so — the same stoic expressions we see as they are being jostled and jammed together while boarding trains prevails in this situation. The only other person to smile about this mishap is the fellow whose lap Carolyn was temporarily astride. His smile is a polite acknowldgement that these things can happen where children and foreigners are concerned. I am unable to determine if his bow, as Carolyn extracts herself from his lap, is an expression of politeness; he may be snapping a vertebrae back in place after being 'sacked' by this tall (by Japanese standards) lady who uses a foreign tongue with which to apologize.

We arrive at Hamamatsu Station where our always-cheer-ful exchange student, Tomomi, now a working gal treating us to a holiday excursion, quickly goes ahead. She then breaks into a brisk run down the train platform, waving for Carolyn and me to follow down a flight of stairs through the exit turnstiles, and then through several glass doors leading to the tour bus counter. *Whew!*

We are ten minutes late but, as fortune would have it in this land where everything runs on time, our bus miraculously awaits. Tomomi apologizes to the driver as we scurry on board to see a small group of about fifteen other tourists on a bus that could easily accommodate three times that many. Our English-speaking guide stands alongside the driver to say, "Good morn-ing. We have a small group for this tour so take any seat you like." I deposit our two overnight bags in an overhead storage bin and we each take a window seat in close proximity. A family of four up front are conversing in a Germanic language, causing me to wonder if our guide is equipped to handle languages other than Japanese and English (but we later learn that this family all speak excellent English).

Carolyn and I exchange relieved smiles with Tomomi, who now fans herself with the tour map each of us has been pro-vided. So, with mutual sighs of relief, we depart immediately. Our tour guide, microphone in hand, introduces himself. "I am Mr. Sato. Sato is the second most common name in Japan. Only the Suzuki name exceeds the number of Sato's, but not by many — sort of like the Smith's and the Jones' in America," he grins, while our driver skillfully maneuvers this large bus through dense Tokyo traffic.

"Sato," our amiable guide continues, "also is the Japanese word for 'sugar,' so you may call me Sugar, if you like." Allowing time for some laughter to subside, this man goes on to say, "This is the Panoramic Tokyo tour, and it is a trip of approximately seven and a half hours. This morning we will be seeing the Imperial Palace East Garden, and the *Asakusa Kannon* Shrine, stopping for lunch at the *Chante Mer* French Restaurant. This afternoon we will visit the *Meiji* Shrine before boarding a boat for a Tokyo Bay cruise. Your bus driver, Mr. Tabata, is very skilled, as you will see now that we're coming into the downtown business and entertainment district. You see, these are the only drivers who manage to survive negotiating traffic like this in one of the world's largest cities. The population of Tokyo, when combined with the sprawling Yokohama and Kawasaki cities adjoining Tokyo, adds up to some thirty million souls, crowded mostly in small homes or apartments. One-sixth of all Japanese live right here in this densely crowded plain."

"Methinks I encountered all thirty million while making it to this tour bus," I whisper across the aisle for Carolyn's amusement. Mr. Sato takes a short breather after suggesting that we might wish to peruse the large fold-out informational map provided each of us.

Carolyn slides over to the center and whispers, "You know who our guide resembles, Tom?"

"Yeah, I was thinking that he looks strikingly similar to your elder sister's first husband, Takashi Kubota."

"He fits Taka to a tee, Tom. His shape of face, hairline, and particularly his eyes when he smiles. Everybody has a double, they say."

We take some time to explain our conversation to Tomomi before the man under discussion begins anew on the microphone, pointing out some highlights along our route. He also frames the historical context of Tokyo's beginnings centuries ago. "We will be stopping at the *Asakusa Kannon* Shrine shortly," Mr. Sato remarks. "Tokyo was once a tiny fishing village, and legend has it, that while two fishermen fished from the banks of this area's *Sumida* River they brought up a golden statue of the goddess of mercy, called *Kannon* (pronounced Kahnohn). Thereupon a shrine was erected at this site to honor the Goddess *Kannon*, in hopes that it will always be a place for good fishing, good health and good living. I don't know about good fishing," laughs our guide Sato, "for our fishing boats must now go afar to meet the needs of this vast population. We find fish very expensive nowadays. Half the cost of fish in our markets is attributable to the petrol fuel needed for fishing boat commerce. And as far as good living — I leave that up to you folks to decide. As far as good health is concerned, Goddess *Kannon* was right on target; we Japanese have the highest standard of longevity among all civilized nations of the world. And, by the way, did you know our birth rate is one of the three lowest in the world? Only one and a half children per family, which translates to two children for every three married couples."

When we depart the bus in the vicinity of the *Kannon* Temple, Carolyn and I say hello to a lady traveling alone from Australia. Also, we become acquainted with the party of four up front and discover they hail from a city in northern Germany. This man and wife and two teenaged children (Mr. and Mrs. Schuettler and daughters, Gisela and Anna) have saved up to tour around the world for one whole year. Mrs. Schuettler teaches French back home in Germany where Mr. Schuettler is a partner in an architectural firm.

Because Carolyn and I visited this shrine during our 1983 trip to Japan, we skip the guided tour to look about the many shops of the *Asakusa* Arcade nearby. "Hurry, Tom. It's starting to rain again." Tomomi has been smart to have brought her umbrella but, having none, Carolyn and I are grateful to the Goddess Kannon that this famous arcade of shops has a roof overhead.

We all enjoy a leisurely look in an antique dealer's shop to view some wondrous objects (with wondrous prices attached). The proprietor is an elderly man with a gentle smile, bidding us welcome and giving us a map of the shops in this Asakusa area. The next stop is a yardage goods store, where Carolyn's eyes light up. "Some of these materials are lovely, Tom. Look at this beautiful pattern. Wow, Tomomi — here's a whole stack on sale! I'm going to pick some out to give to my sis, Jeanne."

I leave the ladies here and cross the arcade to a shop where I can buy some more rolls of film for the camera. Rejoining Carolyn and Tomomi, I signal that we must make haste to return to our bus at the appointed return time of 11:30. A wave of concern washes over Carolyn and me to discover that Tomomi has no better notion than we as to where our bus is parked. We three walk briskly in the general direction we think it is, then Tomomi has the bright idea of making inquiry of a shopkeeper. She doesn't bother to raise her umbrella, so swift is our flight to reach the bus. We make it just in time so that I need not add another chapter in this diary: *Lost in Tokyo on a Rainy Day*.

As our bus leaves the parking area it hits a pothole, and Carolyn's luggage careens down with a clang-bang into the aisle, just missing an Oriental man sitting alone behind us. He tells us in well-spoken English, "No problem. I was by the window, so your bag bounced off empty seat to floor."

This is one *more* reason to be thankful to the Goddess Kannon. After that one collision mishap on the train earlier, it would have been adding insult to injury had this heavy bag of Carolyn's bounced oft this poor fellow's noggin and perhaps cause an international incident!

In any event, this chance encounter called for an introduction, so as soon as efficient guide Mr. Sato announced where we were headed next, I turned around to shake hands and get acquainted. The almost-recipient of our American 'bomb' is Tiianasit Sererat, a dentist working as an Assistant Professor on the faculty of Dentistry at Chulalongkorn University in Bangkok, Thailand. Since he was a Thai, I was pleased to apprise him of an article read in the Armed Forces newspaper David subscribes to. "Just yesterday, I read that the most outstanding graduate award from the Air Force Academy in Colorado was awarded to a countryman of yours. I can't remember his name, but it was as long as yours."

"Most Thai names are very long," he grins. "I am glad to hear of this. It is news to me."

"Well, listen my young friend," I suggest, "if you pick up the next issue of Time or Newsweek, these magazines will undoubtedly have noted that event."

"Good. I read English. In fact, I studied dentistry at the University of San Francisco for two years."

If Carolyn's bag hadn't almost clobbered this dentist just now, I might have inquired about a filling causing me some trouble recently. Instead, I invite him to dine at the table we share with the family from Germany.

We have a gorgeous view of a an irregular-shaped pond of waterlilies here, with a teahouse and veranda situated along the bank to the left. What a view Carolyn and I have while hobnobbing with a professor from Thailand, and an architect and French teacher from Germany — and of course, our bubbly, dear Tomomi from Yokohama. We all conveniently use English as the vehicle for communication while we feast on delicious French cuisine in the *Yayoi Kaikan* (Seaside Hotel), a site we were told is a favorite Tokyo venue for weddings and banquets.

Later that day, we would all get together again at a table on the excursion boat trip around Tokyo Bay. Mrs. Schuettler suggests we toast one another with a glass of wine. And, dear diary, my toast was prefaced to elicit a smile from these friends who hail from the four corners of the earth: "Just how I will explain this moment in time to my countrymen in the U.S. puzzles me. I've spent this day wining and dining with citizens who were World War Two adversaries — namely Germany and Japan — and this at the very time of the fiftieth anniversary of the Normandy Invasion. But what better time than this to set such distant memories aside in the company of dear people like you. Yet, not before we clink our glasses together as a toast to the memory of all the good young men and women on all sides, who met with early deaths due to those terrible days of war."

Carolyn's toast is closer to home: "Here's to all of us, and to my granddaughter, Monica. May we all prosper in health and happiness."

CHAPTER XLIV

Sunday, June 12 (New Sanno Hotel, Tokyo):

This hotel is an American enclave near the 'Embassy Row' section of Tokyo. It is officially designated 'The New Sanno — U.S. Forces Center in Tokyo.' Located along *Meiji Dori* Avenue across the street from The French Embassy, it is accessible by the *Hibiya Line* Subway.

But it is not by subway train that we arrive here on a Sunday morning that threatens rain. As our son's family's two vehicles are too small to squeeze his parents and their combined luggage into, he has seen fit to rent a van from the Base Motor Pool.

David, Isabel and Kirby have a room directly across the hallway from ours on the seventh floor. This is an upscale, but not ostentatiously flashy, hotel, where a sentry box outside the main entrance houses an obese civilian American employee, checking identifications to assure one's entrance here is legit, before one can access an underground parking area or hotel lobby. It's a fact of life that U.S. relations with North Korea are three shades less than cordial, so caution dictates the need for strict security, lest the New Sanno becomes a *cause celebre*.

American dollars are the 'coin of the realm' here, although one can also make purchases with yen at several Japanese souvenir shops sharing space with a military PX.

"Isabel and I have heard what fabulous Sunday brunches they put on here," David told his parents earlier this week, so Carolyn and I immediately thought what a great way to show appreciation for as many of our Japanese friends who could travel here — to join us in that gala Sunday brunch. The Seyamas from Yokohama can't make it, unfortunately; but Mrs. Sudo and her youngest daughter can. Dear Tomomi would have loved to but explained, "I'm sorry to have to work at travel agency. I will come in the evening to say hello, and again your last day in Japan, the day after, to say good-bye."

Another guest at our brunch table is Mrs. Junko Kohno. It is the first opportunity for Carolyn and me to manage a visit with a dear friend of many years. This busy lady was first introduced to us through the auspices of the International Internship Program in Tokyo, as one possessing considerable skill in English and teaching. Mrs. Kohno subsequently was to spend six months as a guest in our Paradise, California home, where she worked school days at Wyandotte Avenue School in Oroville.

I served as principal of that elementary school in 1984, two years prior to retiring. My large instructional staff, cooks, custodians and many parents who made her acquaintance thought the world of Junko Kohno. Carolyn and I shared those same sentiments. Our home has a good-sized guest room downstairs where Junko would stay up late evenings, industriously preparing lesson plans and materials for the next day.

Having alerted the official at the sentry box outside of our

Japanese guests pending arrival, Carolyn and I are delighted to escort them into a huge ballroom where a lavish brunch, including a tall ice sculpture, has been set up. "This is how they air condition the place," I joke with our guests."

This Sunday brunch is both a gourmet's and a glutton's paradise. There are such quantities of meat, seafood, fruit, vegetable, egg, pastry and dessert dishes that one can, if so desired, eat away like there's no tomorrow, and since this has been paid for in advance, I encourage these dear guests and family to do just that! Number-one son takes that advice to heart; where that food is disappearing in that slender body of his is anyone's guess!

Baby Kirby is showered with attention this morning; the waitresses who pour coffee, tea and champagne can't resist giving this child a squeeze, and our guests do likewise on their way to refill their plates. She thinks this more fun than her nursery school. The minutes are fast ticking down before her grandparents must return home to the U.S., and we will miss this dear grandchild. "Son," I muse while sitting here grinning at Kirby, "you've fathered two of our granddaughters, but why is it your mother's and my plight in life, that they both live in Japan? Life's certainly not fair."

David napkins his face after polishing off a second bowl of strawberries with whipped cream, then responds, "I dunno, Dad. But at least you'll be seeing this one in a few more years when we're back in San Diego. But c'mon — let's everybody pose for a picture in front of that ice sculpture before it melts."

On the schedule this afternoon is a trip to the *Edo-Tokyo* Museum. "I want to treat the Drake family," Junko Kohno beams after brunch. "It's closed tomorrow, so we must go today."

"Sounds like a must-see, Son. Coming?"

"We better not tag along, Dad," David responds. "The baby is too young to enjoy a museum trip. And you can see the little rug-rat's ready for a nap. Thanks anyway, Mrs. Kohno."

The sky is overcast as Junko leads the way to the Hiroo Subway Station, two long blocks distant, but it feels good to walk briskly after that brunch. Upon reaching the Ryogoku Station, it's another walk of three minutes past the modern, monolithic concrete structure where sumo wrestling matches are held. Then we see an even more remarkable edifice, situated on a prominence requiring one to take two long flights of escalators before reaching its entrance, or one can do as I, and work off some second helpings by climbing the broad concrete stairs.

A light, misty rain has begun to fall halfway to the top, so I duck under an imposing modern roofline to wait for Junko and Carolyn (who are escalating here) at crowded ticket windows. I see that, if one desires, a payment of fifty yen (about fifty-cents) can also purchase a key to a compartment, where one's umbrella can be stowed, to the left of the entrance of this grand Museum.

It's difficult to envision Tokyo as once being a tiny village, but when it was, it was called *Edo*, and started out the way the universe did (according to the big-bang theory), exploding from insignificance to make its mark as one of the world's greatest entities. Ravaged by earthquake, fire and wartime destruction, Tokyo keeps bouncing back like the *daruma* dolls favored by Japanese children, whose weighted bases automatically swing them back to attention when pushed, pulled or kicked over. But all asides aside..... The window displays of this museum house numerous artifacts from bygone eras. At the left and right of these windows are explanatory commentaries emblazoned on plaques, one in Japanese, the other in English. The first enlightens us that there is no reliable data as to the population of Edo (Tokyo) during the feudal period. Our tour guide, Mr. Sato, told us that this metropolis started out in its infancy as a tiny fishing village, owing to the fresh water from the *Sumida* River, I recall.

Reading on, I discover that, by the early 18th century, the population here had reached one million — higher than that of any contemporary European city. Not all is of antique origin in this fascinating museum (which was opened to the public just last year); there are a number of mock-up structural models of homes and villages. By traversing a full-scale model of the original wooden bridge, called the *Nihonbashi* (Bridge of Japan), one can look below to gain a sweeping view of these quaint models wrought by the hands of skilled craftsmen. "All distances in Japan are measured from the *Nihonbashi*," Junko informs us.

It is so congested with other visitors on a Sunday afternoon, and there are so many rooms, that Junko, Carolyn and I are soon separated. The ladies want to view vintage apparel, and I seek out a display of olden fire fighting equipment. At one point, I hear a clamor to my left and think this stuff on display here better be trotted out to aid some poor soul who's perhaps met with some accident over there, but Junko rushes over to quickly disabuse me of that notion. "Tom," says she, "come look. A *sumotori* (sumo wrestler) is passing through."

By the time we reach where she thinks this behemoth of a man may have gone, we see his broad backsides disappearing in the distance. Boy, could Carolyn and I have used one of these fellows to run interference for us in crowded train stations....

And now, back in the confines of this large, American-style hotel room, I've just scribbled the previous paragraphs, adding a few more lines with the thought, *Much more of this will bring on writer's cramp, dear diary. Suffice it to say, it's been an eventful day. Someday I'd like to return to that splendid museum (and to that super Sunday brunch, now that I think of it).*

On the train returning the three of us back here, Carolyn had much to relate to Junko about her birthday visit with granddaughter, Monica. While Mrs. Kohno has no children of her own, she nevertheless is very close to a number of nieces and nephews, and she and Carolyn both went often to their handkerchiefs during that summation.

Someday, somehow, dear diary, I intend to bring Monica to

see the Edo-Tokyo Museum. Next time I appear on the threshold of that dear's door in Suzuka, however, I plan to bring along something other than a strawberry cream pie. And just what is that? Well, just remember that this diary is the *private* domain of this tired scribbler before I reveal that this grandpa desires to be accompanied by a *sumo wrestler* on that occasion!

CHAPTER XLV

onday, June 13, New Sanno Hotel, Tokyo (Last Day in Japan):

David, Izzie and Carolyn are hot to go shopping, but no way will my son attempt to drive about these streets and find parking on this busy workday Monday. There isn't much shopping to do near this hotel unless one would like to buy an Embassy — the buyer having a choice of the French, South Korean or Australian — all within a short radius of this American Hotel. Not being in the market for an embassy, the family plans to hop on the subway and find other shopping after a hearty breakfast this morning. "Sure, I'll be happy to baby-sit Kirby, Son," I reply to Dave's entreaty (an entreaty inspired after he learns that his dad prefers to remain here and look about the hotel shops, rather than hit the boulevards outside), "as long as I don't have to change her diapers, that is," attaching an important caveat to this consideration.

"I'll change her now, Dad," says Isabel, all smiles, "and we'll be back in a couple of hours, so don't worry."

"Oh, Tom, don't forget," interjects Carolyn, radiating a smile akin to Izzie's, "Junko Kohno will be here at noon. She wants to treat the two of us to the matinee performance of the *Takarazuka* Dance Show."

"Don't count on my participation in that, honey. I heard from some Japanese acquaintance (I forget whom) that those babes in the *Takarazuka* revue are all lesbians."

"Lesbians or not, Tom - I don't intend to miss that spectacle. Everyone says they're terrific dancers, and their costumes will knock you off your feet. Well, we're off and running, Tom. See you in a few hours."

"And if you take Kirby for a walk in her stroller, don't forget to strap her in good," adds Isabel. "She has another bottle in the small refrigerator in the hallway if she acts fussy."

"And there's a bottle of beer in there for you, Dad, if you like," apprises David.

"You *know* I like, sonny boy. I passed up that cotton-picking champagne yesterday at brunch, you notice. That stuff's as evil as the *sake* wine a certain bricklayer tried to pawn off on me on your mom's birthday in your daughter's village."

"Yeah," he chuckles, "I remember you telling me about that. See ya, Dad."

Baby Kirby doesn't understand a word, but I enjoy talking to her anyway. "Listen, kiddo, let Grandpa stand you up on this window ledge, and we'll see what goes on out of this seventh-story window."

Her little eyes dance and her lips grin to look out on the rooftops of smaller buildings than this hotel. There is a drab looking apartment building directly across the street, and a huge pyramid-shaped tower with a red light winking on and off in the distance to the left. The sky is covered with gray clouds. "Listen, Kirby, if you should spot a Baskin-Robbins Ice-Cream

Store out there somewhere, don't get any fancy ideas. Your gramps isn't about to haul you over there." With that, she throws up her little hands and slaps them against the window, knocking my spectacles to the carpeting. "Hmmm...perhaps you understand more than your grandpa gives you credit for. Well, I'll tell you what. Into the stroller you go, dear. Then, while Grandpa fetches his glasses from the floor and cleans your little paw-prints from the window-pane, we'll be off for a stroll to the elevator. I'll share you with other guests in the lobby before we go shopping for some goodies little varmints like you think are peachy-keen."

Kirby's parents and my wife return, out of breath, after several hours. Shortly thereafter, the telephone rings to announce Junko's arrival; she awaits on a bench at the sentry post outdoors, we're advised.

"Honey, I'll walk out with you and greet Junko. But I'll pass, if you don't mind, on seeing the Bazooka Girls with you two."

"*Takarazuka* Girls, Tom. You're quite sure? Look at this pamphlet showing three of them on stage. Woo-woo, Grandpa."

"Wow, Dad, I'll take your place," opines David.

"No you won't," remands his wife. "It's your turn to baby-sit."

At nine o'clock this evening, Miss Tomomi Sudo pays us a good-bye visit. This young lady has threaded her way here via a long series of train and subway rides after putting in a long day at work in the city of Kawasaki. When visiting here for the first time late last evening, Carolyn and I showed her around the shops of the New Sanno Hotel. It being late, however, they were closed, and all we could do was peek in the windows.

This evening we introduce Tomomi to Mrs. Kohno, who met her mother and younger sister at brunch yesterday. Several packets of photos are strewn about the bed, serving now as a couch, so Tomomi sits and peruses them while I fetch her a soft drink. "We have some more rolls of film to develop, Tomomi,"

Carolyn remarks. "We'll send you copies of the ones taken on that grand 'Sunrise Tour' of Tokyo you took us on Thursday."

"Rest awhile and sip your cola, little daughter," I tell her. "In the meantime, Carolyn and I will escort Mrs. Kohno below. She tells us a long train ride awaits her where she resides on the outskirts of this humongous city."

After seeing Junko off with well-wishes, and the hope we will see this dear friend sometime in the future, Carolyn and I return to the elevator. The lobby is quiet this time of evening. A tired-looking lady behind the main desk appears to be struggling to stay awake. In the elevator, Carolyn cautions, "Let's not urge Tomomi to remain very much longer, Tom. The poor dear looks exhausted."

"I couldn't agree more, dear. She has a long train trip ahead of her before reaching her home in Yokohama. I hope the caffeine in that cola serves to keep Tomomi from falling asleep on the train and overshooting her homebase stop."

Before departing, we give a rap at the door of our son's 'headquarters' across the hall, and he appears as sleepy-eyed as Tomomi. After saying good-bye to Dave, Isabel and Baby Kirby (the latter of whom looks so bright-eyed and bushy-tailed, her parents may be in for a rough night), Carolyn and I escort Tomomi to the lobby where she and my wife exchange tearful good-byes, just as happened twice at the San Francisco Airport when she was returning home to Japan from visits with us in the U.S.

"Tell you what, Tomomi. The streets are dark out there. I wouldn't mind a good walk, so permit me to accompany you to the subway station."

"That's nice, Tom. You had a good nap today, didn't you? I'm beat. Farewell, Tomomi. Give our love to your mother and younger sister."

Unlike many large American cities, Tokyo's a relatively safe haven at night. Nevertheless, I regard this errand as a fa-

therly duty. This fine young lady, you will remember, lost her father while still a young child.

The air is damp outside as the two of us tread gingerly over
puddles of water on the sidewalk leading to the Hiroo Subway
Station. Reaching there by a slow ten minute walk, I fish the
telephone calling card from my wallet to present to Tomomi.
"Here, dear, as you can see, this card still has some credits remaining, and you may as well use them. Carolyn and I will be on
the plane bound for the U.S. tomorrow, so we don't need this
anymore. And I want to thank you for your thoughtfulness once
again, in enclosing it with your last letter to us. It came in handy
several times over here."

Tomomi's eyes are as moist as the weather outdoors.
"Good-bye," says she, "I want come Paradise and see you and
Carolyn again sometime."

"Anytime, little daughter. You're welcome any time. And
please don't work too hard. You look awfully tired this evening.
Oh, and by the way, I'm still hoping you and that fine lad,
Takanori Seyama, will get married someday soon. Then, if you
come to America on your honeymoon, Carolyn and I will have
the pleasure of seeing you both. Good-bye for now, dear."

We part with a hug, and I don't know whether the hug or
that last remark is the source of this young lady's blushing complexion.

CHAPTER XLVI

Tuesday, June 14, New Sanno Hotel, Tokyo:

Having taken a long nap yesterday afternoon, I wasn't a bit sleepy after seeing Tomomi off at the subway station. Then, too, the cool moist air invigorated as I returned to this hotel. *This is a good time to set some remembrances down in the old diary*, I muse while waiting for the elevator to reach the lobby level. Just then, however, a door opened to the left, and I could hear music pouring forth as a man and woman approached in quest of this elevator also. I held the side panel of the elevator door, so it would remain open for these two to enter. "Where's the music coming from?" I ask.

"There's a large screen television in a dining area just off the bar," responds this well-tanned gentleman, nattily dressed in white slacks and a sportshirt that could pass for a page in an atlas; a colorful map of the Hawaiian Islands is splashed across its front and back.

While the elevator ascends with the three of us, I note what a stunning blonde lady this is. Tanning may not be healthy for the skin, but one must admit that the combination of blonde hair and blue eyes is enhanced by an even tan like this young lady possesses. "I'll bet you've been stationed in Hawaii," I remark as the elevator pauses for their exit at the 6th floor.

"You guessed right. My wife and I just spent the last three years there. It's expensive, but not like Japan. We'd return in a minute if we could. Have a good one."

Good one of what? I muse, exiting the elevator one floor above and fumbling in a pocket for the room key. It's almost 11:00 p.m. This family of mine on both sides of the hallway are pooped out and sleeping soundly. The thought occurs that to remain awake to pen entries in a diary is not the best way to 'have a good one,' so I return to the elevator and go below to view the scene where the two tanned Americans have just come from.

There are bowls of popcorn and pretzels on the bar counter, so I sit and nibble some of each. The lone bartender is carrying on an animated conversation in Japanese with a waitress and hasn't spotted this newcomer, perched on a stool next to a man in an army officer's uniform. "What deviously sneaky and tricky places are bar counters like this," I remark to him.

The poor chap looks startled to hear this comment and probably thinks it's his unhappy fate to encounter someone who has had 'one too many' earlier this evening. "Why? What do you mean, sir?" he says, looking warily in this direction.

"Forget the 'sir.' The name's Tom. Don't you agree that plying us with these free but salty snacks is trickery? You know good and well that this popcorn and pretzels are calculated to bring on a thirst. *I'm* ready for a beer."

The army man relaxes with a chuckle. "Yeah, how true — free popcorn teamed up with expensive drinks. My name is Richard. Some call me Dick. I considered going by my middle name after Nixon's debacle, but Herbert's worse yet."

"And how do you like Japan, Richard?"

"Great. I've been here just short of a year. It's a safe country, a clean country. I'm even studying a little Japanese. Watch this." He gets the bartender's attention by saying, "*Ano ne - Biru wo motte kite kudasai* (hey there - please bring a beer)."

The bartender breaks away from a jovial conversation with the waitress. "What kind beer you like?"

"None, really. I just came in to sample your popcorn. May I have another bowl? This one's kaput."

"'Nother bowl, sure. But Richard say you want beer. No unnerstand."

"*Joodan deshita. Budweiser ga daijobu* (just joking. Budweiser's fine)."

"You must have been over here a long time. I better shut up. You know more than me," remarks Richard, as the bartender hands me a Bud with a chilled glass.

"Just one month. Tomorrow my wife and I fly home to the U.S. She's Japanese-American and we've been together for over forty years. I undertook a study of Japanese many years ago."

"You must work for the government, then."

"Because I'm staying here at the New Sanno? No, this grandfather is retired. Put out to pasture some years ago. My son's a navy man. I thought about knocking at his door just now to invite him here for a father-son chat. He and his wife and daughter will be here in Japan for at least two more years, maybe longer."

"I'm divorced," says Richard. "The last three months... let's see...since early April, anyway, I've been dating a Japanese lady. Her name is Mariko, and the poor lady is only permitted one day off each week from her job in a department store. She's always tired."

"I know what you mean. A former exchange student paid us a visit this evening. She has to work a six-day week also."

"Would you care for another beer on me?"

"No thanks. I had a couple around noon while baby-sitting the grandkid. It's time to turn in or my family won't be able to pry me loose from the bed tomorrow to catch an airplane. Goodnight soldier, and have a good one — whatever the hell *that* means."

Before hitting the sack at midnight, I returned to you, dear diary, and jotted down a few thoughts after taking note of what transpired on this, our final day in Japan...

There's a book store next to the PX, where I purchased a book upon arriving. It's a paperback entitled *The Japanese*, authored by Edwin O. Reischauer. It's an absorbing, well-written piece of work, and I'll finish it during the long flight across the Pacific.

I know it's not kosher for a backwoods philosopher to disagree with a profound scholar such as Dr. Reischauer, but I take issue with that honorable gentleman's contention (on page 274) that: "The close to 115 million Japanese, crowded into the narrow flat lands of their small islands, are like a party of Alpinists clinging to a narrow ledge and therefore more threatened by the storms of international conflict than are most other peoples encamped on broader bits of terrain."

After ruminating on that lengthy sentence yesterday, it struck me that, on the contrary, a country of small islands is a far safer habitat for ones like the Japanese to have survived as a thriving nation, as opposed to, "people encamped on broader bits of terrain," which areas Reischauer deems less threatened by international conflict.

Warring factions have crossed and crisscrossed the "broader terrains" of Europe and mainland Asia for centuries, while island nations, like England and Japan, have solidified into spheres of relative calm and prosperity, their peoples much *less* threatened, I think, by the destabilizing turmoil of war. The feudal lords thought it prudent to protect their castle domains by the means of water-filled, man-made moats. Japan and England (and the U.S. too, when one considers the Atlantic and Pacific waters) have their own built-in 'moats' courtesy of Mother Nature. For certain, dear diary, as they say in the real estate business: location, location, *location!*

And while on the subject of location, a certain pair of American grandparents are going to have to relocate this morning...

"It's nice out today, honey," Carolyn beams, looking charming for so early in the morning, "Do we have time to go out for a final sightsee?"

"I'd better check with the desk in the hotel lobby to learn what times the airport transporter bus stops here. Our flight leaves at 5:45 p.m. so we should be at the airport by 3:30 or so."

"Shall we go see what Dave and Isabel are doing? I heard Kirby crying during the night. I hope she's not ill."

"Sure. Let's do, babe. We'll invite them to breakfast. I'm starved. Man cannot live by popcorn alone."

"Popcorn?!"

"Yup. Didn't you smell it on my breath as midnight turned into morning while I communed with the ol' diary?"

"How could I when sound asleep? But I could smell beer. You didn't take Tomomi to a bar on the way to the train station, did you?"

"Silly grandma, as beat and tired as that young lady looked then, one drink and she would have had to be transported by means of a large white truck with a red cross painted on its side instead of a subway train."

After breakfast, Carolyn and I were ready to zap upstairs and finish packing. Dave and Izzy remained downstairs with Babe Kirby in her stroller. "I'll check to see what time you need to catch the airport shuttle bus in the meantime," David called to his parents as they bid haste to return to their room.

"Our son doesn't think his dad will have time to make it to the U.S. Embassy this morning, honey. It's the first clear day since we've been here, so I'm hoping so. I have a Minnesota Farm Journal, circa 1939, I want to drop off there for Ambassador Mondale. That magazine has an interesting article written by a Minnesota farmer who paid a visit to Japan back then."

Returning to the lobby, Carolyn anxiously asks, "How much time do we have before I start crying? I'm going to miss you all so much."

Isabel responds, "Not quite two hours, Mom. I talked with the lady at the reservation desk and asked that she save two seats on the bus that comes at 11:40. You'll need to pay her when you pick up the tickets there."

I went directly to that counter but the lady was on the telephone. While waiting, I studied a chart behind her that listed airport bus departure times, and noted that there was one departing at 1:20 p.m. Once off the phone, I inquire of her, "How long does it take for a bus to reach the airport? I notice that you have departure times but not arrival times."

"That's due to the uncertainties of Tokyo traffic conditions. These busses make pickups at several hotels, so that's also a factor. Even the posted departure time here is iffy. Sometimes a bus runs late by fifteen or twenty minutes. It's generally a two-hour run from here to the airport."

"In that case, I'll gamble. Change our reservation to the 1:20 departure if you will. The name is Drake. My daughter-in-law just asked you to reserve two seats for an earlier bus."

David is miffed to learn of the change. "I thought you needed to reach the airport by 3:30, Dad. You better change that schedule back to the 11:40 bus if you can." Ever since number-one son came into this world early, he's had a fetish for being early in all manner of things. It could be genetic as well; Carolyn's mother is never at the middle or back of the line for an appointment. She's always at the front.

As it turned out, I touched bases with the U.S. Embassy while the rest of the family toured this area, presented my gift to a secretary, who took it, explaining that it would be brought to Ambassador Mondale's attention after he returned from a trip to the U.S., and our airport shuttle bus reached our terminal two hours ahead of a scheduled flight. At the embassy, I overheard a young army chaplain inquiring if there were a way to reach the New Sanno Hotel by some means other than a taxi. He carried a baby I learned he had filed adoption papers for, and his wife held the hands of a toddler whom they were also adopting. "Follow me and I'll take you to the subway train from whence I came here. It's a convenient and inexpensive way to reach the New Sanno."

Rejoining my wife at the hotel, we bid tearful good-byes with David, Isabel and Kirby. Our shuttle bus reached the airport two hours ahead of our scheduled flight. Prices for food and souvenir items are doubly steep here at the airport, and I wonder if that's the *modus operandi* at all international airports. I suspect that departing passengers generally have currency and change on them that will be rendered useless once returned to their country of origin. What better way to fleece them of it than to jack up the prices at their point of departure?

In the case of Tokyo International Airport there is a 2000 yen (or $20) tax each passenger must pay prior to departure. It strikes me that an American, whose wallet might be shy of that twenty dollars, must stay on here and take out citizenship papers while looking at the classified ads in the newspaper for employment! In any event, one pays this fee by inserting four 500 yen coins in a vending machine to receive a perforated ticket, then pass through a turnstile to the customs area, where the tickets are collected, and a stub returned to the bearer. The ticket stub, in addition to Japanese writing thereon, states in English: *Bearer to Retain And Show On Demand.* I was cautious, therefore, to place our two stubs in my shirt pocket.

Relieved of $40 worth of coins for airport tax, I discover Carolyn still has some in her purse. "Take these and find us some goodies to eat while I sit with our carry-on luggage, Tom." I hate to tell you, dear diary (writing now on the plastic table tray of this jumbo jet awaiting its take-off) what I just forked over for a Polish sausage, a cheeseburger and two cokes. And, old friend, one must stand in *line* to order items like these at amazingly inflated prices. Gluttonous punishment!

Carolyn and I were just polishing off this snack when a fit, athletic-looking black fellow walked by, dropping his carry-on luggage and stretching muscular arms. "You know something, honey, that man over there is a professional football player. I've seen his face on television in America. After I find a place to unload our trash, I'll go ask him. But isn't that a thousand yen bill you have in your hand? You don't want to throw that away. Here, let's have it. I'll order another cheeseburger and Coke."

"Don't touch. When we get home I intend to enclose it in the first letter I send to Monica."

"You're a professional American football player, are you not?" I asked of the handsome black dude, who returned my smile. He'd been joined by a white kid of about sixteen or so. "What makes you think so, mister?"

"Because I've seen your face on TV. I'm not great on names, but would you mind signing your autograph on the back of this airport tax stub? Here's a pen."

This man obliges with a flourish of the pen more akin to a bookkeeper than an athlete. I can observe Carolyn waving that I return, and hear a crackling voice coming from a loudspeaker: "Will all passengers for Flight...." I scarcely have time to shake hands and thank the man who has just signed: *Best wishes, Herschel Walker # 34.*

"Tokyo Airport was an unlikely place to meet an American football star, Tom," Carolyn remarks as she looks at his autograph while our aircraft is nearing cruising altitude.

"You know, honey, I heard from an acquaintance named Richard, last night over a beer, that O.J. Simpson's ex-wife had been brutally murdered yesterday or the day before. I thought for a minute this was O.J., bound for Los Angeles in the wake of the horrible fate perpetrated on his ex-wife."

The coastline of Japan recedes in the distance now, and the same display screen appears in front as on our flight over one month ago. I view a map of the main island of Honshu, the island of Hokkaido to the north, and the Russian coastline to the west.

"How close Russia is to Japan, huh, Tom?" Carolyn muses while munching on some Japanese rice crackers.

"Those two nations had it out with each other near the turn of this century, honey. I think it was referred to as the 'Russo-Japanese War.' Anyway, it was a real fiasco at the time for Russia. I truly think it ushered in the decline of the Czar's dynasty to cave in to the lure of Communism. And, contrariwise, it was the coming of age for Japan. I was amused to hear your mom tell me how she jumped rope as a young child growing up in Hawaii. The kids of Japanese ancestry like her, would jump rope to the sing-songy verse: *NIP-PON KA-I-TA, RO-SHI-YA MA-KE-TA* (Japan Victorious, Russia Defeated)."

"It'll be neat to see my mom and sisters and brothers in Los Angeles before we drive north to Paradise, Tom. We have so much to tell them."

So much to tell them, dear diary...so much to tell them. Good-bye Japan...Good-bye dear David and Isabel...Good-bye to all our many friends and kinfolk who call that nation home as well. And good-bye Monica, you precious dear! Seeing you was truly the fulfillment of a grandparents' quest....

EPILOGUE

hen the last word of the last chapter had been typed, I pushed the chair back from the keyboard of an out-of-date Brother word processor and breathed a sigh of relief. At 10:30 p.m. on a windy October 15th, I've finally reached the end of a tunnel entered in mid-June. This day and yesterday, winds have kicked up so gustily that I feared an area power outage would shut down any further operations here in a section of our laundry room where I've been sequestered day upon day.

"You've become like a hermit out there, Tom," Carolyn remarked on days when I've put in as many as fourteen hours, cooled only by a small fan during warm summer days, but now chilled by the onset of autumn.

Letters, gifts, cards and photos sent to our granddaughter have gone unacknowledged, as before, during an interim of almost five months since Carolyn and I visited Monica in Suzuka-

Shi, Japan. Close friends, knowing of this heartbreaking alien-
ation, have commiserated with words of encouragement to push
ahead and seek to have this diary published.

"In the final analysis, that's not up to me," I tell these folks.
"I'm to meet with a publisher soon. We'll see what he thinks."

At this point I've made preliminary contact with publishers in New York, Kansas and Southern California. My hunch is
that since California is linked to the 'Pacific Rim' — referring to
the dynamic interaction between Asia and our own Pacific
Coast — a book dealing with Japan will be served best by a California publisher.

Ultimately, I envision that these chapters will be translated into Japanese. I think there is much herein to pique the interest of readers in that nation of inveterate readership. The es-
says of Alexis de Tocqueville in the mid-1900's provided an interesting and enlightening purview for Americans to look at
themselves through the eyes of a foreigner that continues until
this day, with numerous books of that genre reminding that
Bobby Burns poem is as timely today as when written in the
mid 1700's: "Oh wad some Pow'r the giftie gie us · To see oursels
as others see us!"

I was delighted to receive a personal letter from Ambassador Walter Mondale upon returning from Japan:

*"Thank you very much for stopping by the Embassy to
drop off the November 4, 1939 issue of the* Minnesota Farmer
*from St. Paul. I'm sorry we did not have the opportunity to meet.
The newspaper is wonderful. It certainly takes one back to sim-
pler times. Thank you for thinking of me. With best wishes,
Walter F. Mondale."*

At this point, Ambassador Mondale knows nothing of
Tom and Carolyn Drake's quest to visit a granddaughter, whom,
although an American citizen by birth, the intrigues of fate
have willed to live in a remote village of Japan, sealed off as in a
silk cocoon from contact with her American relatives: a victim,

if you will, of a web of intrigue, as the reader of this narrative has come to realize. As the publisher in question is located over 500 miles south of this laundry room workshop of mine, it entails a ten-hour drive tomorrow. "It will be great to visit my family again," exclaims wife, Carolyn.

And it is that, but for every silver lining there's a cloud. During a visit to see Carolyn's kid sis, Jeanne, in Torrance, I run up against the same brother-in-law who teased me, prior to my embarking with Carolyn to Japan last spring, that the airline tickets must have been purchased with a mind obsessed with negotiating the best discount. That aircraft, you'll recall, was scheduled to land in Tokyo on Friday the 13th.

"So you've written a book, eh?" remarks Jim. "Does it have any sex and violence?"

"Come to think of it, no, Jim."

"Well then, you may as well forget the whole thing, Tom. You've wasted your time. Without sex and violence it'll never go anywhere."

"Son of a gun, Jim, you're probably right. Hmmm...I don't see the proposed publisher until tomorrow morning. It's not too late to tag on one more chapter."

"What's that?" asks Jeanne, reaching for a chocolate candy.

"Don't worry about it, Tom," advises Carolyn. Jim's only teasing."

"Of course he teases, honey. Nevertheless, Jim's made a case for adding one more chapter. Jim, listen up — here's the scenario: You and I will head out now for the nearest whorehouse. And since our wives are both raven-haired, the two of us will engage in a knockdown, drag-out fight over the services of an available blonde prostitute."

"*Over our dead bodies!*" protest our wives, in unison.

"Aha," interjects Jim, "*more* violence! Tom, I think you've stumbled onto an answer at this table: sex, a battle over a broad, and finally - TWO DEAD BODIES."